To Jody
To long memories, comradeship and future struggles & collaboration

CULTURAL STUDIES AND BEYOND

Ioz.

Cultural Studies and Beyond traces the origins, growth and diffusion of cultural studies, inside Britain, the United States, Canada and Australia. The book looks at the origins of cultural studies in the early years of the *New Left Review* and the adult education movements, and introduces the central theoretical issues and key personalities over a near forty-year span, beginning in 1956.

Ioan Davies argues that cultural studies, part social movement and part interdisciplinary studies, emerged and developed in resistance to established definitions of culture. He shows that in so doing, it drew on traditions (in particular those deriving from a reading of Marx) inside and outside Britain that articulated this resistance. The debates about Englishness, gender, race and differences are covered as well as the love-hate engagements with aesthetics and popular culture.

Extensively researched, wide-ranging and lively, the book will be essential reading for both students and teachers of cultural studies, and for all those seeking to understand the recent rapid transformations in the culture of the west.

Ioan Davies is Professor of Social and Political Thought, York University, Canada.

D1532344

CULTURAL STUDIES AND BEYOND

Fragments of Empire

Ioan Davies

London and New York

First published 1995
by Routledge
11 New Fetter Lane, London EC4P 4EE

Simultaneously published in the USA and Canada
by Routledge
29 West 35th Street, New York, NY 10001

© 1995 Ioan Davies

Phototypeset in Times by
Intype, London

Printed and bound in Great Britain by
TJ Press (Padstow) Ltd, Padstow, Cornwall

British Library Cataloguing in Publication Data
A catalogue record for this book is available from the British Library

Library of Congress Cataloging in Publication Data
A catalogue record for this book has been requested

ISBN 0–415–03836–7 (hbk)
ISBN 0–415–03837–5 (pbk)

CONTENTS

The two empires which block this cold war are called 'nay-toe' and 'double-you-toe'. This is perhaps because they meet along the margins and are 'toe-to-toe' with each other. Within each toe there are subsidiary tribes, clients and toenails, such as 'Great Britain' (where I am cooped) which is a little satrapy of nay-toe used by its officers for parking their nukes.

(E. P. Thompson 1988: 221–2)

According to some contemporary theorists of literature we are living in an age when books as we traditionally conceive them are no longer possible. The word 'book' implies a degree of coherence and organisation which is neither appropriate nor desirable in a world where the individual voice has been decentred, disinherited, stripped of its imaginary resonances. The shining that seemed in an earlier epoch to surround and sanctify the gush of human utterance in written form melts away as the book and the voice dissolve into a plethora of half-completed 'texts', voices, incommensurable 'positions'. Between the two moments – a world of a difference.

(Hebdige 1988: 7)

While the creeds of both Marxists and feminists contain truths, along with anomalies and absurdities, the business of spotting which are which requires the services of an alert and active brain. Traditionally, the purpose of the best kind of Western liberal education was to train that vital part of our anatomy: to prepare it to think clearly and logically as well as to respond intuitively. The future of agreeable civilisation depends heavily on such human ability, but those who would create more rigid regimes are right in seeking to destroy this facility altogether. . . . Those in authority in doubt about what is happening could do no better than to arrange for the monitoring of courses in fine art at Goldsmiths' College or those in modern art history at the Courtauld Institute or the University of Leeds.

(Auty 1993: 34)

For Diane

ACKNOWLEDGEMENTS

Parts of the first three chapters of the book appeared in earlier versions: 'British Cultural Marxism', *International Journal of Politics, Culture and Society*, IV, iii (1991): 323–44 and 'Cultural Theory in Britain: Narrative and Episteme', *Theory, Culture and Society*, X, iii (1993): 115–54. A segment of the last chapter appeared in *Border/lines* 31 (1993/4): 1. Much of the research was made possible by a grant from the Social Sciences and Humanities Research Council of Canada.

Various people offered suggestions on the manuscript, at different stages of the writing. Comments by Jody Berland, Philip Corrigan, Fredric Jameson and Frank Pierce and anonymous readers for Routledge were particularly helpful. At very early stages I had discussions with Richard Johnston and Stuart Hall about the Birmingham Centre, and Richard allowed me to go through various documents in Birmingham. Of course, none of them are responsible for the final product. In addition, I tried out some of these ideas with graduate students at York University and am grateful for their perceptive comments. Diane, Justin and Benjamin allowed me to go into hiding so that I could break the back of the work, and I still don't know how they put up with my peculiar work habits.

Finally, I would like to thank two editors at Routledge, Chris Rojek for encouraging me to write the book, and Mari Shullaw for being both critical and supportive in the final stages.

Toronto,
November 1994

PROLOGUE

As one of Richard Hoggart's 'uprooted and anxious' (though not quite in the way that he intended), I was born in Zaïre of working-class parents. As one of the *pieds noirs* of the missionary diaspora, sent out to convert the world to the only civilization that seemed to matter, I was born into a nomadic world. Was I really Welsh? (A people with soul and voices, but apparently no bodies.) Was I really African? (A people with body and soul but a voice that was never heard beyond the immediate contours.) Was I an Antipodean? (My parents migrated to New Zealand just as I was getting used to being comfortable in a British cultural *Heimat*. Upside-down the family body is all.) Was I North American, after moving to Canada where the body gestated in a world where the family body is all talk because the real body and the real family have been commodified beyond recognition?

So where is home? Most of Marxist theory is concerned with trying to construct the home we would like to inhabit or, alternatively, trying to construct a home against those that the others want us to inhabit. This is probably no different from any other struggle to find or define *Heimat*, but with one important difference: the Marxist critique suggests that the next home will be better, not because it has more equipment, more space and more art, but rather that the interconnections between art, equipment, space and, above all, people is where we want to be. Most other critiques suggest that these are spaces where we have to be because of the remorseless juggernaut of history.

In his novelette, *Imaginary Cities* (1972), Italo Calvino argued that there are two cities that we all inhabit. One is the city of the imagination, the other is the real city that we have come to define as being ideal for us. We use these two cities to read the others that we encounter, which in a sense contain fragments of the ideal. But there are also those who try to turn cities into inferno, 'the inferno where we live every day, that we form by being together'. The purpose of having ideal cities is to resist inferno, 'seek to recognize who and what, in the midst of inferno, are not inferno, then make them endure, give them space'.

1

The cultural New Left was caught in the paradox of the imaginary, the ideal (based on juxtapositions of the real) and the evident inferno of 'progress'. The imaginary was based on the concepts of a community derived, in part, from Marx, and in part from the English utopians; the ideal was collected from fragments of communities that the various members had lived in or been close to; while 'inferno' was an interlocking of media, politics and economics which had to be encountered in terms of the imaginary and the ideal. This dialectical play led to some surprising conclusions, as in many senses each of the nodal points had different ingredients. This study is concerned with how what might have appeared at one time to be a homogeneous body of work took on a rich diversity which ultimately changed not only how the English viewed themselves, but also the Welsh, the Scots, the Irish, and even the Americans, the Australians and the Canadians.

One of the earliest cultural studies writers wrote that 'The Human energy of the long revolution springs from the conviction that men can direct their own lives, by breaking through the pressures and restrictions of older forms of society, and by discovering new common institutions' (Raymond Williams 1961: 347). In fact new institutions were created (educationally and politically), sometimes replacing the old, but whether they were 'common' or not depended on ideas of commonality: the Open University was perhaps a singular achievement, but ultimately the major achievements might be seen in the particularity of new formations – feminism, black awareness – turning Raymond Williams into an icon of Welshness.[1] Some of the shining moments (*Marxism Today* and the cultural policies of the former Greater London Council) were transitory, and the sheer academicism of the discourse that cultural studies encouraged often seemed to take it along routes which were more likely to create pedanticism than discourse. The idea that the revolution would be long depended on a sense that there were roots of a common culture that had to be nurtured to grow. It did not take into account the possibility that counter-revolutions happen overnight, and that when they happen they hack away at those roots. How can they be re-rooted? Much of the trauma of cultural studies since the mid-1980s can be related to the search for new and old roots and the recognition that the revolution would be a very long one. For this reason it will be noted that I punctuate my epigraphs with clearly reactionary ones.

The richness of cultural studies in Britain came precisely because, for the most part, those who were involved were aware of these contradictions, and of the conflicts of thinking about and making culture. Further, it was international in its conception of reading, watching and thinking about writers, artists and film-makers from around the world who would help to refashion a sense of how the culture of the English should be examined. Because of Britain's previous imperial status, its entry into the

European Economic Community (EEC), its privileged linguistic affiliation with the United States, a wide range of comparative cultural interpretations were not only available, but also seen as necessary for consideration. The ways in which these became part of the work were affected by the particular circumstances of those in Britain who felt the activity was necessary. Certain theorists, until the late 1980s, were largely ignored (Mikhail Bakhtin, Pierre Bourdieu, Alain Touraine, the Frankfurt School), other experiences (China, the USSR, Africa) were zapped into for occasional fixes, but seriously considered only when they became other than taken-for-granted. Debates in Canada, Australia, South Africa and New Zealand were generally ignored. This, of course, does not mean that they were ignored in Britain as a whole, but rather ignored in the central debates on cultural Marxism. The reverse also happened. British debates were entered into abroad, but selectively, as they suited the ongoing debates of the country appropriating them. None of this is surprising. We all pick what we need to use to make sense of ourselves. What is remarkable about the debates around Marxism and cultural studies in Britain was how much of the world's concerns were seen to have relevance for understanding the culture of the English.[2] Every country has some form of cultural studies which tries to come to terms with how the culture has been created from within. The remarkable thing about British cultural Marxism was not only that it was self-reflective, but also that this self-reflection took place with the outsiders looking in and asking the patients to account for themselves.

The book is organized around a set of themes. It begins by arguing that British cultural studies originated in a sense of social and intellectual movement, and that to understand what cultural studies became we have to understand in large part its relation to the social movements to which it was linked. Because the book is about cultural studies, it does not trace all the nuances of the movements (a fuller account for the 1956–77 period is provided by Lin Chun (1993) in her book *The British New Left*). Subsequently, it argues that three themes engaged cultural theorists: the peculiarities of the English, the peculiarities of the un-English, and the particularities of gender. Beyond this, it argues that, to understand the impact of cultural studies we have to understand both how the debates came to be centred in pedagogical practice and why the debate around aesthetics was central to understanding why cultural studies has had such a mischievous press. In Chapters 6 and 7, it encounters two of the most contentious issues in cultural studies – representation and popular culture – but doing so by contrasting the various approaches and suggesting lines of accommodation. In Chapter 8, the sense of 'beyond' takes over. I try to suggest that, although British cultural studies had become an institution, it had also retained the idea of itself as being a political catalyst, inside

3

academia and outside. Understanding what it might become requires understanding not only its peculiar situations within Britain, but also the grounding of cultural studies in societies with quite different traditions. Throughout the book, 'narrative' is interspersed with 'theory'. Theory is not something that comes from on high: it is the (re)making sense of our own stories so that they make sense to ourselves and others.

NOTES

1 At the Hay-on-Wye literary festival in June 1993, participants were invited to a walking tour of the sites of Williams's novels.
2 I use 'British' and 'English' advisedly. The 'English' culture was centrally the object of study because the English had accumulated an empire by, first, colonizing the Welsh, the Scots and the Irish and, subsequently, a large part of the world. 'British' cultural Marxism was, in part, an attempt to come to terms with the problems that the English had imposed on the world.

1

INTRODUCTION

That which one would insinuate, thereof one must speak.

Ernest Gellner, 1959: 265

The English, like any other society, had forms of 'cultural studies' long before the term was coined. Dr Johnson's first *Dictionary of the English Language* was an idiosyncratic venture into providing a lexicon of English habits and rituals, while eighteenth-century writers such as Hazlitt, Addison, Steele and Mary Wollstonecraft tried to come to terms with the nuances of political and everyday life as they saw it from their privileged positions; the historian and essayist Thomas Carlyle, the Scots sociologist Adam Ferguson, the French travelling critic Alexis de Tocqueville, the poet and antinomian rationalist William Blake, John Stuart Mill, the critical political economist of liberal identity and the poet and literary critic Samuel Taylor Coleridge provided a span of ideas to account for the culture of the English at the beginning of the nineteenth century; while, throughout that century, an ongoing array of novelists, theologians, historians, poets, essayists, art critics and dramatists tried to peel away the various layers of the culture. In particular, Matthew Arnold, Walter Bagehot, John Ruskin and William Morris addressed the issues of industrialization, democracy, literacy and artistic value. Equally, by examining other cultures, anthropologists and archaeologists told us as much about the dominating values of their own society as they did about those they were investigating. The diaries, letters, poems and novels of women (mostly of upper-class background) sketched out a potential feminist cultural studies, while the voices of blacks, convicts and workingmen are to be found in the letters and songs that were distributed widely across the empire.

To understand the culture of the English it is therefore enough to read what was written, look at the paintings, wander round the buildings, and engage in one's own self-reflection. Or is it? The challenge of cultural studies was that these readings should be connected – by theory, by political engagement and by being conscious of one's personal situation in relation to that of others. Even though others had argued for this

5

before – notably in the early twentieth century by authors as diverse as the essayist/poet/novelist D. H. Lawrence, the American poet/publisher/essayist T. S. Eliot, the novelist and critic Virginia Woolf, George Orwell, whose journalism was at least as politically significant as his novels, and F. R. Leavis, who tried to argue for which of the writers mattered, all in the field of literature – they seemed a far cry from the great totalizing schemas of the European continent, or even the attempts at synthesis in the United States.

The suggestion by Leavis (and also by many of the other critics) that we should think carefully about what parts of the cultural tradition were essential for understanding ourselves *now* was, of course, the beginning of an appraisal of coming to terms with what parts of past culture were worth preserving. In English literature (and, indeed, in the literature of the rest of the world) this has led to proposals about the canon (see Bloom 1987), that is, which books (or, indeed, films or works of art) that everyone should be familiar with before they considered themselves cultured. The New Left take on this was somewhat different. The issue was not *What Books?* but under what conditions did reading or making books, watching or making films *matter?*

Raymond Williams argued strongly towards the end of his life that cultural studies originated in the adult education movement.

> in the WEA, in the extramural extension classes. I've sometimes read accounts of the development of Cultural Studies which characteristically date its various developments from *texts*. . . . But, as a matter of fact, already in the late forties, with notable precedents in army education during the war, and with some precedents – though they were mainly in economics and foreign affairs – even in the thirties, Cultural Studies was extremely active in adult education. It only got into print and gained some recognition with these later books.
>
> (Williams, 1989b)

But there *were* books. Three at the end of the 1950s established the grounds for a rethinking of the whole cultural tradition of England, all of them written by men who were working in adult education. E. P. Thompson's *William Morris: From Romantic to Revolutionary* (1955), Richard Hoggart's *The Uses of Literacy* (1957) and Raymond Williams's *Culture and Society* (1958) from different angles worked over cultural sources of engagement in English culture which had typically been the preserve either of conservative criticism or of a narrowly focused Communist Party of Great Britain (CPGB) interpretation. Thompson's study of Morris is frequently overlooked in accounts of the early days of the New Left, partly, perhaps, because at the time of the writing Thompson was still a member of the CPGB, and partly because it was overshadowed

6

by the appearance in 1963 of *The Making of the English Working Class*. However, in setting the tone for a reappraisal of a major cultural figure of the nineteenth century, *William Morris* is crucial in being honest to Morris's language, vision and personal development. It was situated against the populist appropriation of Morris by the Labour Party, the turgid rhetoric of the CPGB, and the vacuous sycophancy of the arts community.[1] Its strategic importance at the time, particularly for many intellectuals in the CPGB, was that it showed that a Marxist cultural critique (beyond the study of folk music or classical Greece) could be richer than anything that flowed from party policies. Richard Hoggart's *The Uses of Literacy*, part autobiography, part social history, part study of education, part analysis of the media, had a much more immediate impact. In a review of the book in *The New Reasoner* ('Britain – Unknown Country'), Peter Worsley wrote:

> Unlike many an academic sociologist, Mr Hoggart does not content himself with meticulous description of working-class habits, but tries 'to see beyond the habits to what the habits stand for'. And this is precisely the kind of approach so badly needed. We have now, for example, plenty of valuable material on the way in which a person's chances of achieving higher education are affected by his class position. This is very valuable. But what are people going to *do* with their education? (how will they 'use their literacy?'); what are they being educated for? what are they being taught? can they integrate their knowledge into their lives? can they develop rounded personalities within the confines of the present social order? ... these are the 'further' questions Mr Hoggart raises, and we should be eternally grateful to him that he has done so.
>
> (Worsley, 1957: 62)

Hoggart not only updated the concerns of Matthew Arnold's *Culture and Anarchy* (1869), but also, by situating those concerns in the lives of working-class youth in the mid-twentieth century, set out an agenda for cultural politics and research for the rest of the century.[2]

Culture and Society's organizing principle, wrote Williams, was

> the discovery that the idea of culture, and the word itself in its general modern uses, came into English thinking in the period we commonly describe as that of the Industrial Revolution. The book is an attempt to show how and why this happened, and to follow the idea through to our own day.
>
> (Williams, 1958: vii)

In 'following the idea', Williams tried to establish a nineteenth-century tradition from Burke and Cobbett to Ruskin and Morris, to deal with writers at the turn of the century (including Gissing, Shaw and T. E.

7

Hulme) and to explore what he saw as the major cultural theorists of the twentieth century – Lawrence, Tawney, Eliot, I. A. Richards, F. R. Leavis, Christopher Caudwell and George Orwell. In doing so he argued for the importance of a 'common culture' which was 'a whole way of life' and based on 'equality of being'. Thus Williams provided a framework ('a structure of feeling') within which encounters with culture could be thought through.

The three books operated from different theoretical positions. Thompson's was clearly Marxist (trying to reclaim Marx from the Communists), Hoggart's was humanistic liberal, while Williams's was a socialist Leavisism (*Culture and Society* was in many ways a socialist *Great Tradition*). What the books paved the way for was a theorizing that was not *ad hoc*, piecemeal, fragmentary; a theory that was grounded in a consciousness of practice, and which was capable of making connections across quite discrete areas, but from the inside, as it were, from the situation of the individual as part of a collective on the road to cultural agency. Marxism was the theory that had to be encountered and, if necessary, transcended.

Thus cultural Marxism was officially born in the late 1950s,[3] by being liberated from both Stalinism and a regimental base-superstructure model. It required not only a rethinking of Marxist theory but also of the ways that the story of British society, politics and culture had been told, recorded and interpreted. From the founding of the *New Reasoner* and the *Universities and Left Review* in 1956 and onwards, the debate, theorizing and research on British culture from a more-or-less Marxist perspective assumed remarkable proportions, in which concepts, metaphors, theoretical frameworks and, above all, social, technological and political experiences, unthought of in previous Marxisms, became centre-stage, if only in some cases for momentary existences.

As a postscript to Thatcherism and its not-so-silent minorities, to the 'end' of the Cold War and the decline of the USSR, and the re-establishment of a US hegemony through military but probably not economic means, it is important to take stock of the trajectory of this vast intellectual and political productivity and ask where it leaves us now. What I shall argue is that throughout the late 1960s and the 1970s, the analysis of culture in Britain was firmly anchored in a strategy of political struggle, that its priorities were those of an elaboration of the cultural problems facing the left at the time, that it had created a vibrant, intellectual left culture. By the 1980s, however, British cultural Marxism had entered a new phase. Was it less Marxist and more culturist, carried along by its own academic institutionalization, shadow-boxing with itself and only indirectly contributing to political practice? One of the frequent arguments advanced, particularly using the reformation of *Marxism Today* and the emergence of cultural journals that came into being in the last few years of the 1980s, is that it became caught up in the process which it had set out to criticize. There is something to be said for these critiques, but I would like to argue that the process was much more complex and that the legacy is far more hopeful.

But to do that it is important to begin, as it were, at the beginning.

NOTES

1 Thompson revised *William Morris* in 1977. An indication of the differences between the two versions is found in Perry Anderson (1980), particularly Chapters 6 and 7.

2 Many people simplified the book by taking it to be, ultimately, 'about' the effects of the media. But the book is not primarily about any one cause or any one effect: the relationships are multivalent. For many of us 'scholarship boys', it was our personal search for intellectual, cultural and social identity that Hoggart had hit on. Chapter X, 'Unbent Springs: A Note on the Uprooted and Anxious', was about us. As we read the following paragraph, we looked at our own shelves and found that Hoggart had been spying on us:

For some people the late *John O'London's Weekly* obviously met a strongly felt need, one stronger, I think, than it could have legitimately claimed to meet. Others are proud of reading J. B. Priestley and writers such as him, because they are 'serious writers with a message'. Others have learned that Mr Priestley is a 'middlebrow' and only mention him in tones of deprecation. They tend to read bitterly ironic or anguished literature – Waugh, Huxley, Kafka and Greene. They own the Penguin selection from Eliot, as well as other Penguins and Pelicans; they used to take *Penguin New Writing* and now subscribe to *Encounter*. They know a little, but often only from reviews and short articles, about Frazer and Marx: they probably own a copy of the Pelican edition of Freud's *Psychopathology of Everyday Life*. They sometimes listen to talks on the Third Programme with titles like, 'The Cult of Evil in Contemporary Literature'.

(Hoggart 1957: 253)

No wonder Sir Allen Lane of Penguin Books helped to subsidize the Birmingham Centre for Contemporary Cultural Studies in the 1960s.

3 There was, of course, cultural Marxism in Britain before 'Cultural Marxism', some examples of which are discussed by Williams in *Culture and Society*. Some of this material – for example the literary criticism of Arnold Kettle (1968) – had a rigid conception of ideology which was unhelpful in reading new literary works. Others, however, such as A. L. Lloyd's (1944; 1952; 1967) studies of folksong or Eric Hobsbawm's (1959) early writings on jazz, showed a powerful sensitivity to the making of culture. However, Joan Littlewood, Gerry Raffles and Ewan McCall (Jimmy Millar) had the most acute sense of putting Marxist cultural theory into practice (see Littlewood 1994 *passim*).

2

THE FIRST NARRATIVE

In November 1956, the director of the Hungarian News Agency, shortly before his office was flattened by artillery fire, sent a telex to the entire world with a desperate message announcing that the Russian attack against Budapest had begun. The dispatch ended with these words: 'We are going to die for Hungary and for Europe.' What did this sentence mean?

(Kundera, 1984: 95)

The starting-point, of course, is the shattering of three illusions. The year 1956 was when the Russians destroyed socialist resistance and turned Budapest into an armed camp and also when the British, French and Israelis immobilized the Suez Canal. Thus the various cultural-political movements, so dear to the heart of the British left – international Bolshevism, socialist Zionism and the British civilizing mission (symbolized by the left's relationship with India) – were revealed as little more than fronts for naked imperialism, though in retrospect they might be seen as desperate ventures of powers on the run. Equally it was clear that after 1956 within British political parties there was emerging a consensus at the centre which governed the sense of what politics was about, a consensus which was in many respects a liberal response to complex issues, not least of which was a reaction to the strident Cold War ·tactics of Stalin and the Americans. The term 'Butskellism' (coined from the merger of the names of R. A. Butler, the left-Tory pragmatist, and Hugh Gaitskell, the centrist socialist) became the neologism that was used a little later to express the coalition of like-minded Keynesians in all parties who saw a mixed economy as the core of a British tradition which reached back at least as far as Lloyd George and Asquith, and perhaps even further back to Gladstone. Anthony Crosland brought out *The Future of Socialism* (1956). John Strachey, the erstwhile Bolshevik, with R. H. S. Crossman (whose collection *The God That Failed* (1950) became the bible of Red-bashers) discovered Karl Popper and why the Open Society had philosophical enemies like Hegel and Marx. Meanwhile at the London

10

School of Economics (LSE) Michael Oakeshott was teaching a political philosophy which excluded Marx because, as he told a conference of social scientists in 1960, he only included thinkers who had written 'at least one major theoretical book'.[1]

The appearance of the *New Left Review* (*NLR*) in 1960 was therefore propitious. The merger of the *New Reasoner* (*NR*) and the *Universities and Left Review* (*ULR*) represented the apparent fusion of two distinct tendencies in British Marxist thinking. *NR*, initially edited by Edward and Dorothy Thompson and John Saville from the north of England, was the product of a humanist, oppositional tradition in the Communist Party of Great Britain (CPGB).[2] *ULR* evolved in Oxford out of a 'left student generation of the 1950s which maintained some distance from "party" affiliations.' (Hall 1989b: 15). It was initially edited by a Canadian (Charles Taylor), a Jamaican (Stuart Hall) and two British Jews (Raphael Samuel and Gabriel Pearson). Different intellectual formations, different political backgrounds, different cultural milieux: these were the juxtapositions of fusion. The new journal therefore played at the edge of Marxist theory, releasing it, in the first editor's words, from the 'reductionism and econo-mism of the base-superstructure metaphor' (Hall 1989b: 25). It was also initially a journal of movement. By 1961 there were thirty-nine New Left clubs across Britain, with the London club holding weekly public meetings as well as having a series of discussion groups based on education, litera-ture, new theatre, race relations and science. The clubs also acted in many cases as the organizing centres for the Campaign for Nuclear Disarma-ment (CND), and in many other cases were created out of the local groups of the Workers' Educational Association (WEA) and the National Council of Labour Colleges. The New Left was therefore borne along by the animated presence of existing bodies of labouring intellectuals plus the few middle-class intellectuals who saw the meaning of their work as having presence in the lifeblood of those whose ideas were generated by their everyday experiences.[3] But the intellectual base of the left in the 1950s was very metropolitan-centred, and the Thompsons and Saville had to go north to get *NR* off the ground. The early editorial board of *NLR* included a large number of people who worked a long way from London and Oxbridge: Ken Alexander and D. G. Arnott in Scotland, Alan Hall in Staffordshire, Alasdair MacIntyre and John Rex at Leeds, John Saville in Hull, the Thompsons in Halifax, Peter Worsley in Manchester, Raymond Williams in Sussex, many of them in extra-mural departments or working for the Workers' Educational Association. *NLR* (issues nos 1–12) was a journal devoted both to the sense of social movement and to the exploration of the political implications of a modernist culture. In attempting to pull together the diverse strands of the left in the early 1960s it tried to walk a tightrope between a popular style of writing and a theoretical one, between the exploration of popular culture as well as

11

the nuances of power. The format was that of a magazine rather than a journal and the articles ranged from the journalistic to the carefully researched and theoretical. Each issue also included reports on club activities, though in retrospect it is clear that the idea of a New Left 'movement' was based more on consolidating and exploring the possibilities for action within existing networks than imagining new ones. The idea of the clubs being the intellectual vanguard of the proletariat, the intelligentsia and youth was not very far away. As an editorial in the first issue of *NLR* put it:

> The Labour movement is not in its insurrectionary phase: we are in our missionary phase. The Left Clubs and New Left Centres – the New Left in general – must pioneer a way forward by working for socialism as the old missionaries worked: as if consumed by a fire that is capable of lighting the darker places in our society. We have to go out into the towns and cities, universities and technical colleges, youth clubs and Trade Union branches, and – as Morris said – *make socialists* there.
>
> (*NLR* 1960 1 (Jan–Feb): 2)

In this form it was not to be. After issue no. 12, barely two years after it started, Stuart Hall resigned, the London club closed, and Perry Anderson and a group of younger scholars from Oxford, who had meanwhile been publishing *The New University*, took over. Thereafter, theory, apparently sundered from social movement, took central space. *NLR* changed format to a standard academistic one, though singlemindedly, through the journal and, later, from 1971, its publishing house, pursuing an agenda of translation from (mainly) European texts from the Frankfurt School, the French structuralists and post-structuralists, Italian post-Gramscian Marxists, and a re-examination of the work of Lukács as well as some Latin Americans (though oddly enough no Africans, Asians or even Russians), and attempting to integrate this work into a rethinking of the nature of British society, politics and culture. It was a formidable agenda, announced in Perry Anderson's (1964) article 'Components of the National Culture' (reprinted in Cockburn and Blackburn 1969: 214–84) which made a distinction between those European intellectuals (Wittgenstein, Namier, Popper, Berlin, Gombrich, Eysenck and Malinowski) who provided a 'tremendous injection of life . . . [to] a fading British culture' by being willingly appropriated to it, and those, 'the "Red" emigration, utterly unlike that which arrived here . . . [who] did not opt for England, because of a basic cultural and political incompatibility' (Anderson 1969: 231–3). Thus the Frankfurt School, Neumann and Reich, Brecht, Lukács and Thomas Mann, who chose to migrate elsewhere, were set against those Europeans who came to Britain to be appropriated by the dominant culture and receive knighthoods, thus maintaining an 'insular reflex and prejudice'. 'For the unmistakable fact is that the traditional, discrete disciplines, having missed either of the great synthetic revolutions in European Social thought, were dying of inanition' (Anderson 1969: 232). The task of the new *NLR* was thus to rewrite the agenda of British intellectual life, and to provide the theoretical foundations for 'a revolutionary practice within which culture is possible' (Anderson 1969: 277).

Thus the agenda for the New Left was turned on its head. Movement took a back-seat to ideas. The last clearly political intervention by the New Left was the publication of *The May Day Manifesto* in 1968.[4] The clubs disappeared, with *NLR* playing a role on the British Left similar to that played by *Les Temps Modernes* in France over the previous two decades, though, in many respects, a more exploratory and dynamic one because nowhere was the possibility for creating a vibrant, intellectual culture more inviting, and probably nowhere had a programme been set for re-examining a national culture through a systematic organization of international and comparative theoretical scholarship. But not everyone saw it this way. By 1963 virtually none of the original board members of *NLR* remained.[5] A privately funded magazine, *Views*, for a short time became the writing stable of those who felt that they were publicly disenfranchised by what they saw as the Anderson *putsch*. Many, of course, continued writing for the academic journals started in the 1950s as part of the rethinking of Marxism (*Past and Present* was certainly the most significant of these, and *The Critical Quarterly* played a part in the study of literature) and for a series of weeklies, fortnightlies and other periodicals which acted as the communicative foundation of what many members of the New Left saw as the core of their public presence (magazines such as *The New Statesman*, *New Society*, *The Listener* and *Peace News* were certainly important, but so were the listing magazines *Time Out* and *City Limits* in London, not to speak of the range of 'alternative' papers that appeared in the late 1960s and early 1970s). But by the early 1970s new centres of activity had emerged and with them their own publishing arms. *The Socialist Register*, an annual edited by John Saville and Ralph Miliband, came out first in 1964, in many respects initially catering to the same public as read *The New Reasoner*. *Screen* and *Screen Education* grew out of the Society for Education in Film and Television and became rapidly a source of critical (but mainly post-structural) thinking on film and the other performing arts. The History Workshop was established in 1968 and by 1975 was producing its *Journal* and collections of articles, procedures of conferences (in many respects as a movement, it was the most obvious extension of adult extension and of the New Left clubs). Various feminist journals (notably *m/f*, *Feminist Review* and *Spare Rib*) as well as Virago, the women's publishing house, were established, arguing implicitly that British Marxism was patriarchal. *Radical Philosophy* came into existence in 1971. Several new publishing houses came into existence that clearly had a left (if not New Left) agenda: Merlin Press, Pluto Press, Alison & Busby, Zed, Harvester, Writers & Readers, while Penguin Books and Lawrence & Wishart were transformed into willing vehicles for New Left manuscripts. The Institute for Contemporary Arts in London embarked on a high-profile exercise in public education. Among the caring professions, radical social workers issued the CASECON manifesto in 1975, which set out an agenda for radical social work. Within the universities there were a number of significant developments. In 1962 the Centre for Contemporary Cultural Studies was launched by Richard Hoggart (under the aegis of the department of English) as a graduate research centre at Birmingham and by 1968 Stuart Hall was the effective director. The centre first started publishing stencilled papers, then occasional papers and, later, books which thematically collected material researched by members of the centre. E. P. Thompson and Royden Harrison established the labour research department at Warwick in the mid-1960s. Ralph Miliband moved from the suffocating atmosphere of Oakeshott's LSE to the vibrancy of northern Leeds. At various other universities (notably Essex, Sussex, Warwick, York and Lancaster) new degree programmes or research units owed much to their contacts with the New Left, as did sociology and, later, cultural studies departments in the polytechnics. Finally, the Open University, owing much in its curriculum and personnel to pedagogical ideas worked out on the left, became functional in the 1970s.

The critical feature of all of this was that the left in the 1970s redefined the nature of its activities. It ceased to be based on a set of interconnected clubs related to a central source. New Left culture in Britain became decentred, while at the same time creating new institutions which arose out of the exigencies of time, space and relationships. Above all, it celebrated the liberating power of theory which, perhaps for the first time in British history, could be tried and tested against other people's theory and experiences. A major element in this was the publishing and editorial policy embarked on by *NLR* in 1963. Much of the subsequent debate on the left was on the appropriateness of different theories to the British practice. Without the bold publishing venture of *NLR* it is doubtful if any of that would have happened. An important by-product of this was that, for a Britain that was entering the EEC, the intellectual grounds were established for a discourse between the British and the European left.[6]

> I think that the success of a revolution in an advanced capitalist society will come from the spreading out of political power from a number of strategic localities, where it first emerges, into a nationally co-ordinated process.
>
> (R. Williams 1979: 424)

14

The consequence of all this was an interesting dynamic. First, the idea of the New Left being a movement had to be rethought in what might be seen subsequently as classically postmodernist terms. The social structures, as well as the patterns of thought that were associated with them, that had been transmitted from the 1930s to the 1960s, underwent a transformation. The idea of the New Left clubs, referring back to the Left clubs of the 1930s, were in many respects equally a spin-off from a parallel tradition, that of the Workers' Educational Association and the local centres for some university extra-mural departments. The Campaign for Nuclear Disarmament (CND), with which some of the clubs were closely associated, had its own antecedents in the various peace movements, the Quakers, the Anarchists, the Rambling Associations, the Council for the Preservation of Rural England, probably also the John Howard/Elizabeth Fry Societies, and a host of other groups which interrelated with each other. These parallel histories and multiple temporalities could hardly be fused together by a common ideological concern, though as CND showed, and, later European CND (ECND) and Charter 88, it was possible to provide a common *minimalist* platform from time to time. The 'death' of the New Left clubs was therefore in many senses inevitable.[7] The growth of new universities and the upgrading of technical colleges and polytechnics to degree-awarding institutions (perhaps the single most important intellectual legacy of the various governments of the 1960s) provided not only a realization of much of the educational campaigning on the Labour left (bringing with it the wider opportunities for students to get degrees and also for New Left intellectuals to get jobs), but also a challenge to the self-help education of the extra-mural departments and the WEA who not only lost some of their leading teachers, but also, further down the road under Thatcher, would lose most of their funding.

Strategically, therefore, the decentring of the New Left was a release. It was, in part, a release from the heavy hand of an ex-Communist commitment (E. P. Thompson's vitriol poured over Perry Anderson's apparent coup, is, in large measure, related to the form within which the left could make itself into a presence.[8] Thompson reserved for himself the form, while preferring to couch his arguments in terms of content. In a very important manner, his conduction of the ECND campaign preserved the form of campaign as a dissident Marxist, while occluding content as a phenomenological reality). But it was also a release in that it allowed the left, not only to explore its own roots, but also to examine the possibility of alternatives. If *everybody* on the left was marginalized, then the issue was surely to explore that marginality.

One of the major effects of this was a remarkable output of research in the 1970s, a fair amount of it stimulated by those new research centres and professional associations that had emerged in the 1960s. Of this the moment of culture was a significant and powerful one. Its roots, as Anderson noted in his article on the national culture, did not lie in philosophy, economics, political theory, sociology or anthropology but in literary criticism: 'in a culture which everywhere repressed the notion of totality, and the idea of critical reason, literary criticism represented a refuge' (P. Anderson 1969: 276). In many respects it was the work of Raymond Williams that set the process in motion, though E. P. Thompson's *William Morris* (1955) and *The Making of the English Working Class* (1963) and Richard Hoggart's *Uses of Literacy* (1957) established the groundwork for constructing an alternative narrative of British life.

Williams's early work, in particular *Culture and Society* (1958) and *The Long Revolution* (1961), set the tone for a British critical theory by tracing an ongoing tradition from 1780 to 1950 in cultural writing, while at the same time providing a framework for rewriting conventional accounts of British history, culture and politics. Several studies have explored Williams's work in some detail,[9] and it would be inappropriate to go over the major themes again, particularly as Williams himself, ten years before his death, engaged in a searching reappraisal of his own work which has provided the basis for all subsequent readings of his remarkably wide-ranging output.[10] Williams's achievement (drawing on the literary critical tradition represented by the Leavises, his reading of Marxist critical theory, and his strong sense of colonial marginality derived from his Welsh roots) was to give to cultural studies a focus on text, social movement and subcultural dissidence which became integral to the development of British cultural Marxism from the 1960s to the 1980s.[11] In many respects he was pivotal in creating the cultural/political sociology which Anderson saw as absent in the British intellectual tradition. He did this, not by taking the external theories as the point-of-departure, but by establishing the internal experiential and textual resources as the base from which theorizing might be possible. It was therefore a cultural studies that was always open to external ideas (Williams, after some hesitation at the end of the 1960s, ultimately saw himself as *European* rather than *British*) but which saw the appropriation of other theories as an occasion to bring into sharper focus the understanding of 'home'. Thus, although *Culture and Society, The Country and the City* (1975), *The English Novel* (1970), or even *The Long Revolution* were basically about the *English*, they were about the English with a Welsh/European theorist looking over the shoulder. It was this sense of the insider/outsider that gave Williams's work its most powerful force. Or, as George Simmel, the German sociologist of the late nineteenth century, might have said, Williams's work was based on the stranger who decided to stay, but who also asked, 'How is this society possible?'

From the late 1960s to the early 1980s these questions were central to all the cultural studies' debates in Britain, and thus redefined both the sense of the individual and of the collective in Marxist theory.

16

The thrust of any kind of cultural theorizing is partly based on an engagement with the communications institutions within which we all have to work. Williams's writing provides such an engagement: university, adult education, journalism, television, drama, radio and language. It is also an attempt to connect the fragments of political experiences of others who are concerned with creating emancipatory practices.

The direction of the debate and the writing in Britain took several forms, of which the following three might be seen as initially the most salient.

NOTES

1 Personal conversation with John Rex.

2 For a somewhat breathless account of the founding of the *New Reasoner* and the exit of the Thompsons and other intellectuals from the CPGB see Wood (1960). A much more comprehensive account is found in Lin Chun (1993).

3 This story obviously needs to be told. The institutional base of the New Left came from an intellectual tradition of popular education which had been established by different routes: the Workers' Educational Association, the extra-mural departments of the universities, the National Council of Labour Colleges, the CPGB, the emergence of Penguin Books and the Left Book Club in the 1930s, and Ruskin College at Oxford. In many senses that tradition had become ingrown. The intellectuals used the experiences of working there as catalysts, but the structures themselves were ossified. They were replaced by the Open University, the Birmingham Centre, the polytechnics and the History Workshop, but with an agenda which was based more on the market than on the free flow of ideas in a political world. But, meanwhile, under the old structures, the promise of the concatenations of solidarity persisted: the new displayed rupture, while ghettoizing the intellectuals.

4 *The May Day Manifesto* (1968) was edited by Raymond Williams with an editorial board that included Edward Thompson and Stuart Hall. First published by the May Day Manifesto Committee in 1967, which draft was almost entirely written by Williams, it was revised, expanded and published by Penguin Books in 1968. The contributors did not include any of the then editorial members of *NLR*.

5 E. P. Thompson, borrowing a metaphor from recent cuts in British Rail, wrote in 1965:

Early in 1962, when the affairs of *New Left Review* were in some confusion, the New Left Board invited an able contributor, Perry Anderson, to take over the editorship. We found (as we had hoped) in Comrade Anderson the decision and intellectual coherence necessary to ensure the review's continuance. More than that, we discovered that we had appointed a veritable Dr. Beeching of the Socialist intelligentsia. All the uneconomic branch-lines and socio-cultural sidings of the New Left which were, in any case, carrying less and less traffic, were abruptly closed down. The main lines of the review underwent an equally ruthless modernisation. Old Left steam-engines were swept off the tracks; wayside halts ('Commitment', 'What Next for C.N.D.?', 'Women in Love') were boarded up; and the lines were electrified for the speedy traffic from the marxistentialist Left Bank. In less than a year the founders of the review discovered, to their chagrin, that the Board lived on a branch-line which, after rigorous intellectual costing, had been found uneconomic. Finding ourselves redundant we submitted to dissolution.

(Thompson 1965; reprinted inThompson 1978: 35)

6 There were, of course, different ways of *translating* European writers. By and large the American academic press chose to translate European authors whose works could either contribute to a Cold War freeze-out or whose writing was so eclectically *academic* that it became part of the cultish research of the universities. Prior to the 1980s very few American publishers saw it as their task to translate work which contributed to a sense of radical movement. Even individual authors were sanitized by American publishers: see my article on Walter Benjamin (Davies 1980).

7 In 1960–2, I was the co-ordinator of the London club. It was interesting then to see that many of the 'clubs' existed largely on paper, or had identities which really derived from other groupings: CND in particular, but also some academic departments, WEA centres, Catholic groups, Welsh and Scottish Nationalists, and the Fife Socialist League. Towards the end of its life, the London club co-ordinated activities with the South Place Ethical Society, Unity Theatre and the Fabian Society, all of which, of course, had existences long before 1960. To have effectively organized a New Left club movement would have required a military-style strategy. Fortunately, none of us was a general.

8 There is another story that needs to be told here, but other people may be able to tell it with greater accuracy. As I recollect it, the *NLR* had received various donations from, among others, Bertrand Russell and Barbara Wootton. At some point, after they saw the first few issues of *NLR*, they decided to call in their money. The *Review* and the London club were then on the point of bankruptcy. A Maecenas emerged. The *Review* was saved. The editorial board changed after a brief transition. The fascinating thing about this version of the story is that the early board of the *Review* believed that people like Russell and Wootton were on their side, *then*. John Strachey was definitely on the side of the *Review* and hovered, melancholically, at many of our meetings. Very few people spoke to him or recognized him. But why not? Did he not see us as people who were trying to do what he had been trying to do, alone, all along? On the other hand A. J. P. Taylor came to one meeting and told me afterwards that the current New Left understood a lot about people's feelings and sense of themselves, but nothing about power. The threads that were connected and torn, to put together the New Left, are multiple.

9 See, in particular, Alan O'Connor (1989) *Raymond Williams: Writing, Culture, Politics*, Oxford: Basil Blackwell.

10 In *Politics and Letters* (1979), Williams was interviewed by the editors of *NLR*, book by book, epoch by epoch, political commitment by political commitment. The book is in many ways not merely a study of Williams's own work, but an account of the political growth of cultural studies on the left.

11 Here I am using 'subcultural' not in the semiotic sense employed by Dick Hebdige in his book *Subculture: The Meaning of Style* (1979) but much more in the sense that Williams uses it in his account of the Welsh as a colonial people:

To the extent that we are a people, we have been defeated, colonized, penetrated, incorporated. Never finally, of course. The living resilience, in many forms, has always been there. But its forms are distinct.

(R. Williams 1989a: 103)

This seems to me not very different from Stuart Hall's reclamation of self in a postmodern world:

So one of the fascinating things about this discussion is to find myself centred at last. Now that, in a postmodern world, you all feel so dispersed I become centered. What I've thought of as dispersed and fragmented comes, paradoxically, to be the representative modern condition! This is coming home with a vengeance.

(Hall 1987)

Both of these statements might be read in the context of developments in the Ukraine, South Africa, Latvia, Croatia, and among the native peoples everywhere in the Americas and the Pacific.

3

THE MODES OF DIFFERENCE

History is made by people. The evaluation of the vital forces making present-day history cannot but be active in this aspect. In order to understand what the classes, parties, and their leaders are struggling for and what is awaiting them tomorrow, we must tear our way through the dense wall of political conventions, lies, and hypocrisy, and the all-pervading parliamentary 'cant' . . . The question that we have set ourselves, and to which we shall endeavour to provide the answer, has an objective character: 'Where is Britain Going?'

(Trotsky, 1960: xvi)

THE PECULIARITIES OF THE ENGLISH

E. P. Thompson's article of this title, first published in the *Socialist Register* in 1965, set a critical standard for asking what comparative social theory is *for*. If Thompson's outrageous pomposity was directed against what he saw as the callow and naive appropriations of other societal models by Perry Anderson and Tom Nairn, the net effect of the article was to demand of the British left a reading of its own history against the acquisition of (foreign) theory which seemed to denounce (domestic) tradition and practice: 'what their schema lack is the control of "grand facts", and England is unlikely to capitulate before a Marxism which cannot at least engage in a dialogue in the English idiom' (Thompson, 1978: 64). The most important work of the 1970s was precisely based on rethinking *foreign* theory in trying to understand 'the peculiarities of the English'. The work of the Centre for Contemporary Cultural Studies (CCCS) at Birmingham and of the History Workshop was notable for teasing out theory in the context of English experience. The theoretical collection, *On Ideology* (Hall *et al*. 1978a), and its *empirical* application, *Policing the Crisis* (Hall *et al*. 1978b), were monuments to the working out of Gramscian-derived theories of the state and culture, finding Althusser heuristic but not definitive. What Althusser had done was to codify Gramsci's idea of civil society so that culture might be seen in institutional terms. This

20

allowed a number of writers to get a 'fix' on cultural projects – Paul Willis's *Learning to Labour* (1977) is a notable example, but so too is Coward and Ellis's *Language and Materialism* (1977) – though the danger that Althusserianism might be simply a Marxist version of functionalism was ever-present. What the debate ultimately did was to produce a Marxist cultural studies that seemed to have three interlocking premises: first, 'Cultural processes are intimately connected with social relations, especially with class relations and class formations, with sexual divisions, with the racial structuring of social relations and with age oppressions as a form of dependency'. Second, 'Culture involves power and helps to produce assymetries in the abilities of individuals and social groups to define and realise their needs'. Third, 'Culture is neither an autonomous nor an externally determined field, but a site of social differences and struggles' (Johnson 1986/7: 39)

Most of the work produced at the CCCS, through the History Workshops and in the writing of individual authors, involved a working out of these problems, though often divided between those who saw that it was important to study cultures, as Johnson (1986/7: 50) puts it, 'as a whole, *in situ*, located in their material context', and those who 'stress[ed] the relative independence or effective autonomy of subjective forms and means of signification'. Although the debate between Perry Anderson and E. P. Thompson seemed in many ways to hinge on these dichotomies, in that Thompson clearly adopted a totalistic, situated perspective, while Anderson seemed to argue from a structuralism that owed much to the linguistic turn in Marxist theorizing, the debate on British culture as it evolved in the 1970s and early 1980s was much richer than these abstractions would suggest.

In *The Poverty of Theory* Thompson argued that

> The investigation of history as process, as eventuation or 'rational disorder', entails notions of causation, of contradiction, of mediation, and of the systematic organisation (sometimes structuring) of social, political, economic and intellectual life. These elaborate notions 'belong' within historical theory, are refined within this theory's procedures, are thought within thought. But it is untrue that they belong *only* within theory. Each notion, or concept, arises out of empirical engagements, and however abstract the procedures of its self-interrogation, it must then be brought back into an engagement with the determinate properties of the evidence, and argue its case before vigilant judges in history's 'court of appeal'. It is, and in a most crucial sense, a question of dialogue once more.
>
> (Thompson 1978: 235)

This was written in response to some of the cruder appropriations of Althusserian Marxism, well summarized by Terry Lovell (1980) in her

wonderful argument for the aesthetics of realism against the schematiciza-
tions of abstract Jesuitical/structuralist logic.

The *real* debate on British culture was on which parts of the past made
sense in confronting the present. Thompson ultimately took the late
eighteenth and early nineteenth centuries as the major vantage-point –
both in *The Making of the English Working Class* (1963) and in *Whigs
and Hunters* (1977) – and much of his attack on the writing in *NLR* is
derived from this and from his own experience in the CPGB.[1] For Stuart
Hall, the CCCS and the History Workshops, the crucial period was

> the profound transformation in the culture of the popular classes
> which occurs between the 1880s and the 1920s ... The more we
> look at it, the more convinced we become that somewhere in this
> period lies the matrix of factors and problems from which *our*
> history – and our peculiar dilemmas – arise. Everything changes –
> not just a shift in the relations of forces but a reconstitution of the
> terrain of political struggle itself.
>
> (Hall 1981a: 229)

Corrigan and Sayer (1985) in their superb historical overview argued that
the defining moment was much earlier, using a span from the Great
revolution to the present to argue that the moment of *that* past was now.[2]
It was this sense of the periodization of history that gave full force to
the writings of Gramsci in much of CCCS work and later to the catch-
phrase 'post-Fordism' which dominated the postmodernist writing of
Marxism Today in the 1980s.[3] The Anderson history agenda, as it turned
out, involved neither of these senses of periodization. His own research
involved a comparative study on the nature of absolutism and a rethinking
both of the concepts 'feudalism' and of the 'Asiatic mode of production',
emphasizing the acquisition of private property as the main distinguishing
feature.[4] Subsequently Anderson argued against both a reading of history
as being homogeneous, 'in which each moment is perpetually different
from every other by being *next*' (he was criticizing the work of Marshall
Berman) or evolutionist in which, as in Lukács, 'time ... differs from one
epoch to another, but within each epoch all sectors of social reality move
in synchrony with each other, such that decline at one level must be
reflected in descent at every other' (P. Anderson, 1984: 101–3). Instead he
argued that Marx's conception of time 'was of a complex and *differential*
temporality, in which episodes or eras were discontinuous from each
other, and heterogeneous within themselves' (ibid.: 101).[5]

The net result of the debate on the peculiarities of the English was
therefore both to set the English experience in relation to global ones
and to posit the crucial moments within British culture when ideology,
class formations and the state, as well as capitalism, took different direc-

tions. Much of the most valuable work in the 1970s precisely explored these issues.

THE SPECIFICS OF THE UNENGLISH

It was inevitable in a country whose imperial pretensions had been pricked away that much of the discussion should hinge on the repercussions of imperialism. One of the marked features of writing in the 1970s was a series of exposures on the culture and politics of the English margins. Tom Nairn's *The Break-up of Britain* (1977), Gwyn Williams's studies of Welsh cultural and social changes,[6] and Raymond Williams's novels and periodical articles on Wales (see O'Connor 1989b for bibliographical details) provided some powerful material for rethinking the situation of the Celtic Fringe, topics which had been largely absent in the 1960s debates, and which had tended to be relegated by the English left and right to lunatic politics.[7] In this material the Europeanness of Celtic as opposed to English culture is constantly stressed, but so also is the problematic role of the state, particularly by Nairn, although in his earlier work the idea that the British state was on the point of break-up had a nostalgic ring to it, based largely on the successes of the Welsh and Scottish Nationalists in parliamentary elections.

The other attack on the Englishness of English culture came from studies on blacks and youth in Britain. Two studies by the CCCS, *Resistance through Rituals* (Hall and Jefferson 1976) and *The Empire Strikes Back* (Solmos *et al.* 1982), dealt with strategies of resistance by teenagers, by blacks and by immigrant Asians. For the most part these were ethnographic studies, providing a theoretically based documentation of their subject-matter. The political underpinning of this research was contained in the volume *Policing the Crisis* (Hall *et al.* 1978b), where the general thrust was rather different from Nairn's. The emphasis was on the crisis of hegemony due to an upset in the 'balance of the relations of class forces' and of the increasing 'reliance on coercive mechanisms and apparatuses already available within the normal repertoire of state power, and the powerful orchestration, in support of this tilt of the balance towards the coercive pole, of an authoritarian consensus' (Hall *et al.* 1978b: 217). The strength of this research was that it located the fragments of British society and brought them into the centre. It confronted the problems of nationalism and ethnicity as integral not only to a rethinking of the problem of class in a changing capitalism, but also (through its reading of Gramsci) provided a reading of the state as a vehicle both for coercion and for the genesis of a rejuvenation of capitalist ideas.[8]

One book out of these concerns displayed the problems of taking subcultures as the point-of-departure. One of the contributors to *Resistance through Rituals* was Dick Hebdige. His book *Subculture: The Mean-*

ing of Style (1979) has become something of a milestone in cultural studies. It was based on a study of white rock music and black reggae as the occasion for looking at punk. As with most of the CCCS material at the time it took an interpretation of hegemony as the launching-pad for its analysis of culture and at the same time used the work of Roland Barthes as the basis for exploring style. It thus attempted to connect two apparently discrepant fields in working out the issue of Why the Punks now? The book was literate, drawing on Jean Genet and T. S. Eliot as well as a range of sociological sources on deviance subculture. But in the end it was a Barthean book, exploring the gap between 'reality' and 'myth', the reader and the 'text'. By proposing a merger between a phenomenologically based Marxist cultural studies and a semiological one, Hebdige instead revealed the rift that would dominate the subject for the next decade, where the surface of 'style', 'simulacrum' and 'textual representation' competed with the located specifics and totality of everyday struggle, though Hebdige's own work has tended since to opt for the stylistic.[9]

THE PARTICULARITIES OF GENDER

The debate on the nature of English society and on the culture/subculture of the margins revealed throughout the 1970s the strong patriarchal basis of New Left discourse. Juliet Mitchell's 'Women – the Longest Revolution' (its title a deliberate play on Raymond Williams's *The Long Revolution*) had appeared in *NLR* 40 in 1966, followed by *Women's Estate* (1971) and *Psychoanalysis and Feminism* (1974). Its point of departure was the work of Jacques Lacan and the linguistic grounding of psychoanalysis, and thus a rethinking both of ideology and feminism. In the introduction to *Psychoanalysis and Feminism*, Mitchell approvingly quoted the French feminist manifesto *Psychoanalyse et politique* which argued that Freudian and Lacanian psychoanalysis provided the theoretical equipment in understanding how ideology functions. Her work, and to some extent that of Jacqueline Rose, was concerned with teasing out the issues of 'how adequately does psychoanalysis analyse ideology and sexuality, and if it does so, what is the political practice that follows from this theory?' (Mitchell 1974: xxii).

The keywords of this investigation, superbly set out in Mitchell's two early books, were 'sexuality', 'phallocentrism', 'femininity', 'production', 'patriarchy', 'ideology', 'reality', and, of course, 'culture'. Its centre of analysis was a structuralist, Marxist and Freudian feminism, setting itself quite distinctly against what it saw as a bourgeois North American feminism which repudiated all pre-feminist theory as being not only phallocentric but also pre-modern. This critique ultimately suggests that North American feminism is bereft of theory, dealing largely in mere polemic, precisely because it denies the concepts of consciousness, the unconscious and production: 'When critics condemn Freud for not taking account of social reality, their concept of that reality is too limited. The social reality that he is concerned with elucidating is the mental representation of the reality of society' (Mitchell 1974: 406).

Thus Marxist feminism brought into cultural studies several fundamental issues which transformed the nature of all subsequent analysis. Significant, first, was the rethinking of the notion of the *subject*, which, bypassing the phenomenological issues of the purely *social* construction of reality and, equally, the merely biological base of most accounts of social differences, argued for the subject as being a linguistic construct. But it is a subject that is capable of redefining itself.[10] And that redefinition is contingent on understanding a patriarchal power structure which uses language to appropriate biology to define the social. As Mitchell (1974: 416) argued at the conclusion of *Psychoanalysis and Feminism*, 'It is not a question of changing (or ending) who has or how one has babies. It is a question of overthrowing patriarchy.'

With this agenda, Marxist feminism also developed further the structural analysis of media and a use of semiotics that could not be seen merely as yet another tool for 'reading' texts, but a politically potent one. It was a reading that had far-reaching consequences. Throughout the 1970s and into the 1980s the influence of structuralist/Marxist/feminism became centre-space for *any* study of the media. *Screen*, in many senses, was dominated by the concerns expressed by the opening to the structuralist/feminist left. In female and male production, from Laura Mulvey to Stephen Frears, it is impossible to avoid the sense that the Eye/I sees all, that the task of production is not to manufacture consciousness (as in the social realism of earlier Marxist-derived documentaries), but to assist in the creation of the self-reflexive eye. The task both of producing and making film became much more complex.

But British feminism did not only grow out of a neo-structuralist reading of Freud, even if for a while that seemed like the most pronounced influence. The academic antecedents of British feminism were as powerful as they were for the whole of the left: literature, history, anthropology and sociology (using whatever theoretical equipment that seemed to be useful) were important catalysts. The work of Sheila Rowbotham, Ann Oakley, Angela McRobbie, Terry Lovell, Valerie Walkerdine, Barbara Taylor, Catherine Hall, Caroline Steedman and Judith Williamson has drawn on a variety of disciplines and theoretical perspectives which have siphoned off from their male counterparts a territory which had appeared to be hermetically sealed-off from the institutional practice of the everyday life of the whole. For example, the work of Sheila Rowbotham, while inspired by E. P. Thompson's uncovering of the history of the dispossessed, not only incorporates gender into the exploration, but also begins to write a narrative in which Thompson would have to rethink himself and his work in relation to a wider whole. Valerie Walkerdine's *Schoolgirl Fictions* (1990) reaches into Foucault, Basil Bernstein, Lacan and many others in order to 'represent a journey, a process of coming into being of a woman who, at last, ceased to be a schoolgirl'. Because feminist studies is necessarily innovative, it is not surprising that its work should be innovative, trying to establish connections across an interdisciplinary terrain, unsuspected by masculine theory. At one level, therefore, feminist writing, as with the most imaginative black or Third World writing, is a renaissance exercise: we start by making new connections across an unchartered intellectual landscape. At another level it is not. In some aspects we have been here before. Feminist work not only provides insertions into the ongoing practices of male thought, but also seeks to redirect our entire practices. Such a venture clearly brings with it the problems of relating theory to practice, which are present in any revolutionary activity. Anti-academism is an ongoing battle in feminist writing. Dorothy Smith, writing from Canada in the late 1980s, has produced a succinct account of how biographical accounts might be incorporated into a Marxist/feminist theory.[11] The implications of such work for cultural studies are clearly political. But, following this, she elaborates on the problems inherent in the project:

> Though we might be able to write a method of inquiry and a method of writing texts that will construct a knowledge of society from the standpoint of outsiders to the relations of ruling, we deceive ourselves if we think that the critical moment is complete in finding new methods of writing sociological texts. Methodological strategies, such as those proposed here, do not transform in and of themselves. They make, or should make, texts that will work differently in coordinating discursive relations, hence the relations forming political consciousness and organization. But they do not work magic. Such strategies themselves become merely academic if they are contained within the relations of academic discourse, even a feminist discourse.... The critical force of these methods is contained and 'institutionalized' if they are not articulated to relations creating linkages outside and beyond the ruling apparatus, giving voice to women's experience, opening up to women's gaze the forms and relations determining women's lives, and enlarging women's powers and capacities to organize in struggle against the oppression of women.

> (Smith 1987: 224–5)

The crucial issue about this is that Smith, using the issue of feminist research, has opened up, once again, the question of the relation between having academic bases and having active political commitment. But the

26

issue, surely, is not whether the discourses will be 'contained within the relations of an academic discourse' but by what dialectic relationship the academic and the wider discourses will relate to each other. The solution is by no means determined, though having academic research which is directed to external practice, or alternatively dictated by external practice, has been decided long ago by business and totalitarian governments. Feminists, like everyone else, need to direct themselves to the issue of the ongoing dynamics of academia as the *base* for research, funded by the state or someone else, and the roots of dissenting culture. This book, I hope, displays some of the logistical problems.

The impulse of feminist research has been to elaborate a culture of difference, a political economy of woman in relation to production/reproduction, and an aetiology of the present situation. The issues are necessarily interrelated. What is, perhaps, clearest in this trajectory is that feminism in Britain is less concerned with acquiring power within the given structures (as North American feminism is), or with overthrowing them (as few feminisms anywhere are), but understanding how women cope with their everyday lives. This may have pushed the study of culture, economics and politics a little towards being aware of feminist concerns, and even provided more women in academe or in the higher levels of business, but it is questionable whether it has shifted any society very far on the road towards becoming feminist. Perhaps it should not. But perhaps, also, feminism (or do I mean women?) has a powerful edge on creating a world which is more humane, more sensitive. Shorn of its legal trappings, that is conceivably the world we would all like to inhabit.

NOTES

1 At the end of *Whigs and Hunters* (1977) Thompson sees the paradox of the rule of law as between 'the cultural moment' which provided the sense of what law might be, and the acceptance of the rule of law by the oligarchs and great gentry 'because this law was serviceable and afforded to their hegemony the rhetoric of their legitimacy.' But 'when the struggles of 1790–1832 signalled that this equilibrium had changed . . . rather than shatter their own self-image and repudiate 150 years of constitutional legality, they surrendered to the law.'

2 Phil Corrigan and Derek Sayer's *The Great Arch* (1985) is certainly one of the most graphic accounts of a narrative which is implanted in the institutions within Britain over the past 400 years, dealing with the formation of the state as integral to cultural practice. Its only rival, in conceptual terms, and also in graphic detail, is Tom Nairn's study of the role of the monarchy, *The Enchanted Glass*, 1988.

3 The large majority of History Workshop books dealt with the period and so did the two CCCS studies of history. See, *inter alia*, Samuel (1981) for papers on some of the research issues, and also Samuel (ed.) *Miners, Quarrymen and Saltworkers* (1977) and Samuel, Ewan MacColl and Stuart Cosgrove (eds) *Theatres of the Left* (1985) for representative samples of History Workshop material. The two CCCS books are John Clarke, Chas Critcher and Richard

Johnson (eds) *Working Class Culture* (1979) and Richard Johnson (ed.) *Making Histories* (1978b).

4 See Perry Anderson's *Passages from Antiquity to Feudalism* (1974b) and *Lineages of the Absolutist State* (1974a).

5 Apart from Anderson's own historical writing, which more or less follows his own premises, the most interesting versions which come closest to this *general* principle might be called near-misses, rather than more conclusive validations of a working historical practice of the theory of multiple temporalities: Thompson's *Whigs and Hunters* (1977), J. G. A. Pocock's *Virtue, Commerce and History* (1985) and Corrigan and Sayer's *The Great Arch* (1985). The work of Derek Sayer, in the round, is an exploration of the problem. See also my own *Writers in Prison* (Davies 1990) for an idiosyncratic crack at confronting the issues in relation to an international theme. In general, however, Walter Benjamin's 'Arcades' project was the single most comprehensive, though incomplete, attempt at working out the inherent problems.

6 See, in particular, Gwyn Williams, *When Was Wales?* (1985) and *The Merthyr Rising* (1979).

7 It is peculiar, to say the least, that the Irish question did not loom large in this Celtic debate, although Nairn (1977) gives a chapter to it. The most important book, which he quotes, is in French: Jean-Pierre Carasso, *La Rumeur irlandaise: guerre de religion ou lutte de classe?* (1970). Richard Rose, *Northern Ireland: A Time of Choice* (1976) is a competent, structural-functionalist account of the Northern Irish situation.

8 There was, of course, another tack on the problem of the 'Other', one which, taking a political-economic stand, saw the central issue as that of interpreting imperialism as *the* central cultural force. If this work did not feed directly into the cultural mode, it was perhaps because the culturalists eschewed anything that smacked of base-superstructure. Several studies throughout the 1960s to the 1980s dealt directly with imperialism and its consequences. Peter Worsley (1964; 1984) wrote two books (the second a full-scale revision of the first) fiercely opposed to the thesis of 'development' that still remains in vogue among American sociologists and political scientists. Ernest Mandel (1962; 1975) wrote several studies on the political economy of post-colonialism and post-capitalism. Robin Blackburn wrote a major study on *The Overthrow of Colonial Slavery* (1988). Perry Anderson's (1974a) studies on the routes to the absolute state, and his brother Benedict's (1983) on how the idea of the new state as well as resistance to it is imagined, all suggested alternative fertile grounds for making sense of the stranger in our midst. There is a smattering of some of this material in the later work of E. P. Thompson (1993a), but in general none of it is brought home to Britain, which, until Paul Gilroy's *There Ain't No Black in the Union Jack* (1987), is a country which exists largely without empire or a political-imperial heritage. When C. L. R. James's *Beyond a Boundary* appeared in 1963, it was reviewed by the sports reporters, but not, to my knowledge, in any left journal.

9 Even though Hebdige has, more than anyone else, maintained in his writing the spirit of the origins of the Birmingham discourse, most of his subsequent work has carefully avoided any of the base/superstructure or power issues. Both *Cut 'n' Mix* (1987), a study of black music in Britain, and *Hiding in the Light* (1988), a collection of essays around, through, and beyond the idea of the postmodern, are monuments to a sensitive imagination which is still exploring the *meaning* of style. His photographic essay, 'Some Sons and their Fathers' (1985) stands with Ronald Fraser's *In Search of a Past* (1986) as a model of

self-critical autobiography, though, interestingly enough, in Hebdige's case it is conducted in terms of photographs.

10 Jacqueline Rose makes this point clear in her introduction to Lacan's *Feminine Sexuality* (1982). In discussing Lacan, she writes:

> There is ... no question of denying here that Lacan was implicated in the phallocentrism he described, just as his own utterance constantly rejoins the mastery which he sought to undermine. The question of the unconscious and of sexuality, the movement towards and against them, operated at exactly this level of his own speech. But for Lacan they function as the question of that speech, and cannot be referred back to a body outside language, a place to which the 'feminine', and through that, women, might escape. In the response to Lacan, therefore, the 'feminine' has returned as it did in the 1920s and 1930s in reply to Freud, but this time with the added meaning of resistance to a phallic organisation of sexuality which is recognised as such. The 'feminine' stands for a refusal of that organisation, its ordering, its identity. For Lacan, on the other hand, interrogating that same organisation undermines any absolute definition of the 'feminine' at all.
>
> Psychoanalysis does not produce that definition. It gives an account of how that definition is produced. While the objection to its dominant term must be recognised, it cannot be answered by an account which returns to a concept of the feminine as pre-given, nor by a mandatory appeal to an androcentrism in the symbolic which the phallus would simply reflect. The former relegates women outside language and history, the latter simply subordinates them to both.
>
> (Lacan 1982: 56–7)

11 Dorothy Smith's *The Everyday World as Problematic* (University of Toronto Press, 1987), while ignoring the Lacanian underpinnings of much of British feminist/Marxism, is a consummate argument on behalf of a decentred, subject-based, feminism which takes the phallocentric institutions as the main problem. The terms of reference, however, are a phenomenological Marxism rather than a structuralist one, which creates a wonderful tension in feminist thinking.

4

NARRATIVE TWO: THE POLITICAL, EDUCATIONAL AND MEDIA SITES OF CULTURAL THEORY

Britain had now acquired a new radical intelligentsia. It overflowed from higher education into broadcasting, journalism, publishing, architecture, design and a multitude of white-collar jobs of which computing was the largest. After the war marxists such as John Saville, Raphael Samuel, and later the contributors to the *New Left Review*, had been marginal men. Now in the seventies they appeared as epic figures on campus.

(Annan 1990: 381)

TRANSITION

The ultimate problem, indicated in Dorothy Smith's quote at the end of Chapter 3, was that cultural studies would move from being part of a social movement to being an appendix of academe, so institutionalized that it became simply a continuation of the classics and humanities traditions which had for long acted as the basis of a critique against the disciplinariness of the universities. But, of course, cultural studies had roots which were independent of academe, just as classics had its roots in the church and in the imperial civil service. And yet they were curious roots, part social movement, part the commonsensicality of a *déclassé lumpenintelligentsia*. With one or two individual exceptions (Raymond Williams at Cambridge and Terry Eagleton at Oxford, in both cases under the aegis of literature), cultural studies did not become accepted at the old, established universities, with the exception of Birmingham where it snuck in through the back door, as it were. And yet, its publications and its influences were everywhere, indeed, to such an extent that throughout the 1980s the conservative media (mainly the Murdoch and Conrad Black papers) conducted a systematic campaign against the cultural left and its supposed influence in the media and educational institutions.

Anyone reading this material in, say, 1982 would have been struck by how much the debate which had been generated by cultural Marxism had done to give Marxist thinking an agenda for political action. The critique of the state had been appropriated as a cultural reading/misreading of the space that everyone was inhabiting, writing on the national and ethnic 'margins' of British society suggested what were the problems at the core, feminist writing and group action were undermining the very basis of a patriarchal society, and the general sweep of cultural studies was questioning not only the academic disciplines' sense of themselves (were they a pushover?) but also the conventional wisdoms of the media, the politicians and the apparatus of state, schooling and business. Not only was all of this being debated, but also the idea that the real point of culture was to understand surface appearances independent of the social structures which might ostensibly have given meaning had become part of the rhetoric of both academic and public cultural writing. Gramsci's sense of creating a counter-hegemony became a point of action, and in some ways was put into action (witness the former Greater London Council between 1981 and 1986, and the development of Black Film in the mid-to-late 1980s).[1]

Any critique of British cultural studies has to reflect on its theory and the consequences of action. If most of what has been said before represents cultural studies as it seemed to be in the early 1980s, three other themes, because they became the bread-and-butter of work after 1980, need to be taken into account before we re-collect this argument. The first, because it speaks of judgement and distinction, is aesthetics. The second, because it speaks of power and the reading of hegemony, is representation. The third, because it speaks of the politics of the everyday, is popular culture. Before launching into this, however, it is useful to consider the work of four authors whose work dominated the period from 1956 into the 1980s, as their themes acted as a template for the ways that the discourse around cultural theory was structured. The fact that they are all men (Raymond Williams, E. P. Thompson, Stuart Hall and Perry Anderson) is deliberate, because it was only in the 1980s (see Chapter 3) that the feminist critique established a body of work that was independent of the male-driven preoccupations. But it seems important to consider these authors as educationalists, whose work would affect the ways in which cultural studies would enter the academic institutions.

PEDAGOGY, CURRICULUM, EDUCATIONAL STRUCTURE

The major disputes around the New Left during the 1960s already established the grounds on which cultural theory would develop during the next two decades. In this the work of four authors stands out not only because of their theoretical agendas, but also because of their different senses of the political implications of their work. Those differences, hinted at in earlier parts of this book, became in important respects the ongoing problematics that cultural theory had to contend with in the remaining decades of the century.

Raymond Williams (1921–88), E. P. Thompson (1924–93), Stuart Hall (b. 1931) and Perry Anderson (b. 1940) all wrote about cultural theory, and all contributed to the emergence of cultural studies as an ongoing critique of politics and the preoccupations of the media and of academics. They did this by being necessarily interdisciplinary, though their most important published work had major impact within one or two specific disciplines. Two – Hall and Williams – held regular academic posts, Thompson, with the exception of five years in the 1960s (see pp. 49–54), was more outside academia than inside it, while Anderson travelled around universities – Reading, Birmingham – holding research fellowships before ultimately being given a chair of history at the University of California at Los Angeles (UCLA) in the 1980s. These different affiliations necessarily affected the base of their work. All of them wrote popular political pieces as well as major books. Williams and Thompson wrote fiction and drama as well as their other work. All of them edited magazines or journals at one time or another, and all of them throughout their lives were on the boards of magazines and journals. The disciplinary springboards of their work came from history in the cases of Thompson and Anderson, literature and drama in the case of Williams, and sociology and media studies in the case of Hall (though he progressed from literature to cultural studies to political sociology throughout his career). Both Thompson and Hall were instrumental in establishing academic graduate/research centres. Williams and Thompson started their academic careers as teachers with university adult education departments, Hall and Anderson started theirs as editors of *New Left Review*. Thompson's father was a Methodist missionary who converted to Buddhism, while Anderson and his brother, Benedict, were brought up as children attached to the diplomatic corps; Williams was the son of a Welsh railwayman, Hall came from Jamaica to Britain as a Rhodes Scholar. In terms of generations, Williams and Thompson were born in the early 1920s, Hall in the early 1930s, Anderson in 1940. Thompson and Anderson went to English private schools, Hall and Williams did not. Hall is black, the others are white.

Another way of reading all this is that if Thompson and Anderson came from a somewhat privileged English background, it was one which had been exposed to international contacts, travel, languages and politics. Williams came from a Welsh industrial background, and then proceeded by scholarships to study at Cambridge: he rarely travelled, and his sense of the international was firmly rooted in Britain (the dichotomy between the Celts and the English) and by reading. Hall, coming from Jamaica, went to Oxford as a Rhodes Scholar, saw himself as marginalized in Britain: both the New Left and cultural studies were means of making sense of, and politicizing, that marginalization. Getting to the central pinnacle of British academic life, and then finding the culture of that academe as being at least problematic, at worst as hostile to ideas which were outside its taken-for-granted assumptions, was perhaps the most important bond in their work and their politics.

Thus the reasons why these four sit at the apex of dissident academic culture in Britain has as much to do with their deconstructing of privilege (their privilege) as it has to do with the specific ideas that they generated. Many have found themselves in this position, and there is an important tradition of dissenting elite culture in England which has created an important, if controversial, path through all definitions of what the culture is about. What had probably never happened was that a group of the recipients of the cultural largesse would try to pick it apart, bit-by-bit, in order to create a different culture. The nearest parallel was the adult education movement, which had its impetus in 1867 with the formation of the Northern Council for the Promotion of Higher Education for Women (persuading Cambridge University to 'supply peripatetic lecturers who toured a circuit of northern towns offering lectures to women on variety of topics from astronomy to literature' – Lovell 1990: 25–6) culminating in the establishment of the University Extension Movement in 1873. This was certainly a top-to-base movement, which tried to bring the fruits of elite culture to working people (hence the Workers' Educational Association, Ruskin College and the extra-mural departments of the universities), the last serious radicalization of which was the Oxford Extra-Mural Delegacy under Thomas Hodgkin in the immediate post-1945 period, and the growth of the Leeds extra-mural department shortly thereafter.[2]

The moment of the New Left, as we are considering it, particularly as it inserted itself into the teaching spaces of higher education, was the attempt to combine theory with academic practice. There were four examples, largely all initiated in the 1960s, which set the mark for how the relationship between radical theory and pedagogical practice would unravel over the next two decades. The first was the establishment of the Centre for Contemporary Cultural Studies in Birmingham in the mid-1960s; the second was the creation of new universities (including, in particular, the Open University) at about the same time, which allowed for new programmes both of research and teaching; the third was the conversion of polytechnics into degree-giving institutions, thus also allowing for the creation of new degrees and programmes; the fourth was the creation of networks (History Workshop; *Screen*; *Radical Philosophy*; Writers & Readers; *m/f*) which, although technically outside academia, became an important base for influencing what academics felt that they were about. Beyond this, there were other spaces (in media, community action and social work) which established a stance for a critique which had a direct impact on what happened in academe, and, to a large extent, outside it. This broad-based institutional attack on the pillars of establishment knowledge (created largely by liberals) provided the nexus for the sites of discourses in and around cultural Marxism in the 1980s and 1990s.

Given that the politics and culture of academia were in many respects the point of departure, several written pieces stand out in the analysis that establish the links and differences between each of the four people considered here. They range from the immediately political to the exponentially theoretical, though obviously they are all interrelated. E. P. Thompson's study of Warwick University being taken over by business interests is clearly a gut, though theoretical and well-researched, response to an immediate event.[3] His *Poverty of Theory* (1978) is an attempt at situating ideology not only in its theoretical senses, but also in pedagogical and generational ones. Raymond Williams's long series of pieces on knowledge and power, particularly as they are rethought in *Politics and Letters* (1979), is an attempt to come to terms with the parameters of what determines culture and also those points of resistance that try to redirect it.[4] Stuart Hall primarily at the Centre for Contemporary Cultural Studies in Birmingham, supervised a series of studies which had a direct bearing on the culture of the elite. His *The Hard Road to Renewal* (1989a), written after he moved to the Open University, displays the consequences of a supine radicalism, while *On Ideology* (Hall *et al.* 1978a) lays out the theoretical parameters. Perry Anderson's early essays tried to establish the ideological fragments of what passed for English culture, particularly in academe, contrasting them with the vibrancy of other intellectual traditions, while his later essays, drawing more on the systematizations of pan-Atlantic intellectual holisms, suggested that elite culture had more to say than that of the dissident or dispossessed.[5]

Drawing on the work of Michael Halliday,[6] Pierre Bourdieu,[7] and Mary Douglas,[8] Basil Bernstein, Professor of the Sociology of Education at the University of London, provided a way of understanding the curriculum which became extremely influential in pedagogical circles in the 1970s. In it, he argued, schematically, that most of knowledge was organized both by the way it was classified into discrete areas of speciality, and also by the mode in which the educational structure framed that knowledge. He argued that within schools and universities knowledge was either collected into specialized or non-specialized disciplines because of the bureaucratic rationality of the curriculum or else it was presented as an integrated whole through teachers. The enormous fun of this graphic account of knowledge was that it allowed educational sociologists both to place their own pedagogical practices and also to situate their utopian ideals within other existing models. Unlike Bourdieu, whose power/knowledge nexus was infinitely French in all its examples, Bernstein, by adding the Mary

Douglas equation of rites of purity and definitions of exclusion, and Halliday's network theory and theory of language functions, was able to cast the net wider. In Bourdieu the structure of knowledge boundaries was founded on an almost exact description of what occurred in France: deviations were deviations within the French paradigm. Mary Douglas's appropriation of Lévi-Strauss's structuralism to rituals of eating, hygiene, intellectual life and economic behaviour provided a wider base from which to examine any set of symbolic relationships. The important feature of this anthropological exercise was that it allowed for alternatives to a single mythic structure, but interrelated with an analysis of power relations which was absent from the structuralist format. If, ultimately, all of this theorizing was 'dead' in that it did not allow for subjects being their own agents, at least it provided a map within which the limits of action might be traced. In addition, Halliday's linguistic theories helped to show '*different* linguistic relations of different contexts *and* decide whether each context had evoked either a restricted or an elaborated variant. We now could examine both the emphasis and the range of choices (alternatives) an individual took up in the network' (Bernstein 1971a: 269). What Bernstein did further with this set of interconnecting structures was to create a model of change which distinguished between a moral crisis of society and the state of the educational system. The trend, he argued, was 'away from collection to integrated codes' which symbolized 'a crisis in society's basic classification and frames, and therefore a crisis in its structures of power and principles of control' (Bernstein 1971a: 67). But, in many ways, this suggested that all societies were always in a state of crisis, and thus crisis was a state of stasis. Durkheim's anomie had been turned against either Bernstein's or Durkheim's intentions into a permanent state of affairs. The history of the New Left's involvement in pedagogy exemplified both the critical sense that crisis was a creative catalyst, but also Bernstein's sense that there were limits to how it might grow.

STUART HALL AND THE CENTRE FOR CONTEMPORARY CULTURAL STUDIES/THE OPEN UNIVERSITY

The establishment of the Centre for Contemporary Cultural Studies at Birmingham University is an important place to start both because of its ultimate stamp on cultural studies and because of its unique pedagogical focus. The Centre was founded by Richard Hoggart, who taught in the English department, out of a concern (revealed in his book *The Uses of Literacy*) that English departments did not bother themselves with how the teaching of English travelled beyond the immediate boundaries both of the curriculum and of its teachers. The Centre was therefore initially concerned with 'a more critical engagement between literary studies and the general culture of contemporary society'. This was soon expanded to studying

> cultural values, attitudes, forms and relationships in a period of transition and crisis; paying special attention to the ways this pattern of change expresses itself in, and is in turn shaped and moulded by, expressive forms – language, media, images, symbols and myths – within which the society conducts the dialogue with itself.[9]

By 1966 Stuart Hall had joined the Centre as deputy director and by 1970 was acting director (Hoggart having gone to Paris as assistant director-general for humanities, culture and social sciences at UNESCO).[10] Until it was established as an independent unit in the Faculty of Arts in 1974, Hoggart and Hall were the only full-time faculty at the Centre. After 1974, when Hoggart formally resigned, there were two and a half (Richard Johnson joining from History and Michael Green being split with English). For much of the 1960s Hall's salary was paid through a grant from Sir Allen Lane, proprietor of Penguin Books.

There are several intriguing features of the Centre which deserve comment. They are the organization of work at the Centre; the publications and their influence; the theoretical space that the Centre inhabited; and, ultimately, the relationship of the Centre to the University of Birmingham. Emerging as a postgraduate research centre within the English department, the early years of the Centre were much influenced by Hoggart and the English affiliation, eclectically concentrating on various aspects of popular culture. By 1968, however, a much more systematic agenda began to emerge. A series of occasional papers in cultural studies, and, later, working papers in cultural studies (which were subsequently published as books by Hutchinson, giving them a much wider circulation), and stencilled occasional papers in cultural studies, revealed not only the broad range of thematic concerns but also the attempt to provide a theoretical core to the work of the Centre. The problem was Marx. As Stuart Hall wrote much later:

> the encounter between British cultural studies and Marxism has first to be understood as the engagement with a problem – not a theory, not even a problematic. It begins, and develops through the critique of a certain reductionism and economism, which I think is not extrinsic but intrinsic to Marxism; a contestation with the model of base and superstructure, through which sophisticated and vulgar Marxism alike had tried to think the relationships between society, economy and culture. It was located and sited in a necessary and prolonged and as yet unending contestation with the profound Euro-centrism of Marxist theory. . . . The only theory worth having is that

which you have to fight off, not that which you speak with profound fluency.

(Hall, 1992a: 279–80)

Such a 'contestation' with Marxism was not without its internal and external problems. The internal fights were many: they involved Alan Shuttleworth, the senior research associate in the late 1960s concerned with television research, a feminist caucus (the fight resulted in the departure from the programme of Rosalind Coward and John Ellis, who were seen as hidebound Lacanians, as well as the publication of *Women Take Issue* (Women's Study Group 1978) where feminists at the Centre demanded an issue of the working papers to themselves), and probably, though there is nothing on record, Richard Hoggart. Some student members of the Centre complained that the 'contestation' with Marxism left little time to think about theorists whose stance was implicitly critical of Marx from quite different perspectives: Vico, Nietzsche, Bataille – all missing. Even the great critics of imperialism – Harold Innis, Frantz Fanon, C. L. R. James, Gilles Deleuze and Mikhail Bakhtin (except when he masqueraded as a linguist) – were absent from the roster of international theorists who were central to the agendas of the Centre. Beyond this, for a centre which was concerned with culture, there were other curious blind thematic spots: painting, sculpture, architecture, theatre, museums, theme parks, the colonization of nature. The omissions (though Janet Wolff, who subsequently wrote books on the sociology of art, was an 'attached student' in the late 1960s)[11] meant that issues of the aesthetics of cultural performances and institutions were either ignored or reduced to the analysis of production. Thus, although Marx was contested, he was, perhaps, not contested enough. The language of the work of the Centre was earnestly Jesuitical and Presbyterian, as if the task was to create science rather than gay science, to struggle towards the invention of political correctness than to become politically playful.

The moment of Althusser and Gramsci (a long moment, consuming most of the waking and sleeping days of the 1970s)[12] became the apogee of trying to reach the transcendental while keeping feet firmly on the ground. The tramp through the dialectical minefields produced some powerful dialogue inside and outside the Centre. From inside the Centre, the collection of essays *On Ideology* (Hall *et al.* 1978a) as well as various articles by Stuart Hall and Richard Johnson give a sense of the struggle with structuralist Marxism in the Centre.[13] As an *internal* development it revealed some of the problems raised by Basil Bernstein. The work of the Centre, under Hoggart, was based on an impure version of subject collection: the discipline of English literature acted as the lode-star for the entire exercise. English was the discipline, cultural studies the subdiscipline. That exercise worked as long as it was recognized that cultural studies was a debate around the meaning of what literature (reading, writing, interpreting) meant. In this sense, although the individual teachers mattered as personal catalysts, they mattered less in terms of the *collection* of knowledge which operated in relation to a received body of work. After 1968, however, as Stuart Hall became the effective director, the problem changed to needing a paradigm for what cultural studies meant. This involved knowing who were the cultural students, what was cultural studies directed *towards*, what was the organizing thematic.

The moment of Althusser and Gramsci of course revealed that if cultural studies was to stake out a terrain for itself, it needed a body of interconnecting ideas (and practices) which situated cultural studies not only against the other disciplines but also against the dominant ideas of what British culture was about. The choice of the European Marxists was not only due to Stuart Hall's reading of Raymond Williams, E. P. Thompson and Perry Anderson (see the Fifth and subsequent Reports of CCCS), but also due to the necessity, if a new discipline was being founded, of pulling together threads from other discourses. In spite of the collectivist tendency of the Centre, it was clear that the most important person in leading the Centre from a collection to an integrated mode of work was Stuart Hall.[14] Thus the integration of different themes and subjects was focused on the teacher who collected all modes into a commonly shared conception of what the new 'discipline' was about. Even though Pierre Bourdieu and Roland Barthes were 'doing' cultural studies in Paris, Umberto Eco in Milan, Ma and Pa Brown in Bowling Green and Marshall McLuhan in Toronto, Stuart Hall popularized the term 'cultural studies' (appropriated from Hoggart and Williams) by developing a theoretical paradigm that would stand at the centre of what it was conceived of as being.

In his account of CCCS, Lawrence Grossberg (1993) has attempted to provide a map of how to read the activities at the Centre both as 'normative history' and as 'narrativizing a war of positions'. The central feature of this account is the argument that

> Its history is a history of political engagements and theoretical debates in response to which alternative positions are constantly being taken into account and new positions offered. In this process, the very questions at the heart of cultural studies – its problematic – are constantly being reshaped and reinflected.
>
> (Grossberg 1993: 22)

Thus to create a linear reading of cultural studies is mistaken, although Grossberg under 'normative history' provides a brief summary of such a reading, noting the sequential development from the 'early' socialist humanism (Williams, Hoggart, Thompson), through the engagements with other forms of cultural critique (the Frankfurt School, symbolic interactionism, ethnomethodology, semiotics), to the debates around Gramsci via Althusser, to a Gramscianism which 'defined cultural studies as a non-reductionist marxism which was concerned with understanding specific historical contexts and formations, which assumed the lack of guarantees in history and the reality of struggles by which historical relationships are produced' (Grossberg 1993: 29). A continuation of this linear account would see the development of a debate with postmodernism as the logical extension.

Grossberg contests this reading of the CCCS history as not being open to the 'greater complexities'. To do this, he posits seven theoretical problematics (epistemology, determination, agency, structure of the social formation, structure of the cultural formation, power, specificity of cultural struggle) and places over it a 'reinscribed' narrative structure of the development of cultural studies:

I   the literary humanism (of Hoggart and Williams);
II the early eclectic effort to define a dialectical sociology;
III the first distinctly 'Centre' position' ('culturalism');
IV a structural-conjuncturalist position; and
V   a post-modern conjuncturalist position.

(Grossberg 1993: 33)

Grossberg argues that the point of doing this, while 'artificial', suggests 'something about the multiple sites and vectors along which the wars of positions are constantly fought' (p. 33). The rest of the article uses this revised narrative structure to think through the ways in which the theoretical problematics are worked over and rethought. Its advantage, clearly, is that it does not impose linear narrative on the work of the members of the Centre, nor does it foreclose debates as if the issues that were debated have a finitude because of their calendar sites. On the other hand, Grossberg's interpretation and his appropriation do raise some concerns. These are addressed in the final chapter of this book.

It is important here, before we continue with the narrative, to enter a caution about the ways in which Gramsci and Althusser were *read*. Gramsci's *Notebooks* were written in prison, and much of them in code in order to avoid the prison censors. The text that finally came out in English in 1971 was translated by two British Althusserians, complete with a long introductory essay on how to read him. The Gramsci that Italian-disadvantaged British scholars read was thus both pre-selected (for 'relevance'?) and doubly translated. That Gramsci had a personal life (see Davies 1990: 144–50; de Lauretis 1987: 84–94, for brief accounts of Gramsci's relations with women), a biological (hunchbacked) presence and a social status as an islander (he was a Sardinian) did not figure in the accounts that people chose to read. He had become his translators. In addition there was the important fact that Gramsci's writing was part of another genre (beyond his Marxism), that of prison epistles (along with some of the work of e.g. Rosa Luxemburg, St John the Divine and Boethius)[15] and that the business of 'reading' Gramsci had multiple layers, of which the proto-Althusserian Marxist cultural critique was merely one.

The same is true of Althusser. His life included spending six years in a prison camp in Germany throughout the Second World War, training for the priesthood, working under the supervision of Gaston Bachelard (writing a thesis on Hegel), suffering from manic-depression for the last forty-five years of his life, conducting an internal battle with the French Communist Party, and trying to construct a systematic Marxism which would do for Marxism what Aquinas did for Catholic theology. Within his work, there is much evidence of contradiction and revision, based on taking into account points made by his critics. (See Geras 1971 for a succinct early critique, and Norris 1991 for a measured later one.) A deconstructive and dialogic reading of Althusser would be a major place to start. Thompson's diatribe against Anderson hints at the possibilities, but does not flesh them out.

The appropriation of both of these authors as templates of theory as opposed to people with their own life and social struggles might have been avoided if another voice had been allowed to be heard. Lucien Goldmann's *The Hidden God* was published in English in 1964. If it had problems in terms of deciding why we should read one author rather than another – Goldmann decided that 'Pascal's work marks the great turning-point in Western thought' (Goldmann 1964: 5) – there was much less of a problem if, having decided to read them, we should decide why they were significant and how their significance came about. Goldmann's book was situated in a movement (the tension between Catholicism, Jansenism and Calvinism in seventeenth-century France). It centred on two authors (Pascal and Racine) whose work operated on a tension between their social status and the movements to which they were affiliated. Both authors (in particular Pascal) were concerned with making sense of contradictory social and epistemological realities. The issue was to understand their particular vision, which Goldmann terms 'tragic'. The methodology of studying their work and their times was immaculate, laid out in the first 163 pages of the book. Goldmann also, like the English New Left on Gramsci and Althusser, found key terms in Pascal and Racine which acted as the central metaphors, mythologies. But the difference between the New Left's appropriation of Gramsci and Althusser was that Goldmann left us a text which allowed us to read all, which forced us back to read Pascal and Racine before we could dare to situate them for ourselves. Goldmann's book defies quotation because the whole book is quotable.

Thus the problem with the Althusserian paradigm was that it was imported, and, if decontextualized, immediately recontextualized in a site not of its own choosing. The furious debates in England in the 1970s and early 1980s were focused both on the word 'experience' and on 'structure'. In a derelict church in Oxford in December 1979, Stuart Hall, Richard Johnson and E. P. Thompson faced off. It was clearly not a meeting to express left-wing solidarity. Thompson had published a savage attack on the Althusserian 'turn' in British cultural Marxism. *The Poverty of Theory* (1978), a salvo across the bows of the 'new' New Left, and a response by Richard Johnson (1978a) in *History Workshop Journal* entitled 'Thompson, Genovese and Socialist Humanist History', was the occasion for the event, reported in detail in Raphael Samuel's collection, *People's History and Socialist Theory* (1981: 376–408). There have been several detailed accounts of this dispute, which can be consulted for more intense documentation,[16] but what is important here is how the dispute raised the issue of the status of cultural studies in relation to other disciplines, and to an ongoing tradition of looking at British culture.

In this particular debate the discipline concerned was history. Because the CCCS had placed 'theory' at centre-stage in its engagements with culture, and because much of that theory necessarily involved writing about history (one of the two-and-a-half teachers at Birmingham was a historian whose academic next-door neighbour was Dorothy Thompson), the historians, and in particular socialist historians, were obliged to take this intrusion on their turf seriously. The encounter with History Workshop was, in many respects, the only likely venue for such a debate. History Workshop (HW), founded as a series of seminars and meetings at Ruskin College, Oxford, in 1967, began publishing the *Journal* in 1976. HW was an interlocking series of networks, involving, to quote Raphael Samuel (1981: xii), 'Feminist history groups, community-based publishing projects, local history workshops, regional labour history societies, oral history groups, independent writers and specialist scholars' as well as socialists working and teaching in universities and polytechnics. It was thus, in many respects, an umbrella organization for socialist history (other journals existed – notably *Past and Present*, *Oral History*, *Social History*, *Feminist Studies* as well, of course, as the *New Left Review*, the working papers of CCCS and a series of regional journals). History Workshop, however, combined the work of academics and non-academics, of engineers and schoolteachers, of folksingers and theatre directors. It was, and still remains, the only forum for such encounters and collaborative work, with an influence that extends far beyond Britain. More than cultural studies, for reasons which will be outlined later, it represents an intellectual social movement with resources and a sense of agency which goes beyond history as an academic discipline.

To understand the uniqueness of the passions aroused by Althusser in Britain, it is useful to contrast it with other adaptations. In Slovenia, the work of Althusser (as well as Jacques Lacan) has been taken as integral to rethinking the subject–structure dualism, by debating the issue of subject as substance, and thus providing a fruitful way of rethinking the concept of alienation in Marx. This is developed particularly by Slavoj Zizek in *The Sublime Object of Ideology* (1990), centrally in Chapter 6. Much of this thinking has reclaimed both Lacan and Althusser as rationalists in the tradition of the Enlightenment, while at the same time prizing them away from the label of post-structuralism.

Equally different are the uses to which the American cultural critic Fredric Jameson puts both Althusser and Lacan. His first book, *Marxism and Form* (1971), was a much more generous reading of phenomenological and existentialist Marxism than anything that appeared in Britain then or later, establishing the grounds for reading the Marxists which was both historically grounded and philosophically sophisticated. Later, in his first chapter of *The Political Unconscious* (1981), while Jameson treats these authors as structuralists, it is a structuralism which is crucial to an understanding of the dichotomies that are present in any account of history and narrative. Furthermore, Althusser is no Stalinist (as Thompson would have him), but his work

> may now be understood as a coded battle waged within the framework of the Communist Party against Stalinism. 'Hegel' here is a secret code word for Stalin (just as in Lukács' work, 'naturalism' is a code word for 'socialist realism'.
>
> (Jameson 1981: 37)

In contrast to the canonical post-structuralists, such as Roland Barthes, who deal with

> a random operation of multiple codes, the Althusserian/Marxist conception of culture requires this multiplicity to be reunified, if not at the level of the work itself, then at the level of its process of production, which is not random but can be described as a coherent functional operation in its own right.
>
> (Jameson 1981: 56)[17]

The British issue, of course, revolves around the context of how the theories were appropriated. Although the debate around Althusser in Britain was ostensibly about theory, it was at least as much about academic discipline and political memory. The historians that collected in History Workshop were largely concerned with themselves as agents of history and practice. Thompson's great evocation of reclaiming the working-class dead from the 'enormous condescension of posterity' had a double message: both to reclaim the dead and to give voice to the living. This message provided the animating core to the work of the History Workshop, generating and galvanizing an evangelical sense of purpose. What Althusser seemed to be saying was that what they were up to was only tangentally related to either what other people were doing or to the social and ideational structures that were the determining factors of their everyday lives. If people make their own history, it was important to recognize that it was not in the way of their own choosing. History Workshop was about how people made their history: structural Marxism was about understanding how that sense of making was foreclosed by language, ideological territoriality and political economy. Clearly this implied a functionalist agenda, with a narrative that read like determinism. As in many ways Thompson had written *The Making of the English Working Class* against such a reading of history, the emergence of a Marxist structural-functionalism posed similar questions about agency.[18] More than that, it posed serious questions about the sense of agency of the historians themselves.

It is important to note, however, that the debate around Althusser had a notable silence. Throughout the acrimonious exchanges between Thompson, Johnson, Anderson and Hall, not one woman's voice was heard. Why was this? With the exception of Janet Wolff (whose work is discussed in the next chapter) the core elements of the debate were simply not considered very relevant to women. As Terry Lovell has written:

> This silence was eloquent not of empirical hostility to theory, but of a dissatisfaction with a *Marxist* theory. For there was nothing critically at stake in the debate for the project of women's history. Each rival formation offered some space within which a feminist historiography might be and was developed, but the history of women was not insistently required to be there as a central condition of the theory. . . . Increasingly feminist historians associated with the [History Workshop] Journal were turning to other, or additional sources to meet their needs for theory, and especially towards psychoanalysis. Marxism permits feminist history, but without necessarily permitting it to *make a difference*. While psychoanalysis is every bit as male centred as Marxism, because it theorizes sexual difference and sexed subjectivity, then feminist intervention here *must* make a difference.
>
> (Lovell 1990: 24–5)

The feminist appropriation of Lacan therefore makes a certain conceptual sense. The feminist 'reply' to the Althusser debate in the pages of the *History Workshop Journal* was Sally Alexander's (1984) Lacanian essay 'Women, Class and Sexual Differences in the 1830s and 1840s: Some Reflections on the Writing of a Feminist History' (reprinted in Lovell 1990). Whether ignored or not, the debate around Althusser was ultimately a debate which posed the question 'For Whom (or why) are we doing this?

That was a question which came to haunt cultural studies as a political and academic practice. The work of CCCS was necessarily a positioning of cultural studies against the activities of existing academic departments. To do that effectively, however, it had to establish a connecting thread of critical theory as well as creating a political site within which (inside and outside academia) its work would be taken seriously. The academic departments which came closest to its interests were literature (English, French and German), history, political science, sociology, and the emerging studies of mass communications, film and popular culture. The subsequent development of cultural studies around the world indicates that its presence was largely felt by these disciplines, who either rejected it outright or appropriated it to their own ongoing concerns (see the concluding chapter of this book). As a political agenda, however, cultural studies had no visible agents or actors, no networks, no commandeering heights of the economy: it operated by secreting itself into the body politic, a samizdat of computers, publishing houses, venues, which bent and reformed themselves. If it existed as a political force, it was guerrilla war against the political centre, or else as the avant-garde of the nomadic cultural elite.

There are two contrasting interpretations, from the outside, of what all this added up to. Paul Johnson dedicated his column ('And Another Thing') in the *Spectator* from the late 1980s to the early 1990s to complaining how the 'Left' had taken over television, the *Guardian*, IBM, the British Film Institute, Oxford University, the Institute of Contemporary Arts, the National Theatre, and every other totem of national culture. The paranoid bile spilled out in every column. The 'Left' was unbelievably powerful, its tentacles grasping everything that might be seen as culture. An ugly spectacle of the 'Left' taking over everything was essentially a mode, structured by the Thatcherism of the moment.

The other version, contained in Dan Farson's (1987) book on Soho, which traces the interpersonal accounts of those who lived in this square mile of London from the 1930s to the 1980s, is that the 'Left' did not exist. Although the *New Left Review* has been in Soho since the late 1950s, there is no mention of it in Farson's book. Its members drank in the Coach and Horses and the French, ate in the Gay Hussar (if they were well-off) and Danny's (if they were poor). All went to Ronnie Scott's Jazz Club and the Marquee. They are not in Farson's book because Farson and his ilk did not think that they were important. Wardour Street, with its scattering of the media industry, and the Post Office (now British Telecom) tower gazing down on it all get nary a mention. And yet, and yet: E. P. Thompson, his hair flying in the wind, showing us Poland Street and William Blake's home and purpose, Stuart Hall, talking animatedly with Colin MacInnes and Ray Gosling, Perry Anderson, buying up former strip-joints to furnish the *NLR* with premises that it could live with, Juliet

Mitchell and Jacqueline Rose trying to reclaim the Soho twilight as a habitable communicable space, and Raphael Samuel, Ewan MacColl and Angela Carter on the flying trapeze. If Johnson's Soho was conspiratorial and malevolent, Farson's is marked by its silences, the silence of the apolitical transients who could never make sense of the politics around them. O God! What a droll world. This space, this infinite space of one square mile, still does not have its historian, because the oral history has been left to journalists who, rather than do research, chose to binge with the putatively famous, like Jeffrey Bernard or Peter O'Toole.[19]

The irony of all this is that the real strength of cultural Marxism was its decentredness, its sense of reclaiming the fragments of a culture that had been overcentred. In many respects the incursions of the left into the new media placed it in no more pivotal position than it had ever been. No major heights of the media were 'taken over'. What did happen, however, was that, because of the creation of the Open University, a media/educational site was found which made the debates between members of the cultural studies left much more public than they might have been. Two studies by David Harris (1987; 1992) provide the occasion for examining just how important was this influence on thinking around pedagogy, political action and culture.

In the early 1970s, when the Open University finally got off the ground, there were two centres which provided the catalysts for thinking about the relationship between education, society and culture. These were the Institute of Education at London University and the CCCS. Both of them were engaged in an eclectic search for different models: symbolic interaction, Frankfurt critical theory, semiotics, ethnomethodology, structuralism, Marxism, empiricism and linguistics. The British Sociological Association's annual conference in 1970 displayed this eclecticism, but tended to emphasize phenomenological sociology. Two books (Brown 1973; Young 1971) reflected these concerns, as did the Open University's first sociology reader *School and Society* (Cosin *et al.* 1971). The problems with social phenomenology, as they were worked out through studying Berger and Luckman (1966) and the readings of Schutz (1964) or Garfinkel (1967), seemed to imply a relativism which, in spite of the excitement which was generated by the links between the sociology of education and the sociology of knowledge promising something else, might not create a convincing basis for action. The reading of Gramsci and Althusser which developed at CCCS and the attempts at creating a Marxist humanism at the Institute of Education pushed the concerns of the Open University's sociology of education courses (and especially its second year, Schooling and Society) away from phenomenology in any form to an open commitment to Gramscianism. The work emerging from the Institute (see Whitty and Young 1976, and Young and Whitty 1977) was concerned that its early work had said nothing about class struggle or activism. In trying to

45

remedy this it tried to come to terms with the work of Williams, Thompson and Althusser, as well as Gramsci, though ultimately it came down in favour of an activism that went 'beyond critique'. 'It was for those engaged in the struggle to decide for themselves what they wanted as an alternative. The politics of the analysis emerged as the final test of its adequacy, a development seen, eventually, as Gramscian' (Harris 1992: 55).

From CCCS, four books had a strong impact: Paul Willis's *Learning to Labour: How Working-Class Kids Get Working-Class Jobs* (1977), Hall and Jefferson's *Resistance through Rituals* (1976), *Unpopular Education: Schooling and Social Democracy in England since 1944* (Johnson *et al.* 1981) and Dick Hebdige's *Subculture: The Meaning of Style* (1979), probably because they addressed the issues of everyday life in a way that made sense to students and traditional sociologists. Willis's study of working-class boys resisting formal schooling was an ethnographic study which imaginatively culled a number of theories from several Marxist and non-Marxist traditions. The book had several interrelated themes: the ways in which the 'lads' were able to see through the ideology of school, the limitations of 'experience' in creating a workable alternative, the sense that exploitation and inequality were inevitable (and hence so was manual labour), the ambivalences of racism and sexism in teenage attitudes, and the problems of identifying official policies and attitudes as purely ideological. In its first appearance, *Learning to Labour* was free of Gramscian terminology, or even theoretical concerns, and was probably closer to theories of reproduction (Bourdieu?), of an historicist Marxist humanism (Lukács?), and perhaps also of a structuralist anthropology. One of the delights of the book was its openness to experience as well as an attempt to explore a theoretical basis for activist struggle, and a residual pessimism that working-class culture may, in the long run, not be progressive at all. In many ways, as with Hebdige's *Subculture* (1979), this was an exemplary product of the fluid period of the CCCS's work.

In subsequent writing Willis revised his position, mainly to tie together the loose, open ends and bring his work more closely into line with a Gramscianism which

> succumbs to the delights of purely abstract cultural politics, based on left-wing possibilities of structural looseness in the system. This abstract activism solves theoretical problems too, since it alone fixes and interrelates the multiple possible identities offered by the formal properties of race, class and sex.
>
> (Harris 1992: 62)

In *Common Culture* (1990), Willis ended a study of youth culture with a resoundingly Gramscian flourish: 'Over-ridingly, ordinary people must make themselves as culturally producing citizens before they make socialism. Meanwhile it should be no surprise that theories and plans for their premature, abstract unmaking should be resisted' (Willis 1990: 160).

Resistance through Rituals, out of which both Hebdige's and Willis's work grew, acted as the occasion for CCCS to free itself from earlier, eclectic approaches to the study of youth. In many respects it is the best example of the CCCS laboratory at work, revealing all the tensions of theoretical positions: Althusser, Sartre, Gramsci, Marcuse and feminist politics. The issue of youth and class, previously treated as if they were continuous from generation to generation, or else distinct in each generation, are now seen as subject to 'double articulation' – to age as much as to class. Teasing out the components of leisure, work and education for youth, as being different from those experienced by their parents, led to the coining of the term 'parent culture' to account for the heritage transmitted. The double articulation model was applied unevenly, sometimes involving a Gramscian model, sometimes not. What was impressive, however, was that the collection indicated both the nature of the debates in the Centre, and the move towards creating a creative body of theory based on a (partial) reading of Gramsci. Although the later collection, *Culture, Media, Language* (Hall *et al.* 1980), was a more comprehensive and theoreticist collection of the range of themes studied at CCCS, *Resistance through Rituals* gave a more lively sense of the nuances of the Centre's intellectual relationships.

Subculture (Hebdige 1979), ostensibly a study of the Punks, came to haunt everyone. With it the experiential or the culturalist and the structuralist or semiotic were laid bare as territory that everyone wanted to inhabit, but did not know how. With it the aesthetics of the postmodern were first exposed in all their contradictions.

By the time that *Unpopular Education* appeared in 1981, Margaret Thatcher had come to power, and the sense of optimistic momentum that had acted as a catalyst for much of the work at CCCS was frozen. *Unpopular Education* was the first book that addressed the crisis. It did this both by analysing the problems of social democratic attempts at solving the inequities of job access through the schools, and by arguing that a tradition of populist education had existed long before the introduction of state education in Britain. The argument against social democracy was that the reform of the school system worked only while the economy was buoyant. In periods of unemployment, the argument sounded hollow, and the idea that the Labour Party could both represent labour (or the working class) and be the guardian of capitalism might be seen as a fraud. Voting for Thatcher was therefore the people's just retribution for a party that was inherently dishonest in its loyalties. The book's solution to all this was to recommend that the Labour Party look at a continuous tradition of popular education which had been ignored by the party (Willis's book in its revised state was used as evidence for a continuing version of this). But what were the grounds for thinking, in the second half of the twentieth century, that this tradition was other than either a middle-class romanticization of the working class, or a rationale for the counter-cultural educational activities (the WEA, the extra-mural departments, History Workshop and the Open University) that the middle class already enjoyed? Was popular education not the absent signifier of a latent struggle that could be fully understood only by middle-class radicals? But was this what Gramsci really meant by latent struggle? *Unpopular Education* was the first of the CCCS books which implicitly recognized that cultural studies and educational reform had less to do with the working class than with the 'organic intellectuals' of the middle class who were ultimately homeless.[20] Thus two of the themes of this book (whom is cultural studies directed towards? and the importance of agency and vision as autonomous actions) were born.

In the work of the Open University (OU), [21] the Gramscian took high prominence, though with cleft palate. In 1979 the revision of the OU's sociology of education course appeared with *two* readers: one was symbolic interactionist, the other Marxist, though with attempts to bridge them. The Marxist depended heavily on the work of CCCS, and in particular *Resistance through Rituals* and the books *On Ideology* and *Policing the Crisis* which had established, ultimately, the primacy of the Gramscian model. The politics of constructing a course had never been more evident. Because of the outrage generated by the Gould Report (Gould 1977) which accused the OU of partisanship in learning, the OU attempted to mould its courses in such a way that Gramscianism and the accepted sociological modes would be treated in tandem, but ultimately leaving the last word to the ultimate pedagogue and organic intellectual. The importance of the work that emerged from the courses that were generated was that it was resistant to the modes of teaching and reading, and thus could create resistance in everyday life.

The rise of Thatcher put a quick end to this. The Open University course which had been the centre of it all (E202) was scrapped after Sir Keith Joseph put his *fiat* on the sociology of education as an essential ingredient in pedagogy. The Institute of Education's sociology department went into slow decline; CCCS looked as if it might close down; the Greater London Council and its culturally affirmative programmes were whisked away by the wand of the Wicked Witch. If *Unpopular Education* read like the swansong of a dying movement, the serial events of the 1980s could be seen as the final nails in the coffin.

'Education', wrote Basil Bernstein (1971b), 'cannot compensate for society.' The thesis was ultimately very simple: 'The power relationships created outside the school penetrate the organization, distribution and evaluation of knowledge through the social context. The definition of "educability" is itself, at any one time, an attenuated consequence of these power relationships' (Bernstein 1971b: 65). After the early 1970s no one seemed to remember these lines. The problem was that the professional educationalists saw themselves as the power-brokers, and middle-class parents as the avant-garde of the progressive educational movement. Most of what OU tried to do was caught up with the tangle of whether it was concerned with turning middle-class students into radicals (in which case it assumed that they had standard public/grammar school education) or educating the working class into radicalizing itself (in which case the radicalization might produce zany consequences). Bernstein had argued that ultimately, 'We should start knowing that the social experience that the child already possesses is valid and significant, and that this social experience should be reflected back to him as valid and significant' (Bernstein 1971b: 65). If this was a phenomenological basis for thinking about education, it was, ultimately, a cry for thinking about education which was not imposed from the outside, but which asked for an interpretation of the outside by looking from below.

The consequences for the pedagogical practice of the OU or any other institution were interesting. The carefully crafted, theoretically informed courses did not necessarily produce students who bought the theory. The 'working class' of the theories was predominantly an imaginative construct, much as was the noble savage of the Enlightenment.

> Lo, the poor Indian! whose untutored mind
> Sees God in clouds, or hears him in the wind;
> His soul, proud Science never taught to stray
> Far as the solar walk, or milky way;
> Yet simple Nature to his hope has giv'n,
> Beneath the cloud-topped hill, an humbler heav'n.
> (Alexander Pope, 'Essay on Man', 1985: 120)

What the students did, as anyone else would do, was to raid the courses for what seemed to fit their own experiences, and reconstruct them in frameworks of their own making (see Harris 1987; 1992 *passim*). What the intellectual left did was to go on talking to itself while scattering its ideas willy-nilly to whom would appropriate them. What the political right did was to seize power and try to organize the teachers' training colleges and faculties of education in which sociologists had no power. Ultimately it wanted to organize the curriculum in such a way that only the right books mattered. It was the first stab at deciding what was politically correct.

THOMPSON AND THE UNIVERSITY

Against these intellectual contortions, two moments stand out as trying to come to terms with the evident realities of power in academe (if we accept the Bernstein/Althusserian thesis that education is complicit in the political/economic power system, whatever the actors think they are doing). The first is E. P. Thompson's involvement in Warwick University, the second is the relationship between Raymond Williams as professor of drama at Cambridge and his involvement in cultural studies, Marxism and the Welsh. Thompson's association with Warwick was short-lived. After teaching as an extra-mural tutor for Leeds in the 1950s and early 1960s, he was appointed as reader in social history at Warwick University in 1965, establishing the Centre for the Study of Social History. The centre was an outgrowth of the work that Thompson had been engaged with at Leeds and the bringing up from the underground the work that had been fostered by associations with the Communist Party, the Workers' Educational Association and the extra-mural departments. By 1965 Thompson (then 41) had published two major studies (*William Morris*, and *The Making of the English Working Class*), three edited collections, three brochures, and seventeen articles.[22] His reputation as the samizdat guru of the British left was at its highest pitch. Having broken with the Communist Party in 1956, he had produced the *New Reasoner*, then helped to found the *New Left Review*. He was one of the most active members of the Campaign for Nuclear Disarmament and perhaps the most formidable pamphleteer of his generation. His elevation to a readership at Warwick could be seen either as a bold co-optive strike by the ideological state apparatuses or else as a piece of naivety by liberally minded nincompoops. The commanding feature of Thompson's presence was that he was able to divide his time between writing one major (well-researched) book per decade, firing off at regular moments a series of broadsides (which were collected, ultimately, in books), conducting political campaigns, and also being nurtured by and nurturing a family and a personal/political society. All of this was conducted from a farmhouse or a bishop's palace in Halifax, Leamington Spa or Wick. It was the ideal example of the 'free-born Englishman's' (or aristocratic) radicalism.[23]

Warwick University Ltd (1970) was the moment when this was put to the test. The legal case (and Thompson subsequently spent most of his time arguing on behalf of the law as the substitute for working-class hegemony) was whether the university had the right to transform the heritage of education (struggled and fought for through numerous encounters) into the enclave of a predatorial business establishment. In what way could education be free if it was commandeered by business? Thompson opted, as any of us would, for the cry of the oppressed. When the purloined files were delivered to him by the students who had secreted them to him from the vice-chancellor's office, he *had* to read them. The historian and the editor of left-samizdat came together. What could he do?

I must confess also that, as a historian, I find a certain piquancy in that moment. It is my trade to open files, but the authors of the correspondence have always been long dead. One of the difficulties in writing 'contemporary history' is that, until the files have been opened, the actual thoughts and motives of the actors may be difficult to determine because of their public image. But here, for a moment, the actuality of the image co-existed, giving a sense of double vision: and even when the inertia of institutional routine reasserted itself, there lingered the sense of a new dimension to its reality – what the institution wished to be taken for set alongside one's new knowledge of what it actually was.

(Thompson 1970: 157)

Thompson's account of the events at Warwick as well as his personal involvement stand as one of the most courageous acts by any academic in the 1970s (and certainly more courageous than any in the 1980s or 1990s), although the actual work done on the files and the organization of the protests were in no way masterminded by him, but were rather the work of the Revolutionary Socialist Student Federation. In opening the files, the way in which the vice-chancellor had constructed a parallel university committed entirely to business interests, and at the same time involving a network of spies concerned with monitoring the activities of left-wing academics and students, became immediately evident. The document that was published as a result of the events was a collaboration between Thompson, faculty and students, though ultimately Thompson, Hugo Radice (one of the graduate students) and Robert Hutchison (of Penguin Books) put the final book together. Douglas Hay, now of Osgoode Hall Law School, Toronto, conducted the background research. The whole book was written in a week.

In putting it together, Thompson had to overcome certain prejudices, particularly against 'youth'.

I am not, among my students or acquaintances, notorious for my critical admiration of 'youth'. I have been known to lament that young people do not serve for a term in a really well-disciplined organization, such as the Officers' Training Corps or the British Communist Party. Youth, if left to its own devices, tends to become very hairy, to lie in bed till lunch-time, to miss seminars, to be more concerned with the style than with the consequences of actions, and to commit various sins of self-righteous political purism and intellectual arrogance which might be itemized in some other book. In short, I am disposed to admire youth only if, by their actions, they command admiration. As, in the case of the students of Warwick, they most emphatically have.

(Thompson 1970: 155)

Thompson also had to come to terms with the most extreme instances of *Academicus Supercilliosus*, that genus that 'over-reacts to *any* sign of student self-activity'.

> Even a polite deputation or petition throws him into a tizzy. His life is lived in a kind of Awe of Propriety. Whatever the students or the younger staff do is wrong, since it is always embarrassing him in some delicate tactical manoeuvre on a higher committee. If he disagrees with student demands he will not go out and argue it out with them, face to face, in a rational way, but will thumb through old senate minutes and utter a low disciplinary hiss. He encourages an atmosphere of institutional loyalty... any serious episode of student 'unrest' – a sit-in, a rough music, or a heckling – is received, with lowered voices, as if it were some aboriginal calamity.
>
> (Thompson 1970: 154)

Thompson's account of Warwick (an account which we all share at a gut level, in every educational institution of which we have ever been a part) was a reaction to the pusillanimous kotowing by the academic establishment to the predators of corporate industry, but also an invocation to the new generation to get their act together. If Pierre Bourdieu was right (knowledge is reproduced because of the ritualistic forms of the knowledge, and the power-complexes that keep it in place), Thompson and the students had found the key that would help to keep the spirit of reason intact, in spite of academic bureaucracy. A spirit and form were moving over the face of academia. But how to grasp it?

'What is wrong', he said, 'is the whole system of values – of this insistent managerial propaganda.'

> It is sad to see even the scholars themselves hesitate in their work and wonder about the *use* of what they are doing. Even they begin to feel, defensively, that a salesman or an advertising executive is perhaps a more productive human being than being an actor, or a designer, or a teacher of English. Able and perhaps eminent men in their own disciplines, they capitulate without a struggle ... resigning their wider allegiances ... retreating within the limited area of the manoeuvre alloted within the managerial structure.
>
> (Thompson, 1970: 163)

If this was William Cobbett riding into the academic twilight (Thompson had decided to leave Warwick before the events occurred), he left a sting in his tail. The Bernsteins, the Halls and the Willises had thought about it, theorized around it. Thompson did it. But what, exactly, did he do? Apart from being complicit in a student raid of university archives, four issues (at least) stand out:

First, the right to know is clearly an ongoing issue which dominates all of our concerns; but how much do we have to know before we can make up our own minds?

Second, however we rank them, students are a part of ourselves. But how do we rank *them*? Thompson has his own gradations, based presumably on a synergistic sense of what used to be called copasetic. But how do we know who they are, apart from Thompson's (or any of our own) sense of those whom he wants to talk to?

Third, do we have colleagues? Thompson's sense of collegiality does not involve many with whom he works, but a large number who are outside. Are all our colleagues at our places of work potential enemies? If the space that we have left for friendship and political commitment is commandeered by 'management', then what space is left for us'?

Fourth, Thompson's own work displays a split between doing history in order to give voice to the uncelebrated dead and ignoring contemporary history in order to give voice to the living. The pungency of this dilemma echoes throughout the 1990s.

Ultimately, as Thompson's subsequent work tried to show, the real problem was how we come to terms with the law. But that is a topic for another book. With *Warwick University Ltd* Thompson opened up the possibility of thinking about the scholar who is a nomad in academia and how he or she responds when the institution to which he or she is temporarily affiliated displays itself as venal and afflicted. Thompson's everyday world, unlike most academics, was an activist one, but an activism which was made possible by an aristocratic lifestyle. Thompson's campaigns for the European Campaign for Nuclear Disarmament as well as his stand-offish attitude to the work of other members of the left in the 1970s and 1980s were both in a large part made possible because of the lack of an institutional base (in other words, ultimately, Thompson did not have to depend on paid work for a living, although for a few years in the 1970s Dorothy Thompson taught history at Birmingham).[24] In many ways Thompson was the ultimate member of the left aristocracy of letters. As his generation passes away (there were others: the Stracheys, the Webbs, the Cockburns, the Hodgkins and the Foots at least) the question that remains for socialist critical theory and action is to assess the impact on what the left was able to accomplish. Was Thompson a catalyst or a break on left politics? Most of the people who helped to put together the cultural politics of Britain in the 1970s and 1980s did not operate from bishoprics in Worcester: they operated from tenement houses in Salford, Leeds or north London, or else tried to negotiate mortgages on slender salaries. If Thompson is important in understanding one route that cultural studies took, it is surely as much because of where he came from as for what he said.[25]

So if we move from Thompson, the creative 'aristocratic' *marabout* of British intellectual life, to Raymond Williams, whose roots were in the working class, it is ultimately because Williams tried to make sense of everything that Thompson stood for while trying to resist the elitism that came from privileged background. Both authors worked for the extra-mural departments of the universities in the 1950s, and both were members of the Communist Party, from which they both resigned. They both became involved in the *New Left Review*. There the comparison ends.

WILLIAMS AND THE TENSION BETWEEN EXTRA-MURAL AND ACADEMIC KNOWLEDGE

There is no such thing as a pure unmediated culture, anymore than there is a pure unmediated self. All people, all cultures, are hybrid.

(Said 1993b)

Raymond Williams represents a quite distinct take on the role of both the left and culture in academic life. In the interviews with the editors of *NLR* that were held in 1977–8, he covers his early days as a student at Cambridge and as an adult education lecturer, as well as his background growing up in the Welsh border country. Williams had been in the army (he fought in Normandy in the 1940s) and had been a member of the Communist Party and thus served 'for a term in a really well-disciplined organization'. His decision to become an extra-mural tutor as opposed to university lecturer was based largely on economic reasons: the Oxford Extra-Mural Delegacy offered him £300 a year while Cambridge offered him £200. From 1947 to 1948 with Wolf Mankowitz (novelist and scriptwriter) and Henry Collins (Communist Party historian and, later, economics columnist for *Tribune*) he established a journal, *Politics and Letters*, which tried to tease out the relationships between political organization and writing. The journal lasted for four issues, but in that time it published a debate on political commitment in literature which included R. O. C. Winkler, Christopher Hill, F. R. Leavis, George Orwell, J.-P. Sartre and Williams himself as contributors. The debate was marked by openness to different perspectives and was partly responsible for Williams being taken for a maverick in his political commitment. (It was an attempt at creating a journal which tried to create a different path from those ploughed by Cyril Connolly's modernistic conservative *Horizon* and the Communist Party's social realist, neo-Stalinist *Modern Quarterly*.) But Williams himself was later to comment that the collapse of *Politics and Letters* (due to financial reasons and personal disagreements) was a very personal blow. 'At that point, apart from going on with the actual adult education teaching, I felt I could only write myself out of this in a non-collaborative way. I pulled back to do my own work. For the next ten years I wrote in nearly complete isolation' (R. Williams 1979: 77).

The work that he completed in this decade (the 1950s) was written in Seaford, East Sussex, while he was tutor for the Oxford Extra-Mural Delegacy:

> The social character of my classes was extremely mixed. At one level there was the class that I ran in Hastings, essentially with the local Trades Council, which was called Public Expression and simply involved specific training in public writing and speaking. There seemed little point in teaching the writing of essays; I taught the writing of reports, minutes, memoranda, and committee speaking and oral reports – skills relevant to their work. At the other extreme you would get a class of commuter housewives at Haywards Heath who wanted to read some literature. Perfectly serious in their interest, but an extremely different social composition. Then I had a fair number in which there was a mixture of the two elements, including of course the substantial number of wage-earners one discovers, who at the third or fourth meeting produce their novel or autobiography, short stories or poems – an enormous amount of unknown writing of this sort goes on. It was a mixture I could live with.

> (R. Williams 1979: 78)

While doing this, Williams wrote five books: two on drama, one (co-authored) book on film, one on reading and criticism, and *Culture and Society*. These were books which were written parallel to, rather than with or against his students. If the students fed anything into the writing, there is no evidence from Williams's accounts. There is, of course, much evidence of the importance of the ambience of the teaching, but nothing of feedback. An American/Czech scholar, Jan Gorak, has argued that Williams was the epitome of the 'alienated intellectual' (Gorak 1988: 10). The argument goes something like this. Williams was Welsh, a member of an ethnic minority. Going to Cambridge as a working-class scholarship boy he was therefore doubly alienated. In his work, says Gorak, he never confronts his own alienation, but his obsession for 'an alien culture's monuments, beset by a compulsion to test the authenticity of his own responses' (Gorak 1988: 10) suggest that Williams is a suitable case for treatment. In some ways Gorak is right: Williams *is* marginal to the culture's own perception of itself, but then, with a name like Gorak, so, presumably is Gorak to American culture (or has he bathed himself in American rectitude?). Marginality in relation to the centre is what all of Williams's work is about. Gorak's snide interpretation of Williams's career does, however, raise a profound issue about how does a Welsh working-class boy make an impact on *English* politics, academe and institutions without being complicit in the machinations which made him marginal in the first place. Williams's silences about his teaching experiences in the 1950s might be a way to start.

None of us, who *are* marginal, ever got into academic life the simple way (and this goes for E. P. Thompson as well), otherwise academic life would be the ultimate in the reproduction of culture and society. We live in a world of nomads. The issue is not to deny the nomadism (the House UnAmerican Activities Committee tried to do that in order to deliberately misplace those who did not 'fit' the sense of wholeness that was defined by a committee), but to accept nomadism as the point of engagement. The 'silences' of Williams's 1950s are the 'silences' of trying to work out a place in an 'alien' culture. He is, of course, quite explicit about what the 'silences' meant: they were the coming to terms with the everyday culture of people's experiences. Williams was an ethnographer of *English* culture, but also an ethnographer who tried to understand that making film, writing novels, watching drama being performed, understanding television, understanding writing as being *written* were all parts of *their* sense both of alienation and having fun.

But did Raymond ever have fun? There is a sad, limpid look in those eyes gazing over the hills of Madoc, recreating the past. His novels are an attempt at reconstructing the Welsh experience against the social romantic realism of Richard Llewellyn's *How Green was my Valley* (1939), Jack Jones's *Off to Philadelphia in the Morning* (1938), and Alexander Cordell's *Rape of the Fair Country* (1939). Raymond wanted to put the record straight against the imposition (via a Communist Party stranglehold on Welsh culture) of a Stalinist stamp on Welsh fiction. *That* ambition was not achieved. The early novels are written for and against a theory. The novels that he wrote *against* were driven by a Welsh poetics as much as by social realism. Raymond had not lived in Wales for over twenty years when he started to write the novels, and, in any case, did not particularly like poetry. Living in Wales may not have mattered much as far as the stories went, but being indifferent to poetry did (of all the books that he wrote, only *The Country and the City* (1975), which is not in any direct way about Wales, deals in any way with poetry). But did not the drama, the film, the lyricism of his writing say something Welsh? Of course, in some ways it did. The 'structure of feeling' has a powerful Welsh ring to it, a Presbyterian echo of how people *perform*. Presbyterians are very much caught up with performance: the collective performance of singing, of dressing up, of playing other peoples' sports, of being communally sad about the end of Welsh culture, of celebrating others' imperial monuments. For the Welsh, feeling was structured, repressed, and could only be released by re-enacting the end of the world as an ongoing event.

Understanding Raymond Williams's achievement in relation to all of this is to understand the problems of breaking out of it. In one of his

interviews, he confronts the issue when asked about his attitude to Aneu-
rin Bevan, a response akin to Lévi-Strauss discussing the importance of
French academia on thinking processes:[26]

> I never trusted Aneurin Bevan, for the cynical reason that it takes
> one Welshman to know another. He came from only twenty miles
> away and I'd heard that style of Welsh speaking since about the age
> of two that I was never impressed by it as other socialists were. It
> is a marvellous form of public address which always assumes a faith
> in common. I think it comes out of the chapels where you didn't
> have to argue whether you should believe in God, everybody did
> that, so you could be very witty about the ways of the world, or
> very indignant about its injustices. But it is not a style for serious
> argument, because your beliefs are presupposed from the start. So
> it was very difficult to know what Bevan at the centre believed. . . .
> After all, if you could have been done by talking, Wales could have
> been a socialist republic in the twenties. The Welsh, you might say,
> were so far aggrieved that there was no need to argue through
> fundamental questions. So you get the fine social democrat of the
> Health Service, but also the Labourist metropolitan parliamentarian
> – a stifling figure – and also the final equivocator on the H-bomb.
>
> (R. Williams 1979: 369)

Williams's work was therefore as much a resistance to the dominating
paradigms of Welsh rhetoric as it was to the commandeering presence of
English cultural imperialism. The 'silences' of the 1950s were therefore
necessary silences, that allowed Williams to rethink his relationships to
English literature, Wales, Marxism and popular culture. *Culture and
Society* (1958) and *The Long Revolution* (1961) were the culmination of
that process. Subsequently he worried over where the concepts which
those books made into slogans had come from. 'The structure of feeling'
was based on a thinking of how, in the nineteenth century, novelists and
art critics recognized the evil of industrialization but balanced it with 'a
fear of becoming involved. Sympathy was transformed, not into action,
but into withdrawal' (Williams 1958: 119). In subsequent work – see
the articles collected in *Resources of Hope* (1989a) – it is clear that the
concept is a Welsh one, transplanted to the English. And on the idea of
'community' or a 'common culture' the evidence is quite specific: in
Politics and Letters, after commenting that 'at this time my distance from
Wales was most complete' (R. Williams 1979: 113) he admits that his idea
of community was based on memories of Wales, without recognizing that
that experience 'was also precisely one of subjection to English experience
and assimilation historically. This is what ought to have most alerted me
to the dangers of a persuasive type of definition of community, which is
at once dominant and exclusive' (R. Williams, 1979: 118–19). In later

years, Williams rethought his Welshness as well as his Marxism. Both the notions of a 'structure of feeling' and a 'common culture' went through important transformations as he began to rediscover his Welsh roots.

But he also had to rediscover Cambridge. The years at Seaford had given him time to reflect, read ('I used to put 50 or 75 per cent new literature into my teaching every year': R. Williams, 1979: 83) and write, but had not provided the opportunity to influence the definition of a culture. Influence (however hard one writes) comes ultimately from having a position of power. Because of changes in style at the Extra-Mural Delegacy (the introduction of refresher courses for managers)

> adult education ceased to have enough meaning. It was at that point that I knew that I wanted to move on. Though it happened quite unexpectedly. I got a letter saying that I had been appointed a lecturer at Cambridge, though I hadn't applied for it. But I was ready to go.
>
> (R. Williams 1979: 81)

Rediscovering Cambridge also involved rediscovering that he was pro-fessionally in the business of literary criticism, in spite of the fact that for ten years he was writing cultural studies.

> From somewhere in the early 1950s I ceased to see work in criticism as the sort of book I wanted to produce. I didn't keep up, for example, with what they call 'the literature'. When I came back to Cambridge, I was quite out of touch: I wasn't a professional literary scholar. I had to read all the publications on the major authors which had appeared since I was a student, to bring myself up to date. Even on authors I had been constantly thinking about, like Dickens. I hadn't read those sorts of books, let alone the articles.
>
> (R. Williams, 1979: 243)

When, for example, he published *The English Novel from Dickens to Lawrence* (1970), his first work of literary criticism since *Reading and Criticism* (1950), it was not a written book, but the transcripts of his lectures. ('If it had been a work conceived in current academic styles it couldn't even have been written. For myself, I felt that a period was over and it was now time just to have it on record' – R. Williams 1979: 244).

Working at Cambridge therefore involved being a dual person. The cultural critic doubled as a literary critic. But the literary critic was also a political activist, a pamphleteer, a novelist and a playwright. Ultimately his work was about communications in its widest sense:

> from the beginning, we cannot really think of communication as secondary. We cannot think of it as marginal; or as something that happens after reality has occurred. Because it is through communi-

cation systems that the reality of ourselves, the reality of our society, forms and is interpreted. This is why, now, someone who writes about communication becomes, in a sense without ever intending to have become, a social critic. He starts by writing about the use of the language, or about the press, or the cinema, or the modern popular novel, or the theatre, or television. And you find as you listen, that he is not talking about secondary activities at all. He is talking about society, he is looking at society in a different way, and he may be discovering things about the society which could simply not be seen in the older kinds of political and economic description.

(Williams 1989: 22–3)

In this, as one of his former students, Ken Hirschkop, wrote, he was writing about himself 'more than any one else. For it is sadly a rare thing to find work in which knowledge about culture and communications leads to knowledge about politics and community' (Hirschkop 1989: 22). The influence of Williams at Cambridge can therefore be measured by the way in which he worked at transforming English literature into a form of cultural studies. He himself traced a path from the establishment of 'Cambridge English' (the first degree courses were offered in 1917, though there was no Faculty of English until 1926) to the emergence of cultural criticism in the 1970s. (See, in particular, three essays in *Writing in Society* (1984a: 177–226), in his contribution to Ronald Hayman's collection *My Cambridge* (1977) and his account of his relationship with F. R. Leavis, 'Seeing a Man Running' (1984c)). In all of these it is clear that for Williams the issue was not English as an academic discipline (contrasted, for example, with E. P. Thompson's almost paranoid sense that history *was* the discipline) but that English was the frame that provided the base for going beyond.

In all my work I have tried to be on the other side, but I say 'tried' because to succeed would be a transformation beyond the powers of any individual or small group. Yet this is why I now look beyond Cambridge English: beyond that remarkable but characteristic innovation which settled to self-definition in an important privileged institution. What I believe is beginning to happen, in English studies and in other important parts of the culture, is the first stage of a new project of transformation: taking what has been learned in necessarily difficult work on to testing encounters with all those men and women who have only ever intermittently and incompletely been addressed: going to learn as well as to teach, within a now dangerous unevenness of literacy and learning which both directly and in all its indirect consequences is radically dislocating what had been assumed, in both literature and education, to be stable forms;

a dislocation that is beginning to reach, harshly but instructively, into the old privileged places.

(Williams 1984a: 225)

Pedagogically, therefore, the task was to push English studies to the limits, and to use Cambridge, without apologies, as the place to start. In other parts of this book, I discuss some of Williams's theoretical contributions to the growth of cultural studies, but pedagogically, his great achievement was to create a base from which serious critical thinking could be done. Terry Eagleton, John Fekete, Patrick Parrinder, Ken Hirschkop, Terry Murphy, Tony Pinkney and Carol Watts: these second and third generation scholars are an indication of his continuing influence.

ANDERSON'S NOMADISM AND THE BUSINESS OF CULTURAL STUDIES

In contrast to those who chose to stay and fight within the English educational institutions, there is, of course, a remarkable diaspora of British academics who do their work elsewhere. It is beyond the scope of this book to account for all the many placements and displacements, but theory, as Edward Said has taught us, not only travels by curious routes but also (sometimes) travels back to its country of origin.[27] By the 1990s the number of people who were, in one way or another, central to cultural studies in Britain but who lived abroad was quite remarkable. Their placement in relation to what the British thought were their own issues is equally remarkable. Thus Tony Wilden, who has lived in Canada for over two decades and first 'discovered' Lacan and the 'imagined communities' of Canada, is barely thought of in British cultural discourse (see Wilden 1972; 1985); Dorothy Smith (seminal work on feminist discourse analysis, discussed elsewhere in this book) was barely considered through the 1970s or 1980s; John Fekete, who has taught at Trent University since 1975, and who wrote one of the major studies on literary theory under Williams's supervision (Fekete 1977) as well as several studies on modernism and postmodernism, is never quoted in any text published in Britain that I know of. And yet both Perry and Benedict Anderson (Benedict has not lived in England since 1960, and Perry not since 1980) have instant attention. The issue is partly to do with a power-base. Cultural studies, like any other political/social movement, not only needs to generate discourse, but also needs *sites* for a discourse. Verso was one such site, the group of expatriates congregated around the University of Minnesota was another, the Lawrence Grossberg University of Illinois group was another, and, for a few electric years, so were the CCCS and the Open University publishing ventures. Meanwhile, everything that mattered was either in samizdat (journals like *October*; *Social Text*; *Arena*;

Stand; *Cine Action*; *News from Nowhere*; *Screen* in its various incar-
nations; *Borderlines;* the *Canadian Journal of Political and Social Theory*;
the *Australian Journal of Cultural Studies*; and I'm sure I missed some)
or in 'professional' journals which none of us reads unless we are 'pro-
fessionally' dedicated, doing research or trying to maintain or get a job.
The cultural brokers raided these journals to find out what was publish-
able. *How* they decided is the topic for another investigation. But what
is clear, for those of us who live away from 'home' is that the power-
brokers call the shots.

Even clearer, from wherever we come, is that relationships and political/
academic sensibilities have to be negotiated and it takes even more time
to do this (in spite of modern telecommunications) across continents than
if we live in close physical proximity. Thus, in spite of what I have said
on the sites of cultural power, the examples of how personal, political
and intellectual relations are maintained and developed when people live
in different countries is of the utmost importance. The relationship
between Benedict Anderson and his brother, Perry, seems to me to raise
all of the issues of this displaced, expatriate sensibility.

In an introduction to one of his books of collected essays, Benedict
Anderson gives an account both of their background and of their subsequent relationships:

> Remoter family history – though I became aware of it only later –
> played its own role. On my mother's side there were mainly conven-
> tional businessmen, judges, and policemen, though my great-uncle
> had made what in those days was a daring journey through Central
> Asia, and even wrote a book about it. My father's family, however,
> was odder, and of mixed Irish and Anglo-Irish origins. My grand-
> mother's people, the O'Gorman's, had long been active in nationalist
> politics. Her great-uncle had been imprisoned for joining the United
> Irishmen's rebellion of 1798. Her grandfather had joined, and later
> became secretary of, Daniel O'Connell's Catholic Association, fight-
> ing for Catholic emancipation. One of her cousins became a very
> stout member of Charles Parnell's group of Irish nationalist parlia-
> mentarians at Westminster. Because of all this, though I was edu-
> cated in England from the age of eleven, it was difficult to imagine
> myself English.
>
> (B. Anderson 1990: 2)

If this reads like an attempt to find roots for the rootless, of course in
many ways it is. The Andersons have not been renowned for trying to
make sense of Ireland (as opposed to Williams, whose 'Wales' was always
present in his work). 'Ireland', that 'remoter family history', was tagged
on to the other stuff. As children of members of the diplomatic corps,
their habitus was the terminals of railway stations, airports, shipyards and

the public schools to which they were shunted. 'Ireland' had about as much sense as the laundry list or grocery bill.

But we must pause before we dismiss their work on account of their rootlessness. The Andersons, like some of us whose parents were missionaries in Zaïre, furriers in Winnipeg, or corner-store operators in Beirut, learned to live with nomadology and turn it to an advantage. Being nomads allowed us to explore cultures which no one else dared to enter. We became spies on behalf of/against the Other. The cultural or diplomatic or business or religious corps were the agents of cross-cultural theorizing. As Benedict Anderson writes of the making of his book, *Imagined Communities* (1983):

> As I look back on it now, it seems an odd book to be written by someone born in China, raised in three countries, speaking with an obsolete English accent, carrying an Irish passport, living in America, and devoted to Southeast Asia. Yet perhaps it could only be written from various exiles, and with divided loyalties.
>
> (B. Anderson 1990: 10)

The Andersons are part of a nomadology which has produced both in the nineteenth and the twentieth century some of the most challenging intellects. Marx wrote *Das Kapital* in London, Leopold von Sacher-Masoch wrote *Venus in Furs* in Prague, though the women came from Bavaria and the Ukraine, and James Joyce wrote *Ulysses* in Trieste. Home can be wherever we want it to be. But not quite. We drag around with us the baggage of the *Heimat* that might have been.

But to get around that peripatetic situation, there are several strategies, not all of which, as Walter Benjamin (1970) said, are possible for us.

The unique feature of the nomadic Andersons is that the location of its *Heimat* seems to be largely cerebral. Ireland is a throw-away history, an encounter with a long-lost place which has been replaced by equally cerebral localities: the Russian Steppes, the Philippines, Los Angeles. The engagement is ultimately academic, sundered from social movement, except the putative. It contrasts savagely with the account by Eric Hobsbawm of why eastern European Jews became Communist:

> What could young Jewish intellectuals have become under such circumstances? [He is talking about the 1920s.] Not liberals of any kind, since the world of liberalism (which included social democracy) was precisely what had collapsed. As Jews we were precluded by definition from supporting parties based on confessional allegiance, or on a nationalism which excluded Jews, and both cases on anti-semitism. We became either communists or some equivalent form of revolutionary marxists, or if we chose our own blood-and-soil nationalism, Zionists. But even the great bulk of young intellectual

Zionists saw themselves as some sort of revolutionary marxist nationalists. There was virtually no other choice. We did not make a commitment against bourgeois society and capitalism, since it patently seemed to be on its last legs. We simply chose *a* future rather than *no* future. But it meant revolution not in a negative but a positive sense: a new world rather than no world.

(Hobsbawm 1977: 251)

The Anderson account, spelt out in *A Zone of Engagement* and *English Questions* (P. Anderson 1992b; 1992a), has no *Angst* of history, no sense of conflict, no social process that is continuous with the lives of living people. It is basically a political travelogue of the mind, and, perhaps, an accountant's sense of what matters in intellectual or social life.

Thus Anderson ultimately joins the academic set which contemplates, from a great political distance, on the fate of humankind. That this stance may advantage the dispossessed should be recognized, but not only for what he has written, but also because, by running a publishing house, he made available the writings of others from across the world who might never have been given voice. Radical culture in Britain is much richer for that.

NOTES

1 The most succinct account of the GLC experiment is provided by Franco Bianchini (1987). On Black Film, see Kobena Mercer (ed.) (1988) *Black Film: British Cinema*. ICA documents 7, London.
2 The most exciting work on the history of the adult education movement is currently being done by Tom Steele of the Department of Continuing Adult Education at the University of Leeds. See, for example, Steele (1987) 'From Class-Consciousness to Cultural Studies: George Thompson and the WEA in Leeds', *Studies in the Education of Adults* 19(2): 109–28.
3 E. P. Thompson (ed.) *Warwick University Ltd* (1970).
4 See, in particular, Williams's *The Long Revolution* (1961), his essays in *Writing in Society* (1984a), and the early part of his autobiographical interview with *NLR* in *Politics and Letters* (1979).
5 The spectrum of Anderson's pieces on this topic range from his early essays in the 1960s on 'Components of the National Culture' (1969) to his more recent pieces on 'A Culture in Counterflow' (1990). They are all marked, of course, by a discussion of the products of educational institutions rather than by a consideration of the processes by which culture is produced or how it is made sense of by people at any level of society. In this sense Anderson makes a pitch for theory as above practice, rather than incorporated in it. He therefore stands outside many of the concerns of the cultural debate in Britain, or, indeed, elsewhere.
6 At the conclusion of the first volume of *Class, Codes and Control* (1971a), Bernstein explicitly recognizes the importance of Michael Halliday's *Scale and Category Grammar*, though in his footnotes he refers to Halliday's 'Relevant Models of Language' (1969).

7 See, in particular, Pierre Bourdieu, 'Intellectual Field and Creative Project' and 'Systems of Education and Systems of Thought', in Michael F. D. Young (ed.) (1971) and also *Reproduction* (1977).
8 See, in particular, Mary Douglas, *Purity and Danger* (1966).
9 Centre for Contemporary Cultural Studies, *Fifth Report 1968–69*: 1. This report was written by Stuart Hall, based on a talk he gave to the Conference on Literature and Society at the State University of New York, Buffalo, summer 1967.
10 For a vivid account of his experiences there see Hoggart, *An Idea and its Servants* (1978).
11 See, e.g. Janet Wolff (1981; 1983); and Janet Wolff and John Steed (1988).
12 I remember wrestling with Althusser. I remember looking at the idea of 'theoretical practice' in *Reading Capital* and thinking, 'I've gone about as far as I can go.' I felt, I will not give an inch to this profound misreading, this superstructuralist mistranslation, of classical Marxism, unless he beats me down, unless he defeats me in the spirit. He'll have to march over me to convince me. I warred with him, to the death.

(Hall 1992: 280)

Oh come thou traveller unknown
Whom still I hold, but cannot see.
My company before is gone,
And I am left alone with thee.
All night with thee I mean to stay
And wrestle to the break of day.

(Charles Wesley, Hymn 311, 1935)

13 See, in particular, Hall *et al.* (1978a); Richard Johnson (1979; 1981) and Hall (1981; 1992a).
14 The switch in emphasis was noticed, of course. In the *Times Higher Education Supplement* during 1977 a bitter correspondence dominated its pages. A certain John Gillard Watson writing from Oxford was particularily irate:

The Centre for Contemporary Cultural Studies has abandoned its original concept and become a centre for Marxist theorizing. . . . The work reported year by year, and the published articles, including, of course, the *Working Papers in Cultural Studies*, became narrower in intellectual interest; and eventually confined rigidly within the particular Marxist heresy peculiar to the centre. . . . Public funds should not be expended on the centre until it has been subjected to a thorough investigation.

(*THES*, 15 July 1977).

15 See Davies (1990), for an account of these.
16 See, for example, Bryan D. Palmer, *The Making of E. P. Thompson* (1981, in particular 105–27); Perry Anderson, *Arguments Within British Marxism* (1980); Simon Clarke, 'Socialist Humanism and the Critique of Economism' (1979); Graeme Turner, *British Cultural Studies* (1990: 41–84); and David Harris, *From Class Struggle to the Politics of Pleasure* (1992), which explores how Gramscian theory was used in cultural studies.
17 Jameson, however, is surely misguided in his interpretation of Barthes, though he follows an argument which was to become current in the dismissal of Barthes in England. For a much more sympathetic appreciation of the relevance of Barthes to both cultural studies and Marxist theory, see Philip Corrigan, *Social Forms/Human Capacities* (1990), in particular 'In stead of an

Introduction:"Doing Mythologies" ', (pp. 3–12); and 'The Body of Intellectuals/the Intellectuals' Body (Remarks for Roland)' (pp. 185–98), ultimately concerned with trying to understand our omissions, what is left out of our speech. See also Reda Bensmaia, *The Barthes Effect: The Essay as Reflective Text* (1987) for reflections on similar themes.

18 Thompson wrote, referring to N. J. Smelser's *Social Change in the Industrial Revolution,*

> it is assumed that any notion of class is a pejorative theoretical construct, imposed upon the evidence. . . . Class consciousness . . . is a bad thing, invented by displaced intellectuals, since everything which disturbs the harmonious co-existence of groups performing different 'social roles' (and which thereby retards economic growth) is to be deplored as an 'unjustified disturbance-symptom'. The problem is to determine how best 'it' can be conditioned to accepts its social role, and how its grievances may best be 'handled and channelled'.
>
> (Thompson 1963: 10)

19 There are, of course, books on Soho which sketch the history. Judith Summers (1989) *Soho* (London: Bloomsbury) is as good a romp as any. Colin MacInnes (1959) *Absolute Beginners* (London: Macgibbon & Kee) and Colin Wilson's callow (1962) *Adrift in Soho* (London: Gollancz) give appropriate fictional accounts of the Soho of the late 1950s. Daniel Farson's name-dropping account is *Soho in the Fifties* (1987). For Karl Marx's sojourn in Soho, see, however, David McLellan, *Karl Marx: His Life and Thought* (1973). There are also suggestive accounts of Marx's lodgings in Summers.

20 David Harris's *From Class Struggle to the Politics of Pleasure* (1992, especially ch. 3), has provided some of the basis for this account. But for a critique of the concept of Organic Intellectuals see Raymond Williams, *Culture* (1981), particularly towards the conclusion of the book.

21 At the high-point of the OU's Gramscian faze, one of the students who had worked with both me and Stuart referred to Stuart Hall as 'Aslan', and to the Open University as 'Narnia', that Protestant heaven invented by C. S. Lewis. As for Stuart/Aslan, 'when they tried to look at Aslan's face they just caught a glimpse of the golden mane and the great, royal, solemn, overwhelming eyes; and they found that they couldn't look at him and went all trembly' (Lewis 1980: 117). But, of course, they wanted him back, because they had seen his face on video. 'One day you'll see him and another you won't,' they were told. 'He doesn't like being tied down – and of course he has other countries to attend to. It's quite all right. He'll often drop in. Only you mustn't press him. He's wild, you know. Not like a *tame* lion' (1980: 166).

In such a way does the Protestant heaven become the stubborn reality of the material world.

22 For a bibliography, see Perry Anderson (1980: 209–13).

23 There have been several autobiographical attempts at making sense of upper-class radicalism. Ronald Fraser's *In Search of a Past* (1986) is certainly the most direct. Benedict Anderson's introduction to *Language and Power* (1990) is a good second in accounting for how radicalism was possible out of an upper-class background. Claud Cockburn's *I, Claude* (1975) is surely the consummate account of being well-heeled and radical. Cockburn's son, Alexander, is now one of the prominent radical journalists on the left in the USA and wherever radical journalism is taken seriously.

24 In the introduction to her collection of essays, *Outsiders*, Dorothy Thompson

provides a marvellous and moving autobiographical account of her life with Edward, in order to respond to the accusations of feminist writers who 'have taken Edward to task for exploiting the relationship between historians in marriage in order to privilege his own work' (Dorothy Thompson 1993: 2). The account is graceful and concerned, and spells out the everyday experiences of living together as historians, Communists, lovers. It would be ungracious of me to summarize Dorothy's account, So, perhaps, one quote will do:

What I am trying to explain is how a partnership of historians worked under these conditions. The first thing is that, although we had little money (Edward's starting salary in 1948 was £425 a year), some of it always went to a bit of help in the house and paying for laundry, etc. We have always had some domestic help, and this has to come before new clothes or outside entertainment. One thing about adult education work is that there are very few evenings available for theatre visits or dinner parties anyway, and when we were both teaching in the evenings part of my earnings would have to be used for child-sitters. Although we did not earn a great deal, we both had supportive families and were never in a situation in which lack of money could have been an absolute disaster.

(Dorothy Thompson 1993: 7)

In an additional comment Dorothy adds why Edward's work rather than hers should be privileged:

This story explains why my output has been small for a career covering more than forty years. In a working partnership exact equality is seldom achieved, and I have had less time and space for my work than Edward has. However, I don't think that I resent this at all, since the quality of his work is its own justification. If I did not respect his work I might feel differently, since I don't suffer from undue modesty. If our work is set side by side there is no doubt which is the more important and more interesting. But of course there are marginal matters in the relationship which can be irritating.

(Dorothy Thompson 1993: 9)

25 Perhaps not so curiously, the only person who was able to get the measure of Thompson was Perry Anderson. In *Arguments Within English Marxism* (1980) Anderson was able to take *all* of Thompson's then published work and make a composite sense of it. As the younger version of a similar diaspora (both were products of the British-at-large in the world) it was easier for Anderson to see through the rhetoric of Thompson's *Poverty of Theory* (1978) which attacked the cultural Marxists because they had not had the same biography. Thus Thompson, born in 1924, seemed to have the same background as Anderson (born 1940), but it was a generational gap. Anderson's critique of Thompson was therefore father-son. It therefore had a more immediate tone than all the other critiques of Thompson, who took him as colleague, whereas he was, like Anderson, more the alien interfering in their everyday concerns. The ultimate issue, of course, was *how* each of them interfered.

26 Pierre Bourdieu, 'Systems of Education and Systems of Thought' (1971b).

27 The idea of 'travelling theory' is discussed by Said in *The World, the Text and the Critic* (1983) and has been taken up by many others, e.g.: bell hooks (1992), James Clifford (1992), Ioan Davies (1989a) and Aijaz Ahmad (1992).

5

AESTHETICS AND CULTURE

Men and women do not live by culture alone, the vast majority of them throughout history have been deprived of the chance of living by it at all, and those few who are fortunate enough to live by it now are able to do so because of the labour of those who do not. Any cultural or critical theory which does not begin from this single most important fact, and hold it steadily in mind in its activities, is in my view unlikely to be worth very much. There is no document of culture which is not also a record of barbarism.

(Eagleton 1983: 214–15)

CRITIQUE OF AESTHETIC JUDGEMENT

Take *aesthetics* first (in part because one of the curiosities of cultural studies is how little attention has been paid to having a critique of judgement, but partly because *all* of cultural studies has ultimately been a debate with aesthetics, whether it recognized it or not) and, to begin with, some once prominent cases which ultimately might be seen as dead-ends. In 1971 John Berger produced a series of programmes for BBC Television called *Ways of Seeing*, accompanied by a book of the same name (Berger 1972). In part it was influenced by Walter Benjamin's seminal essay 'The Work of Art in an Age of Mechanical Reproduction' (Benjamin 1970: 219–53) and in part it was a reaction to Kenneth Clark's BBC Television series *Civilization*. The message of Berger's essay was clear enough:

> The art of the past no longer exists as it once did. Its authority is lost. In its place there is a language of images. What matters now is who uses that language for what purpose.... A people or a class which is cut off from its own past is far less free to choose and act as a people or class than one that has been able to situate itself in history. This is why – and this is the only reason why – the entire art of the past has now become a political issue.

(Berger 1972: 33)

In juxtaposition to that interpretation of art, Peter Fuller argued against the 'reductionism' of all aesthetics to 'the prevailing ideology, excreted by contemporary cultural institutions' (Fuller 1980: 235).

> I believe that by learning to *look*, and to *see*, one can – admittedly within certain limits – penetrate the veil of ideology in which the art of the past is immersed. The Mona Lisa may be a good painting or not; but because one emperor, once, had no clothes does not mean that all emperors, or empresses, everywhere and at all times are necessarily parading themselves naked. Indeed, the point of this excellent little story has always seemed to me to be that courageous, empirical fidelity to experience can, under certain circumstances at least, cut through ideology. Experience is not *wholly* determined by ideology: it is very often at odds with it, causing constant ruptures and fissures within the ideological ice-floes.
>
> (Fuller 1980: 235)

What both of these positions ultimately hinged on was the relationship of art to nature, the dichotomy between technology and human liberation, the problems of authenticity and periodization. In the long run, however, the distinction between Berger and Fuller must rest on the separate routes taken from their inherited Marxist phenomenology. For Berger the route is that of the story-teller:

> The act of writing is nothing except the act of approaching the experience written about. . . . To approach experience, however, is not like approaching a house. Experience is indivisible and continuous, at least within a single lifetime and perhaps over many lifetimes. I never have the impression that my experience is entirely my own, and it often seems that it preceded me. In any case experience folds upon itself, refers backwards and forwards to itself through the referents of hope and fear, and, by the use of metaphor which is the origin of language, it is continually comparing like with unlike, what is small with what is large, what is near with what is distant.
>
> (Berger 1985: 14–15)

Painting and photography are other ways of telling, and with painting this telling is a pushing against the limits of medium, ideology and conventions in order to create 'a fully original discovery, a breakthrough. . . . It is intrinsic to the activity of rendering the absent present, of cheating the visible, of making images' (Berger 1985: 203). Berger's critical theory is therefore grounded in collective experience, narrative and personal struggle.

Fuller, on the other hand, was ultimately concerned with establishing a canon of British painters who insist that the roots, if not the branches, of aesthetic value lie in the elements of our experience which have a relative constancy about them – rather than in the shifting movements of history or mechanism. Thus they affirm precisely that of which Late Modernism lost sight. At a time when there is a growing recognition that the roots of both ethics and aesthetics may be ecological, this continuing tradition acquires growing significance.

(Fuller 1990: 23)

Ultimately Berger's art criticism led him to develop a strong identification with the peasantry of France and the Third World, from which he established a vantage-point to examine art and writing. Peter Fuller's Marxism ultimately became an English Conservatism arguing against what he saw was the decadence of all contemporary American art and criticism. That they both seek salvation on the land is not without significance, nor is the attempt to provide ideal types of art. In many respects they display the dangers of a phenomenology which is ultimately rootless, and has to *invent* its base of commitment.

Both Fuller and Berger are very critical of 'theory', by which they mean structuralism, post-structuralism and semiotics, echoing with approval E. P. Thompson's critique of Althusserianism, without much sense of having read either. In this way they manage to bypass most of the critical aesthetic theory of the 1970s and 1980s, though the work of Benjamin, Marcuse and Max Raphael is systematically echoed, while nowhere dealt with in any depth, though Raphael becomes a trope for Berger's book on Picasso. What have they missed? The answer is to be found both in coexisting work on painting and sculpture and in other Marxist-informed writing on aesthetics.

Perry Anderson takes up this issue in his 'A Culture in Counterflow' (1990), though it takes 'art' alone (albeit with side-views at literature) as a special prerogative of the aesthetic.[1] The major disputes in Marxist writing about the arts have operated in the twin influences of Marxist-derived issues of ideology, and post-structuralist issues of decentring the subject. The net effect of this work has been to bypass all questions of aesthetics and either prioritize the ideological content of art objects or to scan all *objets d'art* with relativistic impartiality, from *King Lear* to a collection of sports cards in order to deduce meaning. The subsequent debate in Marxist aesthetics attempted to pull these strands together. Dick Hebdige's *Subculture: The Meaning of Style* (1979) was perhaps the apogee of the debate at the level of popular culture. But the problem has remained that aesthetics has been given short shrift by British neo-Marxists. As Barrett wrote:

Raphael's usefulness, in my view, lies in the fact that he tries to explore the ways in which meaning is connected both to aesthetic

69

form and to the senses. This project is difficult, and one that few contemporary writers address in its complexity: it is not currently considered very important.

(Barrett 1988: 712)

Anderson's quest, to find a return to aesthetics, might in some ways appear close to Barrett's, but ultimately they must be seen as operating on different trajectories. Anderson's project is nothing if not an attempt to find the totalizing theories via a reading which derives from non-popular arts (music, painting, architecture) which 'remain specialized and discontinuous from any common capacities' (P. Anderson 1990: 90). Michelle Barrett, on the other hand, is puzzled by Fredric Jameson's account that 'pleasure is finally the consent of life in the body, the reconciliation – momentary as it may be – with the necessity of physical existence in a physical world' (Jameson, 1983: 13).

She adds, 'This is a curiously grudging description (consent, reconciliation, necessity) that makes one wonder what could constitute un-pleasure.' (Barrett 1988: 700). The distinction between Anderson's search and Barrett's is therefore quite clear: Anderson is concerned with a 'meaning' which is validated through elitist arts, while Barrett is concerned with aesthetic pleasures that we can all share. Thus Barrett, who, like Berger and Fuller, uses Max Raphael as her starting-point, is concerned with a popular conception of aesthetics, while Anderson focuses on an aesthetics which sits over and above that of the common people. The grounds, from Berger and Fuller to Barrett and Anderson, have shifted, of course. Berger and Fuller resist (even defy) the postmodern (Fuller ultimately defying even the modern) while Barrett and Anderson, fully conscious of what is there, take a low and a high road to discussing what to do about it. The problem remains, however, in knowing how to take the sensual and the meaningful together, and whether there is a way of teasing a radical, Marxist aesthetic out of the jungle of contemporary art creations and the reception of past art objects.

AESTHETICS, OTHERNESS, ARTEFACT

The problem of developing a convincing aesthetic is based on a number of substantive issues. If the thrust of contemporary cultural studies has been to study popular culture and to absorb all forms of art into a common schedule in order to more fully understand the politics and interpersonal meanings ascribed to everyday living, aesthetics does not rest merely on issues of 'superior' taste or a sense of beauty and pleasure, but surely on the grounds on which any judgement is made. In making this distinction it is important to rethink how contemporary aesthetics is possible. In the period since the industrial revolution (and even more so since the beginning of the twentieth century) debates on aesthetics have hinged not only on the temporal issues of how art replaces art and whether 'new' art is Art (the perennial struggle of the avant-garde to legitimize its own activities, witnessed at present by the debates on postmodernism), but also on the way that aesthetics is itself integrated into a socio-historical theory of experience, for artists and all of us.[2] The site of this distinction is not only the ideological terrain of fashion, taste, appearances, manners, customs or even the opposition between the various bodies within society (physical, political, linguistic and temporal) but also in the technical continuities and discontinuities that characterize the very specialisms that are at the core of how the aesthetic transforms itself.

The debate around aesthetics therefore involves a pronounced conflict between the ideologically located interpretations of the 'artistic' and the much more materially and historically situated considerations of the matter and skills that the artist employs in creation. Peter Osborne (1989) indicates in his article on Greenberg and Adorno that the distinction between these two issues is blurred by postmodernist critics of modernism, while Perry Anderson levels a similar criticism against Terry Eagleton's *The Ideology of the Aesthetic* (1990): 'one might say that while a rhetoric of the body, as undifferentiated site of experience, does generate an ideology of the aesthetic, it is the discrimination of skills that founds its reality' (P. Anderson, 1990: 97). This reintroduces technology and political economy with a vegeance and clears the ground for indicating what a Marxist aesthetics might be. If this brings us back to Berger and Fuller by a different route (Fuller argued that William Morris was a 'radical aesthetic conservative' engaged in 'creative and decorative labour'), it is a route which makes a radical distinction between aesthetics as the coming to terms with the expression of the body and one which comes to terms with technique and the mastery of technique. However, the actual work in creating such a materialistic aesthetic has barely commenced, in a large measure because the connecting theories have not been explored.[3]

I am standing here, in Kenya, my body painted, a work of art. I am either a mother, warrior, slave, servant. I am dying of AIDS. I am congested, the lungs spit out that rheum which helps me survive. Of course, I'm a work of art.

I am a tombstone in Prague. No. Let us do that again. My tombstone, which you see on this postcard, is made courtesy of Herr Hitler who decided that mine should stand here, as opposed to those in Lvov, Gdansk, or Heidelberg, because Prague had been declared an 'Exotic Museum of an Extinct Race'. Today I am part of the Judaic Disneyland of the Czech Republic. Of course, there are no Jews here, but who needs Jews when you have their artefacts?

I am a New Guinea mask.... But why go on? You know what I mean.

We have, as Peter Wollen (1993) argues in his book on twentieth-century culture, been *Raiding the Ice-box* for a long time.[4]

One way of examining the problem of appropriation is to situate it at that intersection of German and Russian scholarship that evolved in the 1930s and 1940s, a scholarship that received little serious study in British writings on aesthetics during the period considered here, until the latter work of Terry Eagleton and Peter Wollen.

In Germany, the work of Adorno and Benjamin on the one side, and Heidegger on the other, suggests different routes towards considering the aesthetic. The central issue is what do we talk about when we talk? How do we *look* when we look at paintings, sculptures, architecture and films? What is the connection between our looking and our writing or our talking? Where do we look or write or talk? The important feature of writing, painting and making film in the 1930s in middle to western Europe was that everything was interconnected. If aesthetics, as Eagleton would have us believe, is about the body, then the aesthetics of the early part of the twentieth century was, on mainland Europe, about the total body, trying to redeem nature from the bland appropriation of it by the post-Enlightenment romantics. Bakhtin by going back to Rabelais and the Renaissance as well as forward to Freud and Dostoevsky tried to situate the body as a text that was urban, political and tormented, but also the embodiment of joy. The same tensions are evident in the poems and elegies of Rainer Maria Rilke:

> Dance the orange. Who can forget it,
> drowning in itself, how it struggles through
> against its own sweetness. You have possessed it.
> Deliciously it has converted to you.
>
> Dance the orange. The sunnier landscape –
> fling it *from* you, allow it to shine
> in the breeze of its homeland. Aglow, peel away
>
> scent after scent. Create your own kinship
> with the supple, gently reluctant rind
> and the juice that fills it with succulent joy.[5]

In England, D. H. Lawrence, also thrashing around for natural symbols for sexuality, turned nature (and women) into something that had to be conquered:

> The proper way to eat a fig, in society,
> Is to split it in four, holding it by the stump,
> And open it, so that it is a glittering, rosy, moist, honied,
>   heavy-petalled four-petalled flower.

72

Then you throw away the skin
Which is just like a four-sepalled calyx,
After you have taken the blossom with your lips.

But the vulgar way
Is just to put your mouth in the crack, and take out the flesh in
one bite.

Every fruit has its secret.
             (D. H. Lawrence, 'Figs', *Collected Poems*, vol II, 1957: 7)

And then he goes on and on about the mysterious yoni, and why women should keep their secret 'like any Mohammedan woman/Its nakedness all within-walls, its flowering forever unseen,/One small way of access only' ending in a burst of anger against feminism

> *What then, good Lord!* cry the women.
> *We have kept our secret long enough.*
> *We are a ripe fig.*
> *Let us burst into affirmation.*

> They forget, ripe figs won't keep.
> Ripe figs won't keep.

> Honey-white figs of the north, black figs with scarlet inside, of
>   the south.
> Ripe figs won't keep, won't keep in any clime.
> What then, when women the world over have all bursten into
>   self-assertion?
> And bursten figs won't keep?

This misogynistic view of women runs deeply in all cultures, but Lawrence brought it to a fine art. In doing so, the playful, carnivalesque nature of mind/body/nature that we find in Rilke and Bakhtin is turned into a brutalism which was to reach its nadir in the paintings of Francis Bacon.

The task of the critic is surely to take the potentiality of carnival as its point of departure. In carnival the body dresses up, puts on disguises, plays roles, invents roles, acts out a communal script, all in order that the self will appear in a political and *creative* way. In the poems (and fiction) of Lawrence we have carnival of a sort, but it is the carnival of death. The 'ripe figs won't keep'. In Francis Bacon the bodies hang from meathooks, or are distorted, dismembered replicas of earlier art. The 'ripe fig' has been turned into an open wound.

THE PRODUCTION AND TRANSMISSION OF ART

Unless we have an aesthetics which tries to connect all this as a purposeful whole, we have no materialist (let alone Marxist) aesthetics. The idea of a political economy of artistic sensibility has never been more important. Yet where is it? Most political economy of the arts has looked from above – the prices quoted at Sotheby's, and that sort of thing. All of this has almost nothing to do with *producing* art, unless the artist has a genius for acquiring sponsors, which is very rare, and even if he or she does, the sponsorship is only a small part of the political economy. Most artists (or musicians or writers) are really quite dead before they make any large money (and most do not), and if they do make that kind of money while they are alive it does not mean that their art is of any lasting value or influence. The serious political economy has to do with how they negotiated their everyday lives. We read biographies precisely because this is an aspect that intrigues us. And yet, of course, there are various elements here: there is the pleasure/compulsion of going on doing *It* whatever the interpersonal involvements (and much of creativity involves manipulating those whom the creator lives with daily simply in order to get things done); there is the negotiation of a place against the dominant ideas of the arts establishments (dealers, galleries, schools and critics); and there is the appropriation of and experimentation with technique and images from wherever they come.

This involves (again!) contrasting approaches to the creative act and actor. In the Althusserian model, the humanistic conception of 'man' is a metaphysical abstraction, ahistorical and not theoretically thought through. Who we are is constituted through ideology, which is both a category of the subject and in turn constitutes individuals as subjects. This relationship Althusser calls *interpellation* or a 'hailing'. When a police officer calls out, 'Hey, you there!' to a person in the street and the person responds, the person is transformed into a subject. Using this example, Althusser goes on to argue:

> Thus ideology hails or interpellates individuals as subjects. As ideology is eternal, I must now suppress the temporal form in which I have presented the functioning of ideology, and say: ideology has always-already interpellated individuals as subjects, which amounts to making it clear that individuals are always-already interpellated by ideology as subjects, which necessarily leads us to one last proposition: *individuals are always-already subjects.*
>
> (Althusser 1971: 175–6)

He then elaborates by giving the example of the child being born and adds, 'Before its birth, the child is therefore always-already a subject,

74

appointed as a subject in and by the specific familial ideological configuration in which it is "expected" once it has been conceived' (p. 176).[6]

This approach towards establishing the relation of the subject to the ideological formations hinges on the conception of the 'relative autonomy' of the apparatuses of civil society from the economic base. In terms of art, the significant issue is in what ways cultural production can be conceived of as being 'relatively autonomous' and how relative is 'relative.' In her account of the usefulness of Althusser's approach, Janet Wolff (1981) argues that the analysis must be specific to particular societies and periods:

> The conditions under which art may be effective, politically and historically, are determined both by the nature of cultural production at that moment, and its possibilities, and by the nature of the contemporary society, and in particular of its general ideology. In societies where artistic production is highly ritualised, leaving little room for innovation of form or introduction of new or radical content, then the potential effectivity of art is obviously severely restricted. In a society where culture is restricted to a very small minority, or to a dominant group, then again its transformative power is extremely limited, whatever the aesthetic conventions prevailing. This means that any attempt at political intervention through cultural politics cannot be made in ignorance of these conditions, but must be based on an analysis of the specific relations of culture, ideology and society. That is why sweeping demands for cultural activism are both meaningless and pointless. Unless it is firmly linked with an understanding of contemporary cultural production, cultural intervention may be impossible, inappropriate, or completely ineffective.
>
> (Wolff 1981: 85)

Thus if the social and ideological spaces within which art exists form one element of the political economy, the spaces which artists create for themselves form another. These spaces, as some of the work derived from Foucault suggests, may exist quite independently of any conception of art as being progressive, avant-garde, transformative, part of a social movement, etc. The political economy of the artist must surely be partly detached from any conception of the periodization or hierarchic nature of art. Curiously, however, Althusser privileged high art in a way not unlike the work of virtually every critic, Marxist or not, since the Enlightenment.

> Art (I mean authentic art, not works of an average or mediocre level) does not give us a *knowledge* in the *strict sense*, it does not replace knowledge (in the modern sense: scientific knowledge), but

75

what it gives us does nevertheless maintain a certain *specific relation-ship* with knowledge. . . . I believe that the peculiarity of art is 'to make us see', 'make us perceive', 'make us feel', something which *alludes* to reality.

(Althusser 1977: 204)

As Terry Lovell comments, this does not help us much in trying to understand popular culture or mass art, which 'presumably can be dis-cussed entirely within the category of ideology . . . as the artistically worth-less product and instrument of bourgeois ideology' (Lovell 1980: 2–3). Althusser's position might instructively be compared with Marcuse, who goes over the top in assigning to art a liberating potential:

The autonomy of art reflects the unfreedom of individuals in the unfree society. If people were free, then art would be the form and expression of their freedom. Art remains marked by unfreedom: in contradicting it, art achieves its autonomy. The *nomos* which art obeys is not that of the established reality principle but of its negation. But mere negation would be abstract, the 'bad' utopia. The utopia in great art is never the simple negation of the reality principle but its transcending preservation (*Aufhebung*) in which past and present cast their shadow on fulfillment. The authentic utopia is grounded in recollection.

(Marcuse 1978: 72–3)

The distinction between Althusser and Marcuse is important. If Althusser would like to see art as a proto-science of the senses, Marcuse sees it as a saving moment of remembrance, not because it 'alludes' to reality, but because it creates a world which is 'opposed' to reality:

The accomplished work of art perpetuates the memory of the moment of gratification. And the work of art is beautiful to the degree to which it opposes its own order to that of reality – its non-repressive order where even the curse is still spoken in the name of Eros. It appears in the brief moments of fulfillment, tranquility – in the 'beautiful moment' which arrests the incessant dynamic and disorder, the constant need to do all that which has to be done in order to continue living.
The beautiful belongs to the imagery of liberation.

(Marcuse 1978: 64–5)

The problem with Althusser's formulation is that it exists *outside* his general system. If it was once produced, ultimately it survives as an abstraction, existing in an uneasy relationship both to the ideational structures and to science. Marcuse, although he, too, privileges art, gives us clues as to how we can begin to think of why it matters. There are three elements: art is a remembrance, it is the politicization of Eros, and it promises an alternative order of things. This sense of art is essentially a literary one (almost all of Marcuse's references are literary) but the sense of remembrance is central to how the work of art is read. One crucial feature of all the phenomenologically inspired work on aesthetics is based on what survives, why, and how it is remembered. In his 'Theses on the Philosophy of History', Walter Benjamin argued that the act of remembrance was *inevitably* skewed:

> In every era the attempt must be made anew to wrest tradition away from a conformism that is about to overpower it. The Messiah comes not only as redeemer, he comes as the subduer of Antichrist. Only that historian will have the gift of fanning the spark of hope in the past who is firmly convinced that *even the dead* will not be safe from the enemy if he wins. And this enemy has not ceased to be victorious.
>
> (Benjamin 1970: 257)

This sense of pessimism is absent from Marcuse, though his reading of the one-dimensionality of American culture might produce a deeper pessimism, while Benjamin's sense of the liberatory potentials of technology is ultimately more optimistic. In looking at any form of art the idea of what it causes us to remember is crucial. But why, how, and on whose behalf it is produced is equally crucial. How it travels over time and space is another dimension which is generally absent from most aesthetic discourses.

In his seminal essay, 'The Work of Art in an Age of Mechanical Reproduction', Walter Benjamin argued that after photography and film, art ceased to exist in anything like its traditional form: 'By means of its technical structure, the film has taken the physical shock effect out of the wrappers in which Dadaism had, as it were, kept it inside the moral shock effect' (Benjamin 1970: 240). Art could not thereafter be viewed except through the lenses of the new electronic means of communication and the political-economic uses to which they would be put. If Benjamin had a hope that something good would come out of this process, it was not a sense that high art would do it. Any form of art (as in Hitler's appropriation of Leni Riefenstahl to make movies, or Wagner to celebrate the myths of Teutonic folklore, or making Heidegger Rektor of a university, or creating a monument to a dead culture in Prague) could be commandeered to do anything. Hitler and Goebbels invented the Disneyfication of history, to create a particularly crude sense of remembrance. The task of creating a real aesthetic was much more complicated.

> Mankind, which in Homer's time was an object of contemplation for the Olympian gods, now is one for itself. Its self-alienation has

reached such a degree that it can experience its own destruction as an aesthetic pleasure of the first order. This is the situation of politics which Fascism is rendering aesthetic. Communism responds by politicizing art.

(Benjamin 1970: 244)

The real moment of a new aesthetics was therefore the moment of the Berlin Olympiad (if the Russians killed off and then replaced the poets, etc., the Germans tried to use those that they had at hand). After this moment, nothing in art was sacred: everything that had existed before was a commodity to be traded, bartered and reproduced. Henceforth art would be beholden to the media, nationalism, multinational corporations and the decentred politics of our everyday lives. Art for art's sake was a sell-out to posterity, but perhaps the instant carnival of national or political rectitude. The parameters of what to *do* had changed, whether as an artist or as a theorist. Art, after the Americans *bought off* the European expressionists, surrealists, Dadaists, post-expressionists, was in a different politico-economic game. Once art became part of power-politics, of the Disneyfication of memory, of commodity-fetishism, what price art in either Marcuse or Althusser's terms?

Benjamin argued that, because of the technological revolutions, art was, in its traditional sense, effectively dead. The aura had gone. Not only had photography/film provided the framework for a new technology within which art had to redirect itself, as genre, but also that, partly because of film and photography, the political and social context within which art would be viewed thereafter would be inevitably different. This was a perceptual issue, a political one, and a pedagogical one. If art (written, oral, musical or figurative) was, in Marcuse's sense, about the remembrance of stories well told, what price if the stories flitted by 'as an image which flashes up at the instant when it can be recognized and is never seen again' (Benjamin, 1970: 257)? The 'zapping' of the past or art is an electronic feature of our culture. But who makes the images available to us?

In his book on *The End of Art Theory* (1986), Victor Burgin takes this argument further. In the twentieth century, he argues, art criticism is no longer possible.

The art object is no more an *object* than the wine and wafer of Holy Communion are what they appear to our brute senses. The art object is the 'human essence' made form, 'civilization' made substance. . . . The idea of art as *object* began with the commodity connoisseurship in the Renaissance; it further developed within eighteenth century aesthetics, primarily with Lessing, as notion of the 'visual' as against the 'literary'. Greenberg's aesthetics are the terminal point of this historical trajectory.

(Burgin 1986: 38–9)

He goes on to say that

> the study of 'visual art' – for so long confined within artificially narrow intellectual and institutional limits – now ranges across the broader spectrum of what I have called elsewhere the 'integrated specular regime' of our 'mass-media' society. 'Art theory', understood as those interdependent forms of art history, aesthetics, and criticism which began with the Enlightenment and culminated in the recent period of 'high modernism', is now at an end.
>
> (Burgin 1986: 204)

This is not so different from Terry Eagleton's argument on literary studies:

> any attempt to define the study of literature in terms of either its method or its object is bound to fail. But we have now begun to discuss another way of conceiving what distinguishes one kind of discourse from another, which is neither ontological or methodological but *strategic*. This means asking not *what* the object is or *how* we should approach it, but *why* we should want to engage with it in the first place.
>
> (Eagleton 1983: 210)

The strategic issue is that literature, painting, sculpture or architecture are, since the advent of modern technology and the growth of capitalist consumerism, inevitably part of a much wider sense of culture. Therefore the task of a new aesthetics is on what grounds do we have a sense of judgement. Eagleton indicates four strategic sites: cultural imperialism, feminism, the 'culture industry', working-class writing. Burgin adds:

> In our present so-called 'postmodern' era the *end* of art theory *now* is identical with the objectives of *theories of representations* in general: a critical understanding of the modes and means of symbolic articulation of our *critical* forms of sociality and subjectivity.
>
> (Burgin 1986: 204)

This does not mean that texts or works of art disappear but that they take on a different contextual meaning. The fetishization of works of art or literature was a consequence of capitalism, though translated by the Russian Communists, the Nazis and by dictatorships throughout the world ever since into crassly manipulative sites.[7] In all of these cases it was built into a conception of what should or should not be read, seen, heard. But what is read, heard or seen *now* is reticulated through other grids. It is not that literature or art is banned (though there are those around who would do that) but that, because of the way that it is projected or published, it becomes the occasion for a political engagement. And *that* engagement is both an internal and an external one.

Let us take, for example, Shakespeare, an icon if there ever was one. Over the years there have been many attempts to bring Shakespeare 'to the people', from Bowdlerizing him in the eighteenth century to a mass industry in the twentieth century which includes festival theatres across the world, television and film versions (Olivier and Jonathan Miller to Kenneth Branagh). As I write this in Toronto, there are no fewer than fifteen Shakespeare plays in production within easy reach. In a copy of *The Independent on Sunday* (1 August 1993) I read that a group of actors is performing 'comic extracts' from Shakespeare at Gatwick Airport 'in the bold hope that this will distract [the passengers] during flight delays and the subdued tension that fills every departure lounge'. Shakespeare, or his facsimile, also appears in television and print commercials, in stand-up comedy, in various dramaturgical extravaganzas, in Tom Stoppard's plays or every other eastern European author drooling into his or hers Hamlet cups. 'The time is out of joint.' But it always was, my dear.

But Shakespeare is political. Boris Pasternak, when he wrote the 'Hamlet Poems', knew that. But *how* political? In a marvellously ironic essay, 'Shakespeare and the Living Dramatist', Wole Soyinka, Nigerian poet, playwright, essayist and Nobel Prizewinner, speculates on the *Arab* involvement with Shakespeare:

> Among other statistical and factual details of this fascination is this: between about 1899 and 1950, some sixteen plays of Shakespeare had been translated and/or adapted by Arab poets and dramatists. They include plays as diverse as *Hamlet*, the ever-popular *Julius Caesar*, *The Merchant of Venice*, *Pericles*, *A Midsummer Night's Dream*, *King Richard III* and – need I add – *Antony and Cleopatra*. There will have been others by now because even the government of the United Arab Republic, fed up with the number of embarrassingly inaccurate and inelegant translations, set up a committee to produce a scrupulous and complete translation of Shakespeare's works. . . .
>
> But the Arab world was not content to adopt or 'reclaim' Shakespeare's works. M. M. Badawi, in an article in *Cairo Studies* (1964) titled 'Shakespeare and the Arab World', states that the matter goes much further. Apparently it was not simply that Shakespeare stumbled on to an Arab shore during his unpublished perigrinations: he was in fact an Arab. His real name, cleansed of its anglicized corruption, was Shayk al-Subair, which everyone knows of course is as dune-bred an Arabic name as any English poet can hope for.
>
> (Soyinka 1988: 206)

So Shakespeare is the poet of travelling culture. But the space that he inhabits is contentious. As the texts themselves are pulled apart in different locations, he takes on different identities. *The Merchant of Venice*, for example, is centrally a play about Jews. ('For instance, it is claimed – as one of the reasons for endowing Shakespeare with Arab paternity – that only an Arab could have understood or depicted a Jew so "convincingly" as in *The Merchant of Venice*' – Soyinka 1988: 208.) Jonathan Miller, for a while director at the Old Vic in London, a Jew born and bred in London, argued that the play is extremely fluid in terms of its interpretation of the competing claims on loyalty.

There is no single superordinate rule to which characters can refer so that they can say in one situtation 'This must take precedence over that.' Shakespeare constantly shows that loyalties are unstable and unforeseeable. They are in fact *debatable* and the play reveals that it is in the nature of moral issues that they are problematic and require mature judgement and the capacity to evaluate competing claims upon resources – whether those resources are of love or commodity. Having thought about the play for many years, I now believe that far from being a rather trivial and regrettable work, it is perhaps the most complex and interesting of them all.

(Miller 1986: 157)

Miller also notes that in the production (at the Old Vic in 1970) Laurence Olivier had to adjust his performance:

He began with the idea of being a grotesque, ornamentally Jewish figure and bought himself very expensive dentures, a big hook nose and ringlets. I think he had a George Arliss view of himself, but gradually he realized the possible advantage in making himself look much more like everyone else, as it is this crucial question of difference which lies at the heart of the play. With the exception of the teeth, in which he had invested such a large amount of money that I did not feel justified in asking him to surrender them, he gradually lost all the other excrescences, partly because I suspect that he could see that the production could have made him appear like a ridiculous pantomime dame in the midst of the rather ordinary nineteenth-century set.

(Miller 1986: 107–8)

Thus, from the inside of production, Miller talks about the problems of a Jew producing *The Merchant of Venice*. But there are also the Jews on whom *The Merchant of Venice* was dumped, and this raises more critically the socio-cultural context within which, whoever produces or acts in it, the message is transmitted.

As a sixteen-year-old schoolboy in Pretoria, I was required to study *The Merchant of Venice*; it was the prescribed Shakespeare text for matriculating students throughout the Transvaal. In a class of thirty boys, I and two others were Jews and, because of this, much of the teaching and discussion of the play was directed at us – not hostilely, but self-consciously, perhaps as though the class would have been more comfortable if we had not been present.

(Derek Cohen 1993: 32)

Derek Cohen goes on to ask

Why had the Transvaal board of education chosen *The Merchant of Venice* as a required text for grade eleven and twelve students? Indeed, why had it done so quite frequently? The play was placed in the curriculum almost every other year ... I was not able to erase the memory of discomfort that the word *Jew* produced in me in class. The word as I later discovered, and related words like *Jewess* and *Hebrew*, is used 114 times in the play, giving it a concentration in one play matched by few other Shakespearean keywords.

(Cohen 1993: 33)

In a brilliant interpretation of how *The Merchant of Venice* has been produced over the years, Cohen argues that there have been two Shylocks: the suffering Jew as depicted by Edmund Kean in the nineteenth century ('a basically decent man who has been hounded and tormented by a cruel and prejudiced Christian community') and the 'vicious monster filled with hatred who seizes the opportunity to murder a good, kind Christian man whose only crime is a too-great fondness for his friend' (Derek Cohen 1993: 35). But the reading of Shylock is predicated on the history of Jews and their relationships with Germans, Arabs, Christians, the mass media and themselves. It is, necessarily, a fractured reading. *How* we read *The Merchant of Venice* now is based on us also reading Robert Maxwell, the Reichmans, the state of Israel, the Warsaw Ghetto, Bosnia, Barbra Streisand, Woody Allen (his films and his women) and, above all, the Holocaust:

Like Shakespeare, the Holocaust has become an industry on its own. Books, magazines, entertainment of all kinds, tourism, manufacturing, education have all been affected by the fact of this terrible event.

This ought not to be a cause for sorrow. It was an inevitable consequence of the same consumerism which has affected Shakespearean studies and which determines so much about the world we live in.

There is a good and reasonable case for dropping the word in its World War II context from the language. A holocaust is a burnt offering, a holy sacrifice. To describe the murder of six million Jewish victims of Hitler as a holocaust is to endow the event with quasi-religious mystical property that empties it of its dirty political reality, a reality which must be faced if it is to be properly understood.

(Derek Cohen 1993: 39)

'Now Barabbas was a robber.' But the Jewish crowd kept screaming 'Barabbas! Barabbas! Release Barabbas!' That anguished cry has been at the heart of Christian-Jewish relations ever since. One more word from Derek Cohen before we slip back into thinking about aesthetics:

> But towering over all these Jewish giants of wickedness and giants of Jewish wickedness is the lonely figure of Shylock. Jews, gentiles, critics, readers, producers, actors, and schoolteachers have always taken from him what they have wanted and, in all probability, they always will do so. His words will continue to be used as they always have been, to demonstrate the sheer humanity of the Jews: they will also be used, as they have been, to demonstrate Shakespeare's prescient awareness of the twisted Jewish psyche.
>
> (Derek Cohen, 1993: 39)

The work of art is not only mechanically reproduced, but also translated into a context not necessarily of its own choosing. To have any sense of aesthetics we have to recognize that its objects and its situations are always negotiated.

THE MIRROR OF ARTISTIC PRODUCTION

But art *is* produced and in its production it mirrors other forms of production. Peter Wollen (1993) has argued that *all* of contemporary art is salvaged out of the detritus of the productive process. Andy Warhol's factory may have been a 'travesty' of a real factory, but it was, after all, a real factory that it was imitating. Similarily it is clear that most twentieth-century art is based on reclaiming the work of other productive sites. In *Raiding the Icebox* (1993), Wollen discusses several cases where history and other cultures are ransacked in order to create art. Contrary to Berger or Fuller's pastoralism, art is not created out of a reclamation of the land but out of conflict, migration, cultural juxtaposition. The trick of postmodernism is to make us think that any of this is new, just because it is *next*. In his study of Los Angeles, *City of Quartz* (1990), Mike Davis shows how the entire culture of the city was imported, and that this importation creates a *frisson* of disquietude of whether Los Angeles has its own culture at all:

> the arts elites, without any concession to the have-not cultural world, have begun to recognize the evident contradictions in their *nouveau riche* strategy (followed by all Sunbelt cities) of buying culture straight off the rack of the world market. Over the last few years strenuous efforts have been made to discover seductive motifs that can act as brand labels for 'culture made in L.A.'
>
> (Davis 1990: 80)

But, of course, LA does have its own *exported* culture, the culture of Hollywood and Disneyland, which has made its own mark by recycling the histories, experiences and cultures of people from around the world. Any reading of the appropriation of world art must be set in the context of a city industry which is embarked on a project of collecting the artefacts and telling the world how to read itself.

> The new geography of power has concentrated cultural affluence in two overweening arts acropolises. On Bunker Hill, along a Grand Avenue axis, the 1964 Music Center has been joined by Arata Isozaki's Museum of Contemporary Art [1986] (which 'fills the box labelled "Culture" ') soon to be followed by the Bella Lewitzky Dance Gallery and Frank Gehry's monumental Disney Concert Hall. Other world-celebrity architects and artists, including Michael Graves and David Hockney, are involved in private developments focused around the Los Angeles Public Library, at the southern foot of Bunker Hill. Meanwhile, sixteen miles west, in the Sepulveda Pass near Westwood, Richard Meir ('perhaps the world's leading architect') is designing the $300 million J. Paul Getty Center: a museum, library and research center for the largest endowment in history ($3 billion plus). On the other side of the San Diego Freeway, in Westwood proper, octogenarian Armand Hammer is preparing his own megalomaniacal art museum, while the over-endowed, over-built campus of UCLA bulges with the expatriate cream of European postmodernism (including in a recent year Baudrillard, Derrida and Jencks).

> (Davis 1990: 78)[8]

Thus the imperialism of art acquisition and transmission. It is impossible now to think about art without thinking of both the capital and the communication technologies that make acquisition and transmission possible. At the end of *Raiding the Icebox*, after documenting the peregrinations of the Situationalist International, Komar and Melamid, Andy Warhol (and a museum is now being erected in Slovakia to its unsung hero), and of the influence of black music and dance on American post-expressionism, Wollen argues that the art of the twentieth century is essentially a project which revolves around understanding different versions of imperialism:

> As we look back over the twentieth century from our present post-colonial vantage-point and try to understand the ways in which massive culture contact has shaped the history of art, both in the core and in the periphery, we can see three main phases, which themselves correspond to phases in core–periphery relations: colonialism, anti-colonialism and post-colonialism, (though with some

84

tags and leads). The first of these was marked by the ethnographic plunder of Third World artefacts for 'hybridized' use by avant-garde artists as a resource in their overthrow of nineteenth-century academism. Here the emblematic moments were Picasso's visits to the Trocadero ethnographic collection in Paris and the painting of the *Demoiselles d'Avignon*. The second of these phases was characterized by the bold attempt of a group of artists from Mexico (*los tros grandes*: Rivera, Siqueiros, Orozoco) after the Mexican revolution to create a pan-American art in which the southern (Hispanic and Indian) periphery would be hegemonic, rather than the Eurocentric north.... Eventually... we entered a third phase, marked by what we might call the global development of 'para-tourist' art, alongside and as an alternative to the postmodernism of the core.

(Wollen 1993: 191)

Art now is not only necessarily 'para-tourist', it is also inter-media. All the products of failed revolutions, nestling in the California hills, in the silicon valleys of virtual reality, are there because the migrants have settled in trying to reclaim – electronically – past utopias. It is, of course, a lonely, anti-social world, but if we are to think through to a new aesthetics (Glenn Gould in a padded studio in Toronto recreating a Proustian Bach to invisible audiences) it is surely where we have to start. *A la recherche du images perdu* ...

NOTES

1 For a definition of 'aesthetic', Michelle Barrett, using Janet Wolff's work (1983) as her point of departure, wrote:

'Aesthetic' is commonly given three definitions or meanings: (1) received by the senses; (2) referring to beauty; (3) superior taste. The last need not concern us here since sociological approaches have forcefully demonstrated the historical vulnerability of 'taste'. We can usefully translate the other two meanings into the questions of pleasure and value.... The questions raised by the term 'aesthetic' are, briefly: Can we say that there is a distinctive 'aesthetic' faculty or mode of perception, and, if so, what is the nature of the pleasure it affords?

(Barrett 1988: 697–8).

2 Peter Osborne (1989) argued that to understand the current debates on post-modernism, it is important to reconstitute the study of the modern by a re-examination of the writings of Clement Greenberg and Theodor Adorno.
3 One possible route might be found in the work of Pierre Bourdieu, whose writing on aesthetics, as opposed to his work on education, has been little examined in Britain. See, in particular, his *Distinction* (1984) and the essay on 'Intellectual Field and Creative Project' (1971a). In Eagleton's monumental *The Ideology of the Aesthetic*, there is one reference to Bourdieu (on Kant) but no discussion of Bourdieu's own theory of aesthetics, nor, indeed, of the

considerable post-Weber, post-Durkheim writing by sociologists on culture and aesthetics. The important work of Norbert Elias receives no reference whatever. What Eagleton does, however, is to situate aesthetics as a major problematic of cultural analysis.

4 *Raiding the Icebox* (1993) collects Wollen's important critical articles on modern and postmodern art, which provide an admirable balance between a concern for social process, the significance of ideas, and the tactile/visual senses of travelling art in terms of the political economy of the artist.

5 The translation is by Stephen Mitchell of Rainer Maria Rilke's 15th sonnet of the *Sonnets to Orpheus* (1985: 47). The original German is, of course, even more interesting, because the gutteral German has to be read 'slippingly on the tongue', as Shakespeare might have said, to get the full Czech intonation:

> Tanzt die Orange. Die warmere Landschaft,
> werft sie aus euch, dass die reife erstahle
> in Luften der Heimat! Erhlhte, enthullt
> Dufte um Dufte.

And so we invent our nationality by being sexually saturated with the juices of nature.

6 For a sensitive and close reading of Althusser as his thinking affects the study of art, see the writings of Janet Wolff, in particular *Social Production of Art* (1981) which has influenced me in writing this section of this chapter.

7 In my study of *Writers in Prison* (Davies 1990), I have tried to show some of these situations, and how the conditions of incarceration, banishment become sites of struggle. For more, see also Barbara Harlow (1987; 1992). Even the *Morte d'Arthur* was written in gaol.

8 We might also add that, in recent years, LA has also been 'home' to three authors who have become important to the account presented in these pages: Perry Anderson, Peter Wollen and Dick Hebdige.

6

RACE, GENDER, CLASS AND REPRESENTATION

The discourse of radical democracy is no longer the discourse of the universal; the epistemological niche from which the 'universal' classes and subjects spoke has been eradicated, and it has been replaced by a polyphony of voices, each of which constructs its own discursive identity. . . . Juridical institutions, the educational system, labour relations, the discourses of the resistance of marginal populations construct original and irreducible forms of social protest, and therefore contribute all the discursive complexity on which a radical democracy should be founded.

(Laclau and Mouffe 1985: 191–2)

POSTMODERNISM AND RETHINKING REPRESENTATION

Laclau and Mouffe's *Hegemony and Socialist Strategy* should not have come as a surprise when it appeared in 1985. The decentring of Marxist theory had been proceeding rapidly throughout the 1970s and the early 1980s, particularly in the work conducted around *Screen* and, interestingly enough, around *History Workshop Journal* and *Race and Class* (the journal of the Institute for Race Relations). Traces had also appeared in *New Left Review*, whose publishing house issued Laclau and Mouffe's book. In many ways also the publications of the members of the National Deviancy Symposium, which operated through most of the 1970s, had staged a pre-emptive strike on behalf of decentredness by taking the 'deviant' and the 'delinquent' as the point of departure for analysing the systems of control. A series of studies by Stanley Cohen, Mary MacIntosh, Sarah Nelson, Laurie Taylor, Ian Taylor, Jock Young and others in the 1970s, drawing on segments of Marxist, symbolic interactionist, and critical phenomenology (in particular Georg Simmel) provided case studies on how everyday resistances are not just part of criminality but of all of our everyday lives. Stan Cohen and Laurie Taylor's *Escape Attempts* (1978) was a singular attempt at rethinking the practice of the everyday by using the prison metaphor to account for the framework of the society within which we all live, and to trace ways that we plan our permanent or temporary escapes:

> Our heroes though are no longer criminals, outsiders, revolutionaries and cultural critics. Men [*sic!*] in this book are only occasionally to be found at the front of revolutionary armies, fighting in the streets or raving from their asylum cells. More often they are discovered at home with their hobbies, at the pictures with their children, or on holiday with their girlfriend. Their fights against reality are rarely frontal assaults, running battles or planned campaigns. They are more often interruptions in the flow of life, interludes, temporary breaks, skirmishes, glimpses of other realities.
>
> (S. Cohen and Taylor 1978: 24)

Cohen and Taylor's book was curious in that, because it departed from the dominant allegories of structuralism or social evolution, it tried to locate everyday practices as discontinuous from the claims of the meta-narratives, and yet as a consequence of bourgeois individualism. They rejected completely the idea that these 'escape attempts' could act as the basis for a new form of social movement or radical politics.

> For the 'masses' not even the 'liberated enclave' of the commune is a possibility and they will surely not draw much consolation about the poverty, alienation and boredom of their everyday life from being told that it needs a new praxis for its transformation. They've heard that one before – and they are as unlikely to be impressed by it as they were by slogans from that other revolution.
>
> (S. Cohen and Taylor, 1978: 221)

In many ways Cohen and Taylor were the harbingers of a postmodernism which was not only anti-political but also pessimistic in seeing any chance of a revival of utopia. The escape attempts operated entirely in the 'supermarket of self'. One other curiosity is that the book paid no attention to the politics of gender or race or any other form of social difference, with the possible exception of class, and very little to the media, which has to be one of the most important escape routes of all. In many respects it is the British equivalent of 'The End of Ideology' thesis which had been so attractive to American sociologists in the 1960s, though with the difference that Cohen and Taylor's relativistic nihilism is absent from David Bell's work (see e.g. Bell 1960; 1976). Its postmodernism consists in its celebration of failed utopias and misguided commitments in favour of the depressing banality of everyday life. The problem, of course, is in the metaphor it uses to construct a sense of the everyday. The idea that prison is a metaphor for the everyday has been used before, many times (Augustine, Boethius, Pascal, Bunyan, Kierkegaard and Dostoevsky are immediate names) but Cohen and Taylor pay no attention to any of this, and thus their book is a weak attempt at constructing an allegory which is theoretically limited. Its importance, however, is that it displayed one of the blind alleys that exercised cultural theorists in the 1970s and that its presence, alongside the work appearing in the CCCS working papers, *Screen*, *m/f* or *New Left Review*, indicates how little communication there was between social theorists at that time (though Stuart Hall does get some sort of credit in the preface, but, one suspects, as a person rather than as a theorist). Its reprinting in 1992, complete with gender-blindness and indifference to many issues of difference, is therefore something of a puzzle.

In many respects the issues that crystallized in Laclau and Mouffe's work were played out much more thoroughly around the study of film and performance art. Most of those discussions took place in the pages of *Screen*. In the next few pages, I shall explore the ways in which *Screen* evolved its own project, but it is an evolution which ultimately involved different senses of movement, movements which cross-cut with each other. The account is, therefore, part narrative and part theory. But, surely, that is how it should be.

THE SCREEN PROJECT

The project that *Screen* set itself was, in its own way, as ambitious as that of the *New Left Review*, with, inevitably similar controversies and disagreements. The Society of Education in Film and Television (SEFT) was from the late 1950s an autonomous department of the British Film Institute (BFI) concerned with liaising with schools and other educational institutions in order to develop film education. *Screen* was the journal of SEFT. By 1970 SEFT and the BFI governors disagreed totally on what SEFT and *Screen*'s mandate was about. The BFI governors saw the role as to provide 'training' equipment for teachers which reissued existing material, while many of the members of SEFT were concerned with developing a critical film and television theory which would open up a debate. The upshot was that SEFT was established as an independent body, with a grant from the BFI. (The different positions are set out in *Screen* 12(3).) Essentially, the critical Marxisant/semiological issues of *Screen* begin with volume 12.

There were several areas of media studies that had not been discussed in Britain in any comprehensive way. These included the origins of film in the former USSR, surrealism, the influence of structuralism and semiotics on thinking about film, the situationalists, the growth of British film as an adjunct to war propaganda, the role of the director (as *auteur*) versus the importance of collective technology, the relationship between film and theatre as a strategic twentieth-century engagement. In particular, at the time there was the increasing availability in English of major works by Gramsci, Althusser, Brecht, Benjamin, Adorno, Barthes, de Bord and many of the Russian silent screen writers or directors. This early task was clearly connected with the problems of creating a revolutionary cinema. The main problem was Hollywood, and Hollywood's pre-eminence could be read as that of an imperial command of the media. *Screen*'s mandate then, as now, was to explore the alternatives.

For most of the 1970s, *Screen* translated, interpreted and rethought the work of (primarily) the Europeans. It entered into a discourse with *Cahiers du Cinema* in Paris, sometimes reprinting its (translated) articles. One of the issues that became clear was that, after the Nazi take-over in Germany and the Stalin terrors in Russia, the centre of radical media criticism had moved to France. The French sense of a theoretical engagement was one which, for want of any other existing on the fringe of the USA as the central imperial power, allowed it to incorporate the work of the Germans, the Russians and east Europeans, the blacks, the Spanish, the Italian, and the Latin American. It was a rich region, which, need it be added, also included the French writers themselves. But Marxist theory could be considered *then* in a multicultural dimension.

This encounter (much richer – because they were more than 'abstract' theory – than those developed at the time in either *New Left Review* or the CCCS working papers) exposed the readers of *Screen* not only to the problems of thinking about film, but also to the problems of making them. For the first decade of the 'new' *Screen*, two issues were hammered into the ground: the pre-1970s history of Marxist theory and experience of film, image and drama and the explorations of semiotics. Some of the salient pieces are put together in the first two readers that *Screen* published (*Screen Reader 1*: Cinema/Ideology/Politics, 1977; *Screen Reader 2*: Cinema and Semiotics, 1981). In re-reading these two collections in the 1990s (one about the reasons for doing it, the other about how we see) the striking feature is how discriminately political and pedagogical they are (whatever the BFI thought it was concerned about in the early 1970s). In the first collection, which covers volumes 12, 13 and 14 (but it should be coupled with vol. 15 (2) 1974 on 'Brecht and a Revolutionary Cinema') we have a marvellous sense of the problems of making films which are exempt from pure commercialism, but also we have serious, in-depth discussions of some major American films. They should be read alongside two other collections that came out at the end of the 1970s: Bill Nichols's *Movies and Methods* (1976) and Gerald Mast and Marshall Cohen's *Film Theory and Criticism* (1979), which include not only some of the material that *Screen* and *Cahiers du Cinema* pioneered, but also a large amount of the material that anyone specializing in film criticism in the 1970s would have taken as read: Bazin's *What is Cinema?*, Kracauer's *Theory of Film*, Sontag's essay on Leni Riefenstahl, Andrew Sarris's 'Theory of Film History' and Christian Metz's *Film Language*. Sam Rhodie, the editor of the new *Screen*, is represented in the Nichols collection (though not in *Screen Reader 2*) by the paper to the BFI which launched the whole exercise in Britain: a paper which, interestingly for its source, takes a sceptical look at the relevance of structuralism for cinema theory. Finally, Tony Bennett's *Formalism and Marxism* (1979), the translated works of Bakhtin, and the various collections by Peter Wollen are indispensable in understanding the contexts of the debates on the Russian, German and French material.

The issues have become central to our thinking about film. In what ways do films 'reproduce' or 'represent' reality? If structuralism is based on a linguistic allegory, is it not possible that a structuralist 'reading' of cinema reduces film to literary terms rather than cinematic ones? If film is a collective production (and it surely is) how then can we talk about the 'author' of a film? (Is not that whole debate around the *auteur* itself a literary carry-over? Or, perhaps, the debate around the death of the author in literature is a carry-over from film production?) Can structuralism help to tell us why a film is 'good'? Can we distinguish between how meaning is communicated, what the meaning is, and how to evaluate it aesthetically? (Nichols 1976: 469)? The twin projects of the 1970s were to examine the Russian/German discourses of the 1920s and 1930s and to explore the implications of the French discourses of the 1960s and 1970s.

The exercise in the 1920s and 1930s was essentially to subject the concepts of realism and revolutionary practice to close scrutiny. This involved examining those Russian writers and film-makers (Mayakovsky, Vertov, Eisenstein, Jakobson, Shklovsky, Bakhtin, Volosinov and Meyerhold) as well as the cultural journals *LEF* and *Novy Lef* who 'saw the task of art as problematising language and representation, carrying on a work of criticising ideology by disrupting its habitual forms' (John Ellis, 'Introduction' to *Screen Reader 1*: vii). Because of the *sequence* of its transmission and translation from Russia to France to Britain this exercise was largely conducted in structuralist and semiological language. The work was being thought about as the English editions of Barthes's *S/Z*, Althusser's *Lenin and Philosophy*, Lacan's *Four Fundamental Concepts of Psychoanalysis*, Kristeva's *Desire in Language*, Derrida's *Of Grammatology* and Christian Metz's *Language and Cinema* were being read, tortuously. In many respects *our* reading of them is necessarily through the same lenses, as was true of the reading of Gramsci (see Chapter 5), because the structuralist trope has become part of our language, but this should not prevent us from pausing to reflect on what happened to critical theory as a consequence. Of course a linear development can be traced from the Russian formalists through to the poststructuralists and ultimately to the attempts at making sense of gender and race as political and cultural processes. In many ways, *Screen* pioneered this way of reading, because it started off with the issue of representation: after all, that was at least one of the issues that bothered the artists and writers in the Russian revolution. 'Who speaks for us?' and its parallel question 'On whose behalf am I speaking?' are clearly two of the most urgent calls of any revolution. But there is another call: 'What are we trying to do?' And yet another: 'How do our voices come to be transmitted so that you receive them?' And yet (if we are in the process of creating a revolution) another question (from Trotsky, Alexander Blok and both Mandelstams and many others, including Lenin) how much and what parts of the past are worth preserving. Why?

Not all of these questions were posed by *Screen*, except delinquently. The central issue from the early 1970s to the end of the 1990s was representation. Certainly an important question, but one which was ripped out of context by a reading of history which was mechanistically applied. The twin issues of the Gramscian paradox (militarize the party and cultivate an organic graft to create an herbaceous garden) are missed in much of *Screen*, which, in many respects, chose the obvious psychological and political dichotomies (white/black, male/female, hegemony/counter-hegemony, North/South, etc.) as its point of engagement, forgetting the nomad, the delinquent, the marginal or the peripatetic as another crucial issue of contemporary culture. The centring on *visible* differences (gender or race), and cloning them with ideology or hegemony, made it difficult to say anything about the *invisible* differences, or the differences which are based not on the evident realities of physical discrimination but on different lifestyles, ideas and marginalities. The 1990s have become a time when the invisible differences have become manifest. The issue of Salman Rushdie, of the unbelievably real atrocities in what used to be called Yugoslavia, of the terror-wars in Zaïre, or religious fascism in India are not centrally about 'representation' but about the terror that is within. Leon Trotsky was *persona non grata* under Stalin's fiefdom because he was in opposition: he is still *persona non grata* because he was a Bolshevik. That he was Jewish is not immaterial, but hardly central.

And yet the *Screen* project produced a major shift in our sensibilities. Film could never again be taken as a text which could be simply read or viewed. As Anthony Easthope wrote:

> *Screen*, committed to the possibility that radical cinema, in denying a transcendental position to its spectator, could intervene in the direction of social change, necessarily therefore had to expose explicitly the Althusserian account of the unchanging subject of 'ideology in general' and deny Althusser's 'thesis that ideology has no history' (MacCabe 1986: 53). But, at the very moment of making this movement, the *Screen* problematic tries to retain sufficient purchase on the notion of ideology in general to argue that cinema can act as ideology *outside the cinema*.
>
> (Easthope 1988: 66)

In a debate which included Stuart Hall, Rosalind Coward, Colin MacCabe and Stephen Heath in the late 1970s, the issue of ideology and film was worked over in such a way to draw out the problematic relationships. How does film act ideologically outside of its own immediate parameters? Is this a textual presence, an institutional one, a visceral/kinetic one? Because film, like books, lends itself to textual reading, the issue of the relationship between the production and the viewer was central to any consideration of how ideology was formed and how films were made. One of the temptations – which the *Screen* project revealed – was to see ideology as an abstraction, as something that existed in a general form, extra-terrestrial, located in and consummated in film. But this turns around on the notion of the audience, the viewer, the reproducer.

The classic *Screen* position was that the reader was 'inscribed in the film'. That is, that the reader was an 'ideal reader, one who completely conforms to the supposed intentions of the text' (MacCabe 1975: 162). But, as Stuart Hall's essay on 'Encoding/Decoding' (1980a) tried to show, there was a distinction between the 'inscribed' reader and the historical, situated one. Much of *Screen*'s project was based on trying to work out of that knotty dialectical problem. The issue came to centre on the notion of representation: who speaks for us? Before we return to the *Screen* project, it is important to examine the work that came from the historians which established a symmetrical counterpoint to similar problems.

HISTORY FROM BELOW

Although E. P. Thompson's *Making of the English Working Class* (1963) became the standard benchmark for 'writing history from below', its themes had, of course, been mulled over many times before, though perhaps no one had sat down in libraries and with a collective of scholars and actually tried to do it in a manner that was honest and critical. The sounding out of an alternative history had been present since the Godwin family (William Godwin, Mary Wollstonecraft and Mary Shelley) had tried to rewrite men's and women's rights and representations. Virginia Woolf's writings (in particular *A Room of One's Own*) had invited a re-reading of literature as well as the status of women as intellectuals. Oscar Wilde's *De Profundis* was as vivid a defence of gay rights as might be possible under the bizarre circumstances of his arrest, trial and imprisonment (as, indeed, were Roger Casement's diaries from Congo, South America and Ireland). A host of manuscripts (some published, many not) from the colonies, the English, Welsh, Irish and Scottish working class progressively built up another version of the alternative history. In addition to this, the French and Russian revolutions provided case studies on what the problems would be if the dispossessed actually took over the state and tried to speak for themselves. The Jacobins (even the Black Jacobins of Haiti), the attempt at creating Proletcult in the USSR, the Cultural revolution in China, provided the vantage-points for examining how the life-experiences of *les damnées de la terre* would be told and then misappropriated for causes not of their own choosing.

The growth of a critical history in Britain (and also in France, the USA, Australia and India) was therefore one which was conscious from the outset of the problems of giving voice, but also conscious of the problems that any voice that was given would be appropriated by those who wished to traduce them in their own interests. Between the cynicism of those who would take any voice to gain power and the pessimism of those whose voice had always been appropriated by the power-mongers lay a great gulf of credibility. There was a slender hope that the voices of the dispossessed would, at some point, provide the grounding for a genuinely alternative sense of being. 'Causes lost . . . might still be won' elsewhere. The issue, of course, was that no one might listen to the older experiences, or, if they were listened to, not know how to translate the messages into their own experiences. The feminists of North America, the gypsies of Central Europe, the Kurds, the destitute multiculturals of Sarajevo, the blacks in US ghettoes, might not know that they had a common cause, nor on what basis they would create a language of commonality. The work of the historians in Britain, whether they called themselves phenomenologists, Marxists or structuralists, tried to establish the grounds from which people spoke at all. At the same time, they raised the issue of whether any meaningful action was possible, except within the formulae established by the existing orders. If so, what could the action mean? Who or what were the agents of change?

E. P. Thompson's own work was based on the premiss that people were collectively and severally responsible for their own actions, though in conditions not of their own choosing. In a felicitous phrase he talked about the customs we have in common as the starting-point towards creating the sensibility of feeling that Raymond Williams saw as the connecting point of creating a common sociable culture.[1] We never start with a *tabula rasa*, and thus historical research is the occasion both for grasping the moment before it is lost (in Walter Benjamin's words 'to seize hold of memory as it flashes up in a moment of danger')[2] and to recognize that this act involves a rewriting of the dominant narratives in such a way that they reconnect with our present condition ('In every era the attempt must be made anew to wrest tradition away from the conformism that is about to overpower it . . .'). But such work is necessarily collective, and the work of the historians, collective in sensibility, tries to re-collect the disparate others.

Thus there is an issue of representation ('Who speaks for us?' is an ongoing and burning issue) but the 'we' who seek voice are not necessarily

94

entities that can be identified in relation to other peoples' identities, even others who seem to be our clones. The sad saga of Salman Rushdie is surely a warning on that one. The issue is that of the ironic, the parodic, the satiric. Who laughs for us, with us, against us is surely as important as who does the collective warbling. In his studies of Rabelais and Dosto-evsky, Mikhail Bakhtin argued for a dialogic way of collecting discourses. This surely means that the different voices must be heard, but heard in a form which is patterned in such a way that each voice is collected into a meaningful whole. And, of course, there are voices of carnival and humour, independent and mellifluous, robust and antagonistic. Like Walter Benjamin's account of Paul Klee's 'Angelus Novus' they 'brush history against the grain' (Benjamin 1970: 258–9).

> A Klee painting named 'Angelus Novus' shows an angel looking as though he is about to move away from something he is fixedly contemplating. His eye is staring, his mouth is open, his wings are spread. This is how one pictures the angel of history. His face is turned to the past. Where we perceive a chain of events, he sees one single catastrophe which keeps piling wreckage upon wreckage and hurls it in front of his feet. The angel would like to stay, awaken the dead, and make whole what has been smashed. But a storm is blowing from Paradise, it has got caught in his wings with such violence that the angel can no longer close them. The storm irresist-ibly propels him into the future to which his back is turned, while the pile of debris grows skyward. This storm is what we call progress.
>
> (Benjamin 1970: 259–60)

This sense of collective disaster ties in very neatly with Bakhtin's theory of the carnivalesque, though he adds a piquancy of collective pleasures to his account. In the Bakhtinian/Benjamin elaboration of the collective moment, the search for the 'lost people' of history is, of course, necessarily a search for the alternative agents of history, for the putative heirs to the proletariat as the transforming angels of history. But – and it is a big BUT – how will these agents be identified? In the work of the social historians, the task often seems to identify the people in their many guises, certainly, but ultimately to find familiar faces in the crowd. The historian wants to find *us* in *them*. But, because the historian is honest, he knows that we were not always there. Thus there is another search – to find a fixed point of commonality between us and them. Bakhtin tries to find it in carnival and in how we have always handled discourse. E. P. Thompson comes up with another clue:

> the rules and categories of law penetrate every level of society, effect vertical as well as horizontal definitions of men's [sic!] rights and status, and contribute to men's self-definition or sense of ident-

ity. As such law has not only been imposed *upon* men from above: it has also been a medium within which other social conflicts have been fought out. Productive relations themselves are, in part, only meaningful in terms of their definitions at law: the serf, the free labourer; the cottager with common rights, the inhabitant without; the unfree proletarian, the picket conscious of his rights; the landless labourer who may still sue his employer for assault. And if the actuality of the law's operation in class-divided societies has, again and again, fallen short of its own rhetoric of equity, yet the notion of the rule of law is itself an unqualified good.

(Thompson 1977: 267)

If this was not the antinomian response that was expected from Thompson after *The Making of the English Working Class*, it did reflect the *Geist* of a continued sense of ongoing common traditions and where they might be found.[3]

The revolution of history from below was, however, in many ways open to the same criticisms as might be advanced against much cultural and social anthropology, and, indeed, against the work of Bakhtin. These were that the analysis of the lives of the people was, in most respects, not done by them but on behalf of them.[4] In its origins, the *Annales* group of historians in France (whose work was very influential in their formative years on Thompson, E. J. Hobsbawm, Raphael Samuel and Georges Rudé) drew heavily on anthropological conceptions of *mentalities* in order to understand the world-views of ordinary people in Africa, Asia, Australia or the Americas. But whereas the anthropologists in their continuing work (Levy-Bruhl, Lévi-Strauss, Edmund Leach, Mary Douglas) related *mentalities* to the sense of a universal, rational logic that was related to everyday practice, the historians seemed to project something alien on to their subjects. Although Thompson wanted to 'rescue the poor stockinger, the Luddite cropper, the "obsolete" hand-loom weaver, the utopian artisan, and even the deluded follower of Joanna Southcott, from the enormous condescension of posterity', it was, perhaps, more of an appropriation of these people to another cause (Thompson's own) than to fully reveal them as they were. Was 'history from below' another form of 'Orientalism', to use Said's language, a grasping for the 'people' to validate one's own culture?

These observations are not intended to traduce the important work that the historians worked on – far from it – but to raise the issue, in a new form, of 'Who speaks for us?' The agenda of Thompson and of the History Workshop group was to give voice to the dispossessed, but it was a search for a voice which would fit a conception of an alternative current of history, a current of history, surely, that was based on a perception of routes taken/not taken. These are important issues that attend all our destinies. But, once that Pandora box had been broken open by those in the west who cared for an alternative culture, anything goes. Who is speaking for the Aboriginal Australian, the Maori, the Andalusian, the Romanian gypsy, the North American feminist, the Palestinian, the Protestant Irish and the transnational exile? The creative search for voices is more vivid than that which has been imagined by those who simply want to hear tribal voices. And this is why the structuralist voice is important as an alternative. It is a voice which asks 'What do these voices mean?'

The structuralist tries to collect these voices into a coherent whole. Its arrogance is that it poses the possibility of collection, its democracy is that the collection can be made only in terms of the language that we all possess. And, ultimately, the structuralist, because he or she is about language, is about sensuality and the texture of relationships. While phenomenology, because it is concerned with lost pleasures, is despairing of the failed others (places, people, situations), structuralism is concerned with the touch of the here and the immediate. Structuralism is directly related to poetry as the creative voice of man (woman) kind, phenomenology to music as the reclamation of posterity.

A *purely* phenomenological history is necessarily exclusive of some important elements that are germane to its own analysis. As has been often remarked, E. P. Thompson, by excluding the Irish, the Welsh and the Scottish from *The Making of the English Working Class*, excluded both complementary and counter-evidence to his own thesis. In trying to be inclusive of the development of class consciousness in England, he was necessarily exclusive of the bits that did not fit. This process (unintentional and perhaps pragmatic) must ultimately be seen as the construction of a particular *habitus* from which the rest of the world is viewed. In a critique of Raymond Williams's *Towards 2000* (1985), Paul Gilroy hammers home the argument, in a sense hitting Williams and Thompson with the same hammer.

> More disturbingly, these arguments effectively deny that blacks can share a significant 'social identity' with their white neighbours who, in contrast to more recent arrivals, inhabit what Williams calls 'rooted settlements' articulated by 'lived and formed identities'. He describes the emergence of racial conflict where an English man (English in the terms of sustained modern integration) protests at the arrival or presence of 'foreigners' or 'aliens' and now goes on to specify them as 'blacks'. Williams does not appear to recognize black as anything other than the subordinate moment in an ideology of racial supremacy. His use of the term 'social identity' is both significant and misleading. It minimizes the specificities of nationalism and ideologies of national identity and diverts attention from

analysis of the the political processes by which nation and social identities have been aligned.

(Gilroy 1987: 50)

Thus both Williams and Thompson defined a 'space' that we inhabit and out of which we view the world. There is some correction of this in Dorothy Thompson's collection of essays (initially published in different collections in the 1970s and 1980s) *Outsiders: Class, Gender and Nation* (1993) which includes essays both on women and on the Irish in English Radical politics in the nineteenth century. In *Customs in Common* (1993a), E. P. Thompson includes two pieces on 'The Sale of Wives' in England in the nineteenth century, and on 'Rough Music' (the custom of confronting wrong-doers – usually drunks, wife-beaters and adulterers – with a cacophony of sounds made on kitchen utensils or burning in effigy in a form of summary justice).

The problem, of course, is that this kind of historical writing makes it difficult to include others without rewriting their histories as well. As the Indian historian Dipesh Chakrabarty has said:

Insofar as the academic discourse of history ... is concerned, 'Europe' remains the sovereign theoretical subject of all histories, including the ones we call 'Indian', 'Chinese', 'Kenyan', and so on. There is a peculiar way in which all these other histories tend to become variations on a master narrative that could be called 'the history of Europe'. In this sense, 'Indian' history itself is in a position of subalternity: one can only articulate subaltern subject positions in the name of this history.

(Chakrabarty 1992: 1)

One reason for all this is that historians, by and large, write for other historians, and that the dominant historical institutions, associations and research resources are in the west. Thus history from below, even though it uncovers a layer of experience that was formerly absent in historical research, creates an appropriation of its subject-matter that makes 'representation' essentially tokenish. In the preface to *The Making of the English Working Class* Thompson argued against the developmental approach of structural-functionalists, but the idea of courses not taken by European 'history' and the expectation that they may be taken up in Africa or India itself implied a developmental approach to them. The same problem arises in the ways that black American writers conceive of Africa. The task, it seems, is not to find out what is actually happening in Africa, but to find in Africa validations of (or alternatives to) what is happening to blacks in America.[5] This is perhaps not so far away from the general thesis advanced by Edward Said in his book *Orientalism*, whose ultimate message is not so much about giving voice to people in the Third World but in deconstructing the use to which the concept of the Orient was put by western scholars, politicians and writers. As James Clifford (1988) has written, after indicating the problems in Said's hermaneutical short-circuits and the attempt at finding a textual unity in his material,

> Beyond these problems (faced by any interpreter of constructed, complex cultural ensembles) lies a substantial and disquieting set of questions about the ways in which distinct groups of humanity (however defined) imagine, describe, and comprehend each other. Are such discourses ultimately condemned to redundancy, the prisoners of their own authoritative images and linguistic protocols? Orientalism – 'enormously systematic,' cosmological in scope, incestuously self-referential – emerges as much more than a mere intellectual or even ideological tradition. Said at one point calls it 'a considerable dimension of modern political-intellectual culture.' As such it has less to do with the Orient than it has to do with 'our' world.
>
> (Clifford 1988: 260–1)

And this takes us on a strange roller-coaster ride. Said's work, with its blend of Foucault, Lukács and Sartre, is precisely the critique that must be ridden in order to come to terms with the ways that the critical west encounters its internal and external others. And yet, as Said himself asks at the end of his book, there is, perhaps, the ultimate question: 'How does one *represent* other cultures? Is the notion of a distinct culture (or race, or religion, or civilization) a useful one?' (Said 1978: 325). The question is, in most respects, the auto-critique of Said's own work up to that sentence. His subsequent writing culminates

> in the insistence that the double task of responsible knowledge is to resist the pressures of the dominant culture and of what would now increasingly be dubbed 'system', 'theory', 'grand theory', 'disciplinary knowledge', and several even more colourful epithets – referring frequently to Marxism in particular, but also to any other way of being-in-the world which seeks to establish theoretical as well as narrative intelligibility of history as such, and then identifies collective agents (such as class, gender, nation) as bearers of resistance and political action. All such *systems* are rejected ... so that resistance can only be personal, micro.
>
> (Ahmad 1992: 199–200)

Ultimately, Said's debate around representation, for all its arguments around hegemony and a Foucauldian concern with knowledge as power, takes us on a divergent route from Thompson's. Thompson's *intent* clearly is to give a voice to the forgotten actors in history, and through most of

99

his life he wrestles with the idea of various collectivities. If he holds on to an identification with the English, and the creating of its culture, and its historical struggles, it is because the texture of the relationship between historial experience and everyday struggle must be felt, inhaled, seen. During the miners' strike of 1972 the miners were itemized by the press and the government as 'a special case'. Thompson wrote:

> The 'special case' turns out, after all, to be the general case of the working nation. It is never safe to assume that any of our history is altogether dead. It is more often lying there, as a form of stored cultural energy. The instant daily energy of the contingent dazzles us with brightness. What passes on the daily screen is so distracting, the presence of the status quo is so palpable, that it is difficult to believe that any other form of energy exists. But this instant energy must be reproduced every moment as it is consumed; it can never be held in store. Let the power be cut off for a while, then we become aware of other and older reserves of energy glowing all around us, just as, when the streets are dowsed, we become aware of the stars.
>
> (Thompson 1980: 75)

In the case of Said, however, the issue of representation is ultimately a game to be played inside a particular sense of what constitutes a global, radical intelligentsia. For all the claim to seeing 'representing' culture as a problem, for all the espousal of a nomadological critique, and for all the Foucauldian concern about the marginalization of other cultures, the 'bottom line', as they would say in business circles, is what constitutes the community of the literate in which the itinerant intellectuals have common cause with each other in order to define an alternative world-view which is *necessarily* the condition of the present age. In a long chapter titled 'Resistance and Opposition' (1993a: 191–281) in his collection *Culture and Imperialism*, Said tries to write a manifesto for a global intelligentsia who have a common radical cause, stretching from the beginning of the twentieth century to the present. There is a problem, however. As with the arguments advanced in *Orientalism*, the cases are entirely literate, and the debate couched in terms of common causes between those who have common linguistic and philosophical heritages. There are no social or existential experiences which are not part of an intertwining text. With Thompson, at least there is the search for an alternative experience which has not been mediated. With Said, the experiences make sense only in terms of a theory which all have in common.

But even historians rely on documents for much of their work, and documents are written by the literate, who, in most Third World countries, have been educated through a colonial system which put a premium on what Basil Bernstein (1971a) termed 'elaborated codes' of language. Therefore history from below in the Third World, if it is not to be elitist history, must be oral history, a history which has all the pitfalls of cultural anthropology. The history that has barely been attempted is a global subaltern history written for, and on behalf of, the oppressed in Africa, India, Britain, the United States and Russia on themes of common concern: migration, gender, trade and war. With new, electronic means of communication it should be possible to establish the networks for such research if governments and institutions of learning are prepared to devote resources to people who need them most. Meanwhile there continues to exist the oppression of particular forms of expression, or, as Trinh T. Min-ha has written, 'Clarity is a means of subjection, a quality both of official, taught language and of correct writing, two old mates of power: together they flow, together they flower, vertically, to impose an order' (Minh-ha, 1989: 16–17).

IDENTITY

Perhaps not surprisingly, one of the twists taken in the debate on representation has been on the issue of identity, and this, in part, returns us to some of the topics explored by *Screen*, and provides an opportunity to consider some nuanced issues that have been only sketched so far. In 1986 the Institute of Contemporary Arts (ICA) in London organized a conference on 'The Real Me: Postmodernism and the Question of Identity'. The stimulus for the conference was a television opera/documentary made by ICA called 'The Man Who Mistook His Wife for a Hat', directed by Chris Rawlence, as well as a book of the same title by Oliver Sacks. ICA published as 'ICA Documents 6' various papers that related to the theme of the conference (see Appignanesi 1987). Of the entries in the book two pieces (by Rawlence and Jacqueline Rose) spin off directly from the film/book, while the others establish their own spaces. The film included the dissection of the human brain of a man who had died of Alzheimer's disease, thus setting the scene for the ultimate biological encounter with the 'real me'.

In the published version, apart from the authors noted above, contributors included Homi Bhabha (who provided a theoretical summary of the other contributions), A. S. Byatt, Cornelius Castoriadis, Terry Eagleton, Bernard Edelman, John Forrester, Richard L. Gregory, Stuart Hall and James Lingwood. The significance of the whole event, perhaps, was that it focused several themes which had been in the air throughout the 1980s, but here confronted by a cross-section of radical theorists and creative artists. It also indicated how many of the questions that had dominated cultural theory in the 1970s had either been abandoned, or had been reformulated.

Jacqueline Rose is perhaps the most useful entry-point because she directly questions not only the inherent logic of the Sacks/Rawlence project, but also the implications of feminist psychoanalytic work for our sense of both the visual and the literate in confronting the latent gender biases in some contemporary critical writing. The issue is centrally that if the psychic is to be taken as 'a model of the social (as diagnosis and/or metaphor)', then the issue of sexual difference must be seen as central to the account if there is not to be a minimizing of the importance of the woman's fantasy. Further, the conception of terror must not be pushed to the edge of such accounts, because if it is we will not be able to come to terms with the ways that 'violence functions as a fantasy of the social today'. Finally, the question of the visual is addressed using the work of Barbara Kruger and Cindy Sherman. The visual, far from having any inherent 'innocence', is centrally 'distorted and subject to the psycho-sexual in the full range of its effects' (all quotes from Rose 1987: 30–3). In doing this Rose resists what she sees as the nostalgia for a reintegrated fantasy of the male self that she sees in the work of Fredric Jameson, among others.

This feminist Lacanian reading of the issues of identity provides a clue for why the search for a core identity in the politics of representation is so fraught with conflict. Most of the papers in the collection are concerned with presenting concise accounts of work for which the author has elaborations elsewhere: Richard Gregory, author of *Eye and Brain*, discusses the Self, by considering how the brain perceives certain kinds of patterns, making a distinction between perception and conception; James Lingwood discusses the consequences of photographic self-portaits on self-image; Antonia Byatt provides an autobiographical account of her own identity as a writer; Bernard Edelman discusses legal issues arising from contested appropriations of fictional characters; and Cornelius Castoriadis outlines his theory of institutions, organizations and the historical constitution of autonomy. These pieces could have been put together in other collections (some were) without the subject of identity being remotely close to the theme of the book, even though they *do* bear directly on it. What gives the book (and presumably the conference) its unique force are four papers which jump right out of the cultural studies/representation debate, and which compel the reader to rethink the other papers (mentioned above) in the collection.

These papers – by Bhaba, Forrester, Hall and Eagleton – establish a bridge from the politics of representation to the debates around postmodernism and post-Marxism to which we return in the final chapter. What is unique about them – and what would set them apart from any conference on a similar theme organized in, say, the USA or France or Germany – is the extent to which the idea of identity is seen as inherently problematic, even by the most politically committed of the authors. While in the

United States the issue of identity might be infused with a stronger sense of possessive individualism, anti-statism, ethno- or gender centrism and national arrogance, all washed down with a comfortable swill of the bubbly generic drink of 'progress', in the British debate the issue of being decentred, marginalized, and possessing minimal identities is far more important across the board. Thus the idea of identity becomes marvellously problematic rather than furiously entrenched. In the ICA papers, Forrester reminds us that the idea of identity is bound up with a debate around the subject which has slowly evolved since the early Romans, but more clearly since Pascal, culminating in Foucault's critique of Freud for 'producing' the subject. It is an argument which is grounded in over 5,000 years of history, rather than taking the contours of the present as the only parameters worth considering. If there is a tendency to schematize history into epochs or epistemic moments (particularily in Bhabha's introduction), it *is* however an attempt to come to terms with historical experience in more than a dismissive way. The sociological problem of identity is ultimately how 'Cultures come to be represented by virtue of the process of repetition through which their 'meanings' are vicariously addressed to – *through* – an Other' (Bhabha 1987: 9). What is referred to throughout the documents as 'the postmodern perspective' is in fact more of a critical perspective which tries to confront the multiple means by which identities are formed, experienced, articulated, mediated and transmitted. The central ingredients to this analysis involve not only the reformulation of the language of the self via Lacan, but also the tasks of translation (with perspectives that range from Walter Benjamin to Clifford Geertz), the experience and image of social movement, the ideas of 'globalization' which are related ultimately to communications, monopoly capital and migration, the common accord between the 'subalterns' of the Third World and those of the first and second ones, the suspension of identity between the search for meaningful communities and the prophylactic self constructed to ward off appropriation of *me* as fetish. It is an agenda for considering identity in a world of great social fluxuation.

In all of this Eagleton argues that we have 'no political theory, or theory of the subject, which is capable in this dialectical way of grasping social transformation as at once diffusion and affirmation, the death and the birth of the subject' (Eagleton 1987: 48). Stuart Hall takes up this issue directly. The idea that the 'minimal self' holds sway, that the politics of *Me* is supreme, is bizarre.

it seems to me that it is possible to think about the nature of new political identities, which isn't founded on the notion of some absolute, integral self and which clearly can't arise from some fully closed narrative of the self. A politics which accepts the 'no neces-

103

sary or essential correspondence' of anything, and there has to be a *politics of articulation* – politics as a hegemonic project.

I also believe that out there other identities *do* matter. They are not the same as my inner space, but I'm in some relationship, some dialogue, with them. They are the points of resistance to the solipsism of much postmodernist discourse. . . . I do think, theoretically and intellectually, it requires us to begin, not only to speak the language of dispersal, but also the language of, as it were, contingent closures of articulation.

(Hall 1987: 45)

The centre-point of Hall's talk was when he recognized that, as Britain had become politically and economically marginalized, his own biography became more important:

Thinking about my own sense of identity, I realize that it has always depended on the fact of being a *migrant*, of the *difference* from the rest of you. So one of the fascinating things about this discussion is to find myself centred at last. Now that, in the postmodern age, you all feel so dispersed, I become centred. What I've thought of as dispersed and fragmented comes, paradoxically, to be *the* representative modern experience! This is coming home with a vengeance! Much of it I much enjoy – welcome to migranthood.

(Hall 1987: 44)

Thus the experiential and the political and the global become linked to each other. Only Said and Diawara come close to situating themselves in a similar way in the USA.

The framing of the discourse around identity is therefore important. However, it is equally important, to recognize that the communities to which we think we belong are all imaginary, and thus that we live in a world of the 'double' – the community to which we thought we belonged and the everyday, economic, political reality which we have to contest in our everyday lives (and not surprisingly many of the papers at this conference dealt centrally with 'doubling'). Media is one one of our imaginary communities, but so is religion, psychiatry, literature, computers, ethnicity. As Hall interpellates to his own discourse,

So the notion that identity is a simple – if I can use the metaphor – black or white question, has never been the experience of black people, at least in the diaspora. These are 'imaginary communities' – and not the less bit real because they are symbolic. Where else could the dialogue of identity between subjectivity and culture take place?

(Hall 1987: 45)

With this discussion, the issues of representation take a 180 degree turn. The issues of experience and the structuring of my experience are placed on an agenda which allows us to contest the imaginary communities and the facticities of the everyday without giving priority to either. Not only does this avoid the banalities of the Dead White Male syndrome (which is antithetical to any serious politics or academics) but it puts our collective human histories as negotiable territories, to be wrestled over as we try to come to terms with the world within which we live.

THE MASK OF THE OTHER

British cultural studies started off in the late 1950s/early 1960s (mainly through the work of Williams, Hoggart, Hall, Thompson, and so on) in arguing that there was a British (or English) cultural dominance that had to be broken down in order to show that, however brilliant were the writings or the dramatical performances, they were not 'representative' of what was actually happening in Britain, or at least to the majority of the people who inhabited the islands. The task could be split up in different ways: first, why were the dominant writings (media presentations, works of art, etc) not representative? (i.e. what were the rest of the people actually saying or doing, not only now but over time?). Second, was there a Britain to which all of this related? Was Britain (or Scotland or Wales or Ireland) all purely imaginary? In which case, how to relate to the state, economics, real power and real violence? Third, what were the networks or catalysts of creativity? If the dominant modes were patriarchal, elitist, non-representative, etc., was there a way of being creative without being patriarchal, etc., but in such a way that people would read, look, listen? Fourth, if we are torn between the subjective and the cultural, the politico-economic and the ideational, how can we or anyone else act? And yet other people (either with terror or self-effacement) do act and change things dramatically: how do they become the agents of change? Is it social structure or personal charisma? These, as sociologists have told us, are the figments of our imagination. Should we even think of becoming agents for change, or should we see ourselves, rather, as the court jesters at the court of change. Ultimately, after I have written all this about you, why are you bothering to reply instead of throwing it into the trash can?

In the end, the issue of representation is related directly to the question of who is being represented by who to whom, and under what auspices. Interestingly enough the early and later members of the British New Left were conscious of their nomadology. Thus almost all of this work is conscious of different constructions of reality that would exclude or include the transient. But, as Stuart Hall says, 'welcome to migranthood'. For Americans who largely believe that the world is where they have arrived, this is an alien message which makes them unsure of how to understand transience as a fact of life. They are not Bosnians, Israelis, Palestinians, Ghanaians, Irish or Mexicans, except vicariously. This could be why Americans spend so much time watching television shows where the home territory is defended against those predatorial others. No country is so much concerned about using the Other in order to defend its own territorial space, which it calls gender, race or identity.[6]

For all the drawbacks of the way that the British constitute the issues (in particular the treatment of self through language-metaphors) it is perhaps more direct in seeing self through the Other. 'I am not sure of myself', is what the British critics seem to be saying, but that is perhaps not so different from the Greek myth of Medusa. Was I raped (by my husband, my sea-god employer)? Is this my face or a mask? Do I have another face, or is that face that you see merely a reflection in the mirror of Athene's shield, me reversed? What face are you lopping off to claim your inheritance? Does all of this matter over time? How? British cultural studies is the study of masquerade, the writing of the face behind the mask. 'The play's the thing/Wherein I'll catch the conscience of the King.'

NOTES

1 In his collection of essays, *Customs in Common* (1993a), Thompson elaborated on how popular culture was formed in the eighteenth century. In doing so he takes issue with the idea of 'culture' itself:

> we should not forget that 'culture' is a clumpish term, which by gathering up so many activities and attributes into one common bundle may actually confuse or disguise discriminations that should be made between them. We need to take this bundle apart and examine the components with more care: rites, symbolic modes, the cultural attributes of hegemony, the inter-generational transmission of custom and custom's evolution within historically specific forms of working and social relations.

(Thompson 1993a: 13)

2 Walter Benjamin, 'Theses on the Philosophy of History', in *Illuminations* (1970: 257).

3 Thompson clearly felt a certain affinity for the antinomian position, while rejecting it. In fact, many sections of *Witness against the Beast* (1993b), his interpretation of William Blake, read like a critical autobiography:

> Blake did not achieve any full synthesis of the antinomian and the rationalist. How could he, since the antinomian premised a non-rational alternative? There was, rather, an incandescence in his art in which the incompatible traditions met – tried to marry – argued as contraries – were held in polarised tension. If one may be wrong to look for a coherent intellectual system, there are certainly constellations of related attitudes and images – connected insights – but at the moment when we attempt a rational exegesis we are imposing bounds on these insights. Certainly there are moments when Blake denies the values of rationality, but one can also see why, to preserve the 'divine vision', he had to do so.

(Thompson 1993b: 228)

Now *that's* an antinomian statement, if ever there was one, though from an alternative angle it reads as if it was penned by Lucien Goldmann, writing a sequel to his book on Pascal and Racine, *The Hidden God*:

To find God, we therefore need to distinguish the real meaning of the Scriptures, to identify the real Church and the real priests from the worldly clerics and time-servers. And the real tragedy of Pascal's position lies in the fact that the believer cannot rely on his own powers of judgement to do this. No real Jansenist ever believed that he could find truth by trusting in his own reason or intuition, or by submitting himself wholly to the Church. The believer finds God 'through prayer', by the need which he has of God, and by his decision to devote the whole of his life to His service.

(Goldmann 1964: 85)

Within the Pascalian Universe

There are only three kinds of person; those who, having found God, seek Him; those who, not having found Him spend their time seeking Him; and those who live without having found Him and without seeking for Him either. The first are both blessed and reasonable, the last both mad and unhappy, and the second unhappy but reasonable.

(quoted in Goldmann 1964: 293)

Thompson displayed a particular kind of unhappiness, a variation on the first form of rationality: 'Those who, having found Him, seek Another.'

4 I am indebted to Victoria Heftler of the Graduate Programme in Social and Political Thought at York University for her insights on some of these questions. Her unpublished manuscript, 'Finding a Familiar Face in the Crowd: "History from Below", "Orientalism", and the Politics of Knowledge' (1993) is a model of critical, scholarly research.

5 This is one of the underlying topics of Wole Soyinka's *Art, Dialogue and Outrage* (1988), which attempts to deconstruct the appropriation of African culture by others. But see also V. Y. Mudimbe, *The Invention of Africa* (1988), and Kwame Anthony Appiah, *In My Father's House: What does it Mean to be an African Today?* (1990), for discussions around similar themes. Appiah, in particular, systematically discusses the Afro-American appropriation of Africa through a 'Euro-American cultural matrix' (1990: 116).

6 For a feisty, but cryptic, account of these traumas see Robert Hughes, *Culture of Complaint* (1993), and in particular Lecture 2.

7

POPULAR CULTURE AND ITS POLITICS

Intellectuals today are unlikely to recognize, for example, what is fully at stake in the new *politics of knowledge* if they fail to understand why so many cultural forms, devoted to horror and porn, and steeped in chauvinism and other bad attitudes, draw their popular appeal from expressions of disrespect for the lessons of educated taste. The sexism, racism, and militarism that pervades these genres is never expressed in pure form (whatever that might be); it is articulated through and alongside social resentments born of subordination and exclusion. A politics that only preaches about sexism, racism and militarism while neglecting to rearticulate the popular, resistant appeal of the disrespect will not be a popular politics, and will lose ground in any contest with the authoritarian populist languages that we have experienced under Reaganism and Thatcherism.

(Ross 1989: 231)

What we call 'popular culture', for example a set of generally available artefacts – films, records, clothes, television programmes, modes of transport, etc. – did not emerge in its recognizably contemporary form until the post-Second World War period when new consumer products were designed and manufactured for new consumer markets. Paradoxically, in many of the debates about the impact and significance of popular culture, these profound social and economic transformations have been mediated through aesthetic

concepts like 'quality' and 'taste'. These words are passionately contested. Different ideologies, different discourses – we could cite at random here the 'sociological', the 'art historical', the 'literary critical', as well as the discourses of marketing and industrial design cut across these words at different angles producing different meanings at different moments. Underneath the discussion of an issue like 'discrimination', complex moral, social, even economic options and strategies are more or less openly examined and the issue of taste – of where to draw the line between good and bad, high and low, the ugly and the beautiful, the ephemeral and the substantial – emerges at certain points as a quite explicitly political one.

(Hebdige 1988: 47)

WE, WHO STUDY THE POPULAR

The study of popular culture is not really about the 'people' but about intellectuals, just as the vast amount of research conducted by anthropologists in the nineteenth and early twentieth centuries was not about the Trobriand Islanders or the Nuer but about the ways that colonial intellectuals tried to map out their sense of themselves in an alien world. This is not to say that the information collected or the theories developed are useless, but it does raise the question of for whom are they useful. And it is therefore important to put the whole of the discourse around popular culture into a similar category as the current, ongoing, debate around 'Orientalism' or 'Representation', a discourse which is now at least as bitter as was anything that attended the moment of Althusser. (I am referring, of course, to the acrimonious words between Edward Said, Ernest Gellner and Aijaz Ahmad, and contrasting it with the alternative discourse around the work of Trinh Minh-ha, Teresa di Lauretis, Himani Bannerji, Chandra Mohanty and Gayatri Spivak, but I return to that topic in a later chapter.) The question of the thrust of studying popular culture (and, to some extent of cultural studies as a whole) comes in part from a journalistic curiosity of 'how the other half lives' – Henry Mayhew's accounts of *London Labour and the London Poor* (1861), or George Orwell's *Road to Wigan Pier* (1937) – and in part from sociological investigations of living conditions (from Booth and Rowntree's studies of the early twentieth century to the ethnographic monographs of Young and Wilmott's Institute for Community Studies in the 1950s). Most of this work was directed towards alleviating these conditions.

The Marxist interest was more complex. While Marx himself was clearly interested in the dichotomy between religion being both 'the opiate of the people and the cry of the oppressed', the overriding question (indicated in the 'Introduction' to the *Grundrisse*) was how identity was formed by the relation between production, consumption and distribution.

> The object of art – like every other product – creates a public which is sensitive to art and enjoys beauty. Production thus not only creates an object for the subject, but also a subject for the object ... But before distribution can be the distribution of products, it is: (i) the distribution of the instruments of production, and (ii), which is a further specification of the same relation, the distribution of the members of the society among different kinds of production.
>
> (Marx 1973a: 96)

The problem with culture was how its objects were qualitatively distributed, as well as how they were produced and consumed. Further, there was the issue of how to deal with literature or other forms of art which had been transmitted from the past. Again in the *Grundrisse* Marx addresses the problem by using Greek art:

> the difficulty lies not in understanding that the Greek arts and epic are bound up with certain forms of social development. The difficulty is that they still afford us artistic pleasure and that in a certain respect they count as a norm and as an untranslatable model.
>
> A man cannot become a child again, or he becomes childish. But does he not find joy in the child's naïveté, and must he himself not strive to reproduce its truth at a higher stage? . . . The Greeks were normal children. The charm of their art for us is not in contradiction to the underdeveloped stage of society on which they grew. [It] is its result, rather, and is inextricably bound up, rather, with the fact that the unripe social conditions under which it arose, and could alone arise, can never return.
>
> (Marx 1973a: 111)

The final, crucial, element in Marx's formulation of culture is his appropriation of the Hegelian notion of *alienation*, which is both a structural and a psychic phenomenon. In this, ultimately, the alienation from nature and self and labour is bound up with the phantasmagoria of images which, derived from the objects that surround him/her, are turned into a substitute for nature. As Lukács noted in *History and Class Consciousness* (1971), culture and historical images become 'a second nature'. Furthermore, what is an activity of alienation for the worker appears as a state of alienation for the non-worker, and the worker's real practice in his job appears to the non-worker confronting him as a theoretical attitude.

Thus, to understand culture, there are four fundamental sets of issues: (i) that the belief-systems are both soporifics and act as the language which the people will use to transform themselves ('Men make their own history, but not of their own free-will' – Marx 1973b: 146); (ii) that the relations of production, consumption and distribution provide the matrix by which culture is formed; (iii) that there are certain forms of culture from pre-modern eras which (as the species enters its adulthood) are intrinsically important because they preserve for us the sense of harmony and unity which are the hallmarks of childhood; (iv) that the banalities and traumas of everyday life are turned into a common-sense, taken-for-granted account of 'what will be, will be' by those who control and want this to appear to be so. The Russian Communist heresy, of course, played fast and loose with these distinctions, choosing elements which suited the exercise of power,[1] but the most elaborate European theorizations were in the works of Lukács, of Adorno and Horkheimer, of Benjamin, of

Bakhtin, of Gramsci, of Sartre, of Althusser, and, in some eclectic ways, in the practice of Bertholt Brecht and his circle of women collaborators.[2]

Thinking about the people's culture had certain problems associated with each and all of these interpretations. The Frankfurt School, as well as Lukács, as Marxists who were not afraid of dipping into the Kantian and Hegelian bags, basically argued around the problematics of (iii) and (iv) as ongoing universals, while seeing (i) as a transitory issue, and (ii) as indicating how the problematics of capital made a truly popular culture unlikely as long as capitalism persisted. The difference between Lukács and Horkheimer/Adorno, however, was the issue of how to connect (i) and (iii). Lukács, to the end of his life, saw hope in the rethinking of the forms in terms of the great Greek mythical and neo-realist totalities. Adorno, using music as his main point-of-departure, wanted music not only to be politically resistant but also to be innovative. But resistant to what? There is, however, a clue in the concept of *Schein* ('show', 'aesthetic appearance or illusion') which Jameson saw as a key word in Adorno, because it implied constantly pushing beyond the show. But a point might be reached where the show might end where art had no more meaning. The only space where *Schein* might live on is the culture industry where production, consumption and distribution is all. As Jameson writes:

> The deeper motive . . . is the ultimate social guilt of art itself, as that was revealed nakedly and without comment at the very dawn of 'Western' culture in the story of the Siren's song. But this 'original sin' is evidently intensified in class society by rationalism and secularization . . . with the only result that the only place where 'aesthetic appearance', 'aesthetic illusion', lives on with a clear conscience, is the Culture Industry.
>
> (Jameson 1990: 166)

Trying to fight within or against the culture industry therefore became an important project. There are, however, other theoretical versions of how the show may, or may not, go on. In Walter Benjamin the real tension was between the childish and the technical, suggestively displayed in his exploration of the story-teller and the Paris Arcades.

> All great storytellers have in common the freedom with which they move up and down the rungs of their experience as on a ladder. A ladder extending downward to the interior of the earth and disappearing into the clouds is the image for a collective experience to which even the deepest shock of every individual experience, death, constitutes no impediment or barrier. . . . The wisest thing – so the fairy tale taught mankind in olden times, and teaches children today – is to meet the forces of the mythical world with cunning and high spirits.
>
> (Benjamin, 1970: 102)

111

Susan Buck-Morss (1989) situates this childish, mythic world in the context of its technological, capitalist and architectural appropriation, inviting us to *use* Benjamin to understand our contemporary world.

Today the Paris arcades are being restored like antiques to their former grandeur; the bicentennial celebration of the French Revolution has at least threatened to take the form of another great world exposition; Le Corbusier-inspired urban renewal projects, now in decay, have become the desolate setting for a film like *Clockwork Orange*, while the 'postmodernist' constructions that reject his heritage bring both wish image and fetish into quite different constellations; 'Walt Disney Enterprises' is constructing technological utopias – one on the outskirts of Paris – in the tradition of Fourier and Saint-Simon.[3] When trying to reconstruct what the arcades, expositions, urbanism, and technological dreams were for Benjamin, we cannot close our eyes to what they have become for us. It follows that in the service of truth, Benjamin's own text must be 'ripped out of context', sometimes, indeed, with a 'seemingly brutal grasp'.

(Buck-Morss 1989: 340)

To this we should add the ways in which Benjamin tried to

decode and interpret what he called the expressive character of phantasmagoria as well. He contrasted his conception with the orthodox model of base and superstructure, and not only on the relative autonomy of culture:

The question is this: if the base determines the superstructure in what might be called the material of thought and experience, but this determination is not simply a mirroring, then how – quite apart from its originating causes – is it to be characterized? As its expression [*Ausdruck*]. The superstructure is the expression of the base ... just as for the sleeper a full stomach is not mirrored but expressed by the dream content, though the stomach may causally 'determine' that content. At first the collective expresses its conditions of life. Those conditions find their expression in dreaming and in awakening their interpretation.

(McCole 1993)

This sense of the play of culture, though, is relatively unique in Marxisant theorizing. Only Mikhail Bakhtin, operating on a treadmill, reading *against* Soviet culture, comes close. But in his case the issue of the popular is foremost. In his study of Rabelais, in his work on Dostoevsky's Poetics, and in his work on linguistics, Bakhtin outlines an approach to culture which stands aside from the normal Marxist encounters with culture, but probably in order to get closer to the central issues. The issue in Bakhtin is how the people are integrated/played with in dominating narratives. The central thesis of his work is the distinction between the monologic and dialogic form of discourse. In other words, whether I talk *at* you or whether I have conversation *with* you. In the books on Rabelais and Dostoevsky, and the fragments from books on Goethe and Freud, as well as the essays on language (probably not written under a pseudonym but as an act of real collaboration with students and colleagues), Bakhtin tries to establish both the literature that gives form to the dialogic, and also the social spaces within which dialogue is possible. He traces the process from the epic (Marx iii above) through to the conditions of production/consumption/distribution (ii), via the circuits of alienation (iv) to the cry of the oppressed (i). The crucial issue of language is that it is grounded in history, which encompasses all of the above. Bakhtin's work is centred around how the people survive through their practices and their language. (It is perhaps not surprising that the English – via Tony Bennett – appropriated the carnivalesque Bakhtin, probably because the English have had no carnivals since Cromwell, while the Welsh – via Raymond Williams – were more interested in the history of language, because language, or the absence thereof, has been a central preoccupation of the Welsh since the days of Edward the Conqueror. The French, partly through the influence of Julia Kristeva, and partly because of the intellectual climate when he was translated and lived there, cloned him as an earlier Lacanian. The Americans, of course, saw him as an important adjunct to the Europeanizing of literary theory.) If Bakhtin's work is therefore the work of someone who asks under what conditions is dialogue possible, each society has, more or less, appropriated him to their own concerns.[4] The monologic has taken over.

In retrospect, Sartre's commandeering presence throughout the period from the 1930s to the 1970s has now been overtaken by Simone de Beauvoir and Jean Genet, she because she made more sense by situating herself in her gender, and he because as a gay prisoner, appropriated by Sartre as a symbol, he lived a rough, trammelled walk through the minefields of dissent. And yet, and yet. It was Sartre who, when called on, introduced both Aimé Cesaire's *Return to my Native Land* (1956) and Frantz Fanon's *Wretched of the Earth* (1962) to an unsuspecting public. It was Sartre who helped to found *Présence Africaine* as well as *Temps Modernes*. It was Sartre who, after thinking through the inauthenticity of Heidegger's Nazism, worried us all with the concept of being authentic, in spite of all that rhetoric of being for itself. The Sartre who taught us that 'L'enfer – c'est les autres' was also the Sartre who made us think through the possibility that, after the nauseous sense of the pitiless nonsense of the everyday, there might be a grounded, materialistic humanism. The Sartre of cultural studies was the Sartre who tried to say that, in the chaos of the everyday, there was an essence which pulled us together. In

Marx's terms it was the 'species man' asserting itself against the condescension of the structural definitions. It was not enough, of course. Camus,
the Algerian *pieds noirs*, could buy the absurdity of being, but would
ultimately shy away from the commitment to political authenticity. He
could not deny himself.

Thus enter the structuralists (from Rousseau through Durkheim and
Marcel Mauss to Lévi-Strauss, via structural linguistics, to Althusser – a
straight path to the ultimate myth). Not quite a straight line, of course.
Roman Jakobson (1930) gave it a few squiggles:

> We strained toward the future too impetuously and avidly to have
> any past behind us. The links in the chain of time were broken. We
> lived too much in the future, thought about it, believed in it; the
> self-generating evils of the day did not exist for us. We lost a sense
> of the present. We were witnesses in the great socialist, scientific, and
> other such cataclysms. *Byt* remained. Like that splendid hyperbole of
> the young Mayakovsky, 'the other foot was still running along a
> side street.' We knew that the thoughts of our fathers were already
> in discord with their surroundings. We read harsh lines alleging that
> our fathers fought in the hire of the old, unventilated commonplaces.
> But our fathers still had remnants of faith in their convenience and
> social utility. To their children was left a single, naked hatred for
> the ever more threadbare, ever more alien cast-offs of the vulgar
> reality. . . .
>
> Nor is the future ours. In several decades, we shall be cruelly
> invoked as the children of the last century. All we had were compel-
> ling songs of the future: and suddenly these songs were transformed
> by the dynamics of the day into a historico-literary fact. When
> singers are killed and their song is dragged into museums and pinned
> to the wall of the past, the generation they represent becomes even
> more bankrupt, orphaned and displaced – disinherited in the most
> authentic sense of the term.
>
> (Jakobson 1930, quoted in Ehrmann 1970)

The blush of culture, in its most dedicated sensibilities, as the shadows
cross the inventiveness of structural theory, should help us remember
those lines.

But *then* there was structural Marxism. One of the more extravagant
features of the influence of Althusser was how a phenomenologist, such
as Gramsci was, could be turned into a structuralist. The Marx of (i), (iii)
and (iv) was reduced, ultimately, to (ii). It is not surprising that Marx
himself could be so appropriated; after all, nine-tenths of his own writing
was linked to variations of (ii). But Gramsci? Gramsci, student of Croce,
the Italian Hegelian, was concerned, ultimately, with how the Italian
Communist Party, after the failure in Turin in 1919 and the rise to power

of Mussolini shortly after, could transform the idea of working-class control into reality. Gramsci chose culture (ideas of nationality, religion, education, the family and the work ethic) as the prerequisite for revolution. His stance on each of these was quite specific, and his attitude to what would constitute the preliminaries for a proletarian cultural revolution was equally specific. In the course of thinking this through (in prison) he appropriated two concepts from Hegel. The first was the idea of 'civil society' (that area which existed in any society as relatively independent of both the state and the economic controllers or producers), and the second was the idea of 'common sense' (the notion that in industrial society there is a commonality of discourse which everybody agrees on because it is taken for granted).

The problem with all this was that it was *fuzzy*. For example, Gramsci wanted Italian students in the 1920s to go on studying the classics because it gave them a holistic sense of life and its connections, as opposed to the reforms initiated by Giovanni Gentile, Mussolini's minister of education, which wanted to make education practical. As he wrote:

> In the old school the grammatical study of Latin and Greek together with the study of their respective literatures and political histories, was an educational principle – for the humanistic ideal, symbolized by Athens and Rome, was diffused throughout society, and was an essential element of national life and culture.... The end seemed disinterested, because the real interest was the interior development of personality, the formation of character by means of the absorption and assimilation of the whole cultural past of modern European civilization.

> (Gramsci 1971: 37)

As far as possible, Gramsci wanted the culture grounded in institutions which were secular, rounded and politically impartial. If there is an element of idealization of the old system in Gramsci, his concern is obviously with the values that education transmits. Although traditional culture was largely for an elite, it was mainly about pedagogical discipline and allowing the student to make living connections from a 'dead' whole. The function of 'liberal' education (and Gentile's reforms were based on the ideas of the Italian liberal-Hegelian Beneditto Croce) is to mirror the division of labour in society by fragmenting knowledge, while at the same time leaving 'integration' to courses on 'civics' and the like, giving enormous power for thought control to the regime and individual teachers:

> A date is always a date, whoever the examiner is, and a definition is always a definition. But an aesthetic judgement or a philosophical analysis?

> (Gramsci 1971: 36)

Gramsci's alternatives are never clearly spelled out (unlike the Russian Communists and their imitators) but the issues that must be taken into account are. The strategies leading up to the revolution must encourage the idea that intellectual life is as tough as manual labour. Only within a formal, connected system of knowledge will the individual be able to generate a system of thought which makes him or her self-reliant. Without it there will be neither a common language nor a basis for political action. Education has the task of creating, not individual but collective freedom. Liberal education works within the assumption that individuals will create their own liberation, while leaving the task of social reform to others. For Gramsci the task is to change society, culture and education *simultaneously but before the revolution*. 'Our aim', he wrote, 'is to produce a new stratum of intellectuals, including those capable of the highest degree of specialization, from a social group which has not traditionally developed the appropriate attitudes' (Gramsci 1971: 43).

The idea of creating the new intellectuals is based on a metaphor borrowed from horticulture (Gramsci's work is replete with metaphors, but the organic and the militaristic are the most pronounced). The military metaphor (applied generally to the role of the party, but also, in an extended way to the analysis of Fordism and the Soviet mode of production) was double-edged. Military structure and the sense of strategic engagements were clearly important in thinking about how the party could manage itself. But, as the Russian revolution had shown, the militarization of people and culture had displayed a literalness of the military metaphor which created the illusion of success, but which ultimately was frozen in a metaphorical cul-de-sac. The idea of the organic is a much more powerful metaphor in Gramsci, which sets his work apart from other Marxist writers of the interwar period. Horticulture is 'trained' culture: 'wild' culture is 'impassioned pedantry' and 'wild demagogy'. The organic political garden has to have its gardeners (the 'organic intellectuals') but it must operate within a structure which playfully engages with the military sense of discipline. All of this is a discourse around the relationship between the metaphorical and the positivistic, a discourse which is older than Gramsci or even Marx. As Gary Genosko (1992) has written:

> Gramsci relies heavily upon metaphors of organicity and produces them in very much the same manner as do such nineteenth-century German poet-philosophers as Johann Gottfried von Herder and August Wilhelm von Schlegel: organic form is innate, essential, living, and grows from within; mechanical form is imposed from the outside, accidental, dead and increases by addition.... For example, Gramsci distinguishes democratic centralism on the basis of the following paired differences: organic/mechanical, fluid/stagnant, real

movement/policed movement, progressive/regressive, bottom up influence/top down influence (*Prison Notebooks*: 155, 189). Ultimately, Gramsci cannot be saddled with these dichotomies which do not respect hybrids, mechanomorphic mutants and cyborgs. The idea of an organic army is not a form of military darwinism.

(Genosko 1992: 65)

The task that Althusser set himself was to make this fuzziness coherent. Thus was ushered in the structuration of the phoneme and the metaphor. Although this has been discussed in previous chapters, it is important to elaborate on a couple of issues which affect the study of popular culture. The Marxist take on popular culture was clearly part of a much wider project, and in many respects the debates around the whole issue of culture necessarily *had* to be able to deal with institutions, language, processes, ideology, the issue of agency with or without the Marxist agenda for transforming society. The move towards creating a new sociology was an essential element of this. The history of sociology has largely been the history of the creation of meta-narratives, but all based on the same Franco-German sources from the nineteenth and early twentieth centuries. The card-pack has been shuffled a number of times, but always in order to create a legitimation for a particular status quo. The frozen neuoro-biology of Talcott Parsons has to be set against the rigid Marxist sanctities of, say, an Ellen Wood or a Michael Apple. To create a new sociology, other voices have to be heard. The electric nature of the debate on popular culture in Britain, in particular in the 1970s and early 1980s, was that other voices *were* heard. The dispute between Althusser and Gramsci was essentially around how they would be heard.

If we want to take the conversation slowly so that we can listen to the inflections – as opposed to David Harris's (1992) book which tries to hit the whole exercise over the head with a bludgeon – we hear a discourse about how difficult it is to conceive of the popular. On the one side we hear Gramsci, talking from a prison cell, meditating on 'common sense' and the possibility of changing all this. And, as an echo, a representation of the importance of Gramsci now, the voice of Teresa de Lauretis (1988):

First I want to situate myself as a non-white American woman, who came of age in a country which, although marked by rigid class differences, had virtually no internal racial differences and was relatively homogeneous culturally. In spite of its location in the First World, Italy is and has been for most of its history – a colonial preserve or a vacation spot for other countries of Europe, the Catholic Papacy and, since WWII, for the US as well. Many Italians today refer to themselves as citizens of a Third World country, which they are in many ways, not simply economically. And I would add that part of the appeal of Gramsci for the critique of colonial

117

discourse may come from his consciousness, as a Sardinian (an islander), of colonial economic oppression within the Italian context. [When people here speak of Europe as synonymous with the West, as the homogeneous place of origin of white supremacy and imperialism toward 'the rest of the world' (as it is typically put), they ignore the histories of internal colonialism, not to mention various forms of class, sexual and religious oppression, within Europe and within each country of Europe. . . .].

(de Lauretis 1988: 127)

Gramsci was not an abstract theorist. As with Raymond Williams, he came from the fringes of a country, which was on the fringes of yet a wider empire. His project was to help the colonized fringe take power. The Althusserian project was predicated on a Jesuitical frame of trying to rethink the world on lines which were organized, symmetrical, coherent and (ultimately) mischievous. The New Left was caught up in the symmetry of this perfect dichotomy. On the one side, the phenomenology of being (Roman Jacobson's sense of *Byt*) and transforming being into a happier sense of otherness (Camus's Outsider beyond the outsider), and then, on the other side, the world made together so that we know where our place is in the great scheme of things.

So the culture of the people, the study of popular culture, was caught up in this sense of doing it from the inside in order to transform, from within, the certainty of everyday experiences, but, from the outside, a system to give us the comfort to work inside. Another way of putting this is that Gramscian phenomenology gave us a sense of where we place ourselves as people who have our own cries of anguish, whereas Althusser told us where we have already been placed. Gramsci gave us our own collective agency, Althusser imposed on us the structural limitations. The two routes are important. We live our lives between the determinating and the determinant, and, of course, they both have their roots in the religious discourses. Which brings us via Gramsci and Althusser, to Bourdieu, and Lacan and Freud. We live in the fictive self, disturbed, alone. Popular culture is, ultimately, about allowing us to make our own fictions, either collectively or alone, and then standing back and wondering why we were given such freedom. Historical materialism provides the clue towards doing this, stripped of all the other fictions of extra-terrestial beings who are destined to 'save' us.

PARADIGMS

In the British discourses on popular culture following the 1960s, there were vigorous discussions and research exercises around what constituted the 'popular', though the major lines of disagreement focused on how or whether the Gramscian notion of hegemony was useful. Stuart Hall (1980c) argued that there were 'Two paradigms' in cultural studies – 'culturalism' which had evolved from an indigenous British tradition (Hoggart, Williams and Thompson as the main names) and 'structuralism' (Lévi-Strauss, Barthes and Althusser) which had been brought in from France after the late 1960s (Hall 1980c). As Jim McGuigan (1992) has noted

> Culturalism can be aligned with Karl Marx's 'men [*sic*] make their own history', and structuralism with 'not in conditions of their own making'. This is the basis for Hall's particular neo-Gramscian synthesis, subsuming the respective strengths of culturalism and structuralism. Culturalism's 'experiential pull' enables it to stress human agency and expression in concrete historical circumstances without, however, adequately specifying the conditions of action. On the other hand, structuralism's linguistic model, which posits that language speaks us, draws attention to structured conditions (not only language but ideology and class relations) within which action is generated. The influence of Louis Althusser's anti-humanism is crucial here in advancing structuralism's case. The key term for culturalism is 'culture': for structuralism it is 'ideology', conceived as the subject's imaginary relation to its condition of existence.
>
> (McGuigan 1992: 30)

The essay also introduces three other paradigms: two post-structuralist ones (a Lacan-derived one emphasizing the reintroduction of the subject, decentred, and a Foucauldian derived one, which emphasized decentred power/knowledge relationships) and the political economy of culture which Hall dismisses as reductionist.

Hall's (1980b) parallel essay in *Culture, Media, Language* (Hall *et al.* 1980) shows how these 'paradigms' and others were part of the ongoing work of the CCCS throughout the 1970s. Thus they should be read in tandem. The 'paradigms' essay (Hall 1980c) is a distilled version of the CCCS discussions, while 'Cultural Studies at the Centre: Some Problematics and Problems' (Hall 1980b) is much looser, displaying the working projects and their theoretical concerns (see Chapter 4). The net effect, however, is to demonstrate the importance of Gramscian theory for cultural studies throughout the 1970s. Hall concluded the second essay by noting:

> There is no social organization without the intellectual function, in its widest sense, Gramsci argued: no organic intellectual formation 'without the theoretical aspect of the theory-practice nexus being distinguished concretely by the existence of a group of people – "specialized" in conceptual and philosophical elaboration of ideas'.

119

But also there is none without 'an analogous movement on the part of the mass' who 'raise themselves to higher levels of culture and ... extend their circle of influence towards the stratum of specialized intellectuals, producing ... groups of more or less importance'. To produce work which is progressively more 'organic' in this reciprocal sense has been, throughout, the Centre's task and goal.

(Hall 1980b)

Nothing could be more explicit. The study of popular culture was thus integral to this higher mission. 'Horticulturalists of the World unite! You have nothing to lose but the weeds!'

THE PERILS OF THE TEXT

The temptation, always, even in pre-Marxist days was to find salvation in the text. But what text? Writing books was one sense of textuality, but dancing, making music, theatre, carnival, sport, talking in bars, walking the streets, shopping, eating, making film, 'doing' television, painting the walls on the streets, painting the body, creating and designing buildings, building, and riding trains, automobiles, making a brain into a machine, using that mechanized brain to transmit this message to you, and the voluble body, speaking and connecting more than it knows? The study of popular culture includes all, and more, of this. Because these are all our creations, we feel we have to read them as part of our intimate selves. We are wrong, of course, unless we believe we are reading ourselves as history. What we did, then, has already gone. The study of popular culture is the study of our past articulations, but believing that there is a moment, now, that we must grasp before it is gone forever. 'The moving finger writes, and having writ, moves on. Nor all thy piety nor wit will move it back to cancel half a line, nor all thy tears wash out a word of it.'

The work of the Fiskes, the Morleys and the Willises is committed to thinking ourselves into that moment when the livable is within our grasp. The feminist work, particularly that of Angela McRobbie, Valerie Walkerdine and Meaghan Morris, suggests that we are grasping the *wrong* moment, an issue that will be taken up in more detail in the next chapter. In Fiske and Morley (and to a degree in Willis) we have texts that matter (television, film and school) but ultimately the texts walk away from us because we know that, although we might have been there once, we are not there now and, if we are, it is because we choose to live in a world which is closeted away in our own sense of finitude. It does, of course, make perfect sense if we want to live in a state where sense consists of permanency as a perception of continuity. *Reading Television* (Fiske and Hartley 1978), *Profane Culture* (Willis 1978) and *Family Television* (Morley 1986) are so clearly situated in place and time that only a

120

Presbyterian God would know how to resituate them. But the idea of popular culture is a shifting one. To concentrate on the text is to deprive the whole idea of popular culture of its dynamism.

The problem with the debate as it developed in Britain and, ultimately, the United States was that the notion of the popular was read in relation to a conception of culture which was independent of economics and, to some extent, of politics. The attempt to escape from the base-superstructure crassness of orthodox Marxism involved a strong resistance to economics in any form.[5] In many respects, this necessitated a return to Gramsci, as the single major Marxist theorist who was both an active participant in events and who also was opposed to Marxist economism. Further it involved a play on the Raymond Williams conception that 'Culture is Ordinary', a sense of culture that was as much anthropological as it was political. If culture was essentially that which was experienced, then a central issue was who did the experiencing and how was the experiencing in part masterminded by those who claimed a more lofty experience than others. And yet, Gramsci was a curious man to whom to turn. In many respects Gramsci (like Adorno or Lukács) had a firm sense of the discipline that was necessary to acquire culture. The culture of the everyday had to be tamed, trained, or else it was simply the inchoate, particular culture of the dispossessed.

The problem therefore came to rest on three issues: first, what were the people experiencing and making as culture? Second, how was the culture of the centre determining what 'voice' they could have? Third, what strategy could the left have to harness the first against the second to create an alternative, more democratic culture? Not surprisingly, the emphasis varied according to the predelictions of the author or the collective. If Gramsci was essentially concerned with creating a 'counter-hegemony' against the 'hegemony' of the existing cultural system, then the analysis had to centre on the issue of hegemonic culture, creating alternative cultures (from an existing 'base', surely?) through 'agents'. Alternatively, energy could be spent on finding 'voices', or on analysing the components of the hegemonic culture in its texts, presentations, performances. Or, alternatively ... The combinations are endless. Essentially, popular cultural studies have been fixated on finding the right combination. (The resistance of the conservative right has been driven by the same agenda: in order to ensure that the computer printout does not yield the same result as that which the left seems to be trying to achieve, it has, as in *Public Interest*, or *The New Criterion*, or the writing of the late Allan Bloom, been playing the same game *in negative*).[6]

By missing out economics and its global presence, the popular culture debate has ignored the *flow* of what affects culture. (Even in its static Marxist phase, a reading of Rosa Luxemburg and Trotsky might have helped.) The issue might be rethought by putting the study of popular

121

culture into a historical context, over the whole period (1956–93) discussed here, and by using material which is as much derived from the students of popular culture as from the culture itself. In this I shall be seen to differ from the approaches of most other writers on the subject (e.g. Grossberg 1983; 1984a; 1984b; 1993; Harris 1992; Turner 1990) but closer, perhaps, to McGuigan (1992). One of the problems of the transmission of cultural studies from Britain to the United States (see O'Connor 1989a) has been its decontextualization, because of Americans' unfamiliarity with the specific examples peculiar to Britain. Thus segments of the work of Hall or Williams are gutted to find graspable gobbets of theory. This argument is developed in the final chapter. But it is also true that much of the British writing has been so particularistic as to make it difficult for most people to make connections across and between the particularities. The flow of the culture, including intellectual responses, is missed in such a thinking. The British, too, have trouble with the details, largely because much of the work discussed as 'cultural studies' is an analysis of particular segments of specifically British media culture, even though methodologically these have much wider implications.

Take, for a moment, the debates that developed around the media, from the time of Hall's essay 'Encoding/Decoding' (Hall 1980a, but first presented at CCCS in 1973) to the work of Hartley (1988). Essentially all of this work, although based on a political agenda that was concerned to show how people asserted themselves against the impositions of the media, was a debate on reading particular segments of the media (the news, game shows, James Bond films, soap operas, teenage magazines, etc.). Much of the debate was around the status of 'text' in the analysis, its relation to the context of both production and consumption, and to the analysis of audience. In some cases – for example in Dick Hebdige's study *Subculture* (1979), Dorothy Hobson's *Crossroads* (1982) or David Morley's *Family Television* (1986) – the studies are more rounded because issues of audience, text, context are bound up with an ethnographic location of the study. (For discussions of some of these, see McGuigan 1992: 125–68; Turner 1990: 87–167.) The problems of what the media are *for*, however, produced as many responses as there were writers. In Dorothy Hobson's study of the soap opera *Crossroads*, pursuing a feminist argument on audience, form and content, there is the clear argument that soap is a progressive genre because the audience is always in control. Morley, whose work was in part based on ideas suggested by Hobson, finds that, with television as the central focus, the home becomes the site of leisure and thus the occasion for gender–power conflicts: the issue is therefore the social forces that produce the audiences rather than the programmes themselves. In all of these cases, attempts to give 'voice' to a population who are otherwise voiceless is hardly successful. In fact, Fiske and Hartley take this process further. Fiske has argued that

122

we may be developing a semiotic ethnography [where] there are no texts, no audiences. There is only an instance of the process of making and circulating meanings and pleasures.

(Fiske 1988: 250)

Hartley (1988) goes even further, but in another direction. In criticizing Morley's work, he argues that the idea of 'audience' is a fiction, conjured up by academics, journalists and pressure groups, by the television industry, and by the legal/political bodies that regulate the media. The curious feature in all this is that if the 'people' disappear in the study of the media, then most of the questions raised by the earlier formulations of cultural studies are either unanswerable or else were the wrong questions. Fiske's solution to the problem is to accept television *in toto*, and to see how as a consequence 'meanings and pleasures' circulate. Fiske ultimately depoliticizes cultural studies, depriving it of any trace of radical critique. The only legacy here is to study the fanzine societies and see how they create their sub-carnivals of meaning and pleasure out of the 'polysemic' nature of the text.

This seems to be a rather pompous way of saying that we should go on doing what the American Popular Culture Association has been doing all along.

THE POLITICAL ECONOMY OF POPULAR CULTURE

Interestingly enough, however, a second stream of writing about popular culture was developed parallel to these other works on audience and text. This alternative set of concerns clusters around what might be seen as a political economy direction. Simon Frith's *Sound Effects* (1983, first issued as *The Sociology of Rock* in 1978) is perhaps the single most successful attempt to take a popular genre and weave together a thread of interconnecting strands which invokes *everything* that might seem to make sense – history, meaning, production and consumption – with a whole set of cross-cutting reticulations (technology, money, youth, sexuality, work and leisure). The book had a major advantage over the work of Morley, Fiske and the other media writers. Frith is a musician as much as he is a social theorist (there is a performing space that he inhabits beyond the classroom or the word-processor). The perceptual difference is important in knowing how critical theory meets creative practice. So, what have they done to my song, bird? What have they done to my song? (Most of the important cultural theorists had an instrument that they played, and against which they read the culture that shifted as they tried to go on playing: Bertolt Brecht, Theodor Adorno, T. S. Eliot, John Berger, Osip Mandelstam, Virginia Woolf and Wole Soyinka.) Starting with the song that I was singing until you interrupted me is at least the beginning of another way of singing.

Frith's book, and his subsequent essays, is an exercise in understanding why some songs are possible only in certain circumstances, and what happens when they are translated to other locales, by translators not of our choosing. The political economy of the transmission is an essential ingredient of that process, but it is an ingredient which has to be coupled with the aesthetic. In a later essay on jazz in Britain, Frith (1988) traces the means by which jazz was transmitted from black American ghettoes to British suburbs. The processes include a series of multiple 'readings' and performances of the relations between black and white music which go at least as far back as the 1850s with the barrel organists replaying black minstrel songs in London. The importance of the communications technologies available is crucial to this, but so also is the relationship between the commercial and the popular, the sense of the 'native' and that of the 'cultured', the marginal and the mainstream. We will not understand why Kingsley Amis, Philip Larkin, John Wain or a whole host of suburban racists like 'jazz' until we try to come to terms with these processes. Frith's account concludes with the following:

> the fact [is] that the major changes in the US music business have always been argued in terms of civilization (Europe) vs. barbarity (Jews, blacks, workers), whether we examine the battle between the young tin-pan alley men and the established parlour song publishers at the turn of the century, or that between the rock'n'rollers and the ASCAP establishment in the 1950s. The point is that so-called 'American' music emerges from these conflicts. It reaches the rest of the world as something that has *already* moved from the margins to the mainstream (this was true of minstrelsy and ragtime, jazz and rock'n'roll). To hear it as corrupting or subversive is, then, to *reinterpret* the sounds, to read one's own desires into them, and in Britain the dominant desires – the ones that set the terms of jazz (and rock) criticism, formed musicians' jazz (and rock) ambitions, determined what it meant to be a true jazz (or rock) fan – have been suburban. To understand why (and how) the worlds of jazz (and rock) are young men's worlds we have, for example, to understand what it means to grow up male and middle-class; to understand the urge to 'authenticity' we have to understand the strange fear of being 'inauthentic'. In this world, American music – black American music – stands for a simple idea: that everything *real* is happening elsewhere.

(Frith 1988: 22–3)

In this account a number of issues are carefully woven together: music as social conflict, music as commercial appropriation, music as a solution to male (middle-class) gender crises, music as an appropriation of the *Other*'s pleasures which are much more real than one's own. What is clear is that music has a whole trajectory of meanings, expressions, points of departure which are now brought to bear on a single issue: why has jazz in Britain become a suburban, reactionary, racist middle-class phenomenon? How does the music of the cotton fields, the bayou of New Orleans end up as the personal preserve of an aged misogynist wanking off before a wine bottle in Hull, England?[7] Not only do people *make* their culture in conditions not of their own choosing, but also it is *taken* to destinations they may not have anticipated.

This is, of course, not a new story. The Jerome Kern-Oscar Hammerstein *Show Boat* appropriated gospel music, jazz and the blues to create a musical whose narrative thrust was quite the opposite of the original singers. Elvis Presley actively reworked black music to make it palatable for white teenagers. But, equally, much of American black music owed its origins as much to Irish and Scottish 'blues' as it did to any African sources. 'Amazing Grace' was composed by an English slave-trader. What this suggests is that the study of popular music and perhaps popular culture as a whole has to delve deeper into its origins and its transformations.

In an instructive piece in the latest Grossberg compendium, Simon Frith (1992) spells out what such an exercise entails. The marginality of the theorist is surely part of the problem but perhaps crucial to the theoretical solution. If the audience is itself marginal (seeking the *other* as a solution to its own marginality) then, of course, the musician was also marginal, creating and transforming his or her own marginality. In contrasting the work of Raymond Williams and Dick Hebdige, Frith found, in reading them together, that they both had a commitment 'to a particular sort of humanistic, communal, *lived* politics' (Frith 1992: 179) but that the differences in their work and lives was even more dramatic than their commonalities. Williams's work resonates with the idea of occupying a border country, but it is a sense of the border where he knows what the parameters are, and what are the senses of roots (both as a person and in relation to political and intellectual traditions) which mark out his personal confidence in sitting on the border. Hebdige, on the other hand, particularly in *Hiding in the Light* (1988), reveals his rootlessness, and his anxieties about being rootless, as a white, English, middle-class male. 'If Williams has no doubt about the need to speak, Hebdige wonders why anyone should listen' (Frith 1992: 179). Further, Williams 'draws easily, unconsciously, from so-called high culture, on the one hand (the usual canonical texts of literature, art and music), and from the practices of working-class culture, on the other' while Hebdige's references are 'almost exclusively pop: even the intellectuals he refers to are intellectuals-as-commodities, the latest French theorists packaged as fashion goods' (Frith 1992: 179–80). Frith concludes:

if Williams is clearly placed in a tradition (literary culture), a geography (the border country), a kinship system (his family), and a political collectivity (the Labour movement), which in combination, give him a confidence to speak, Hebdige is placed simply (as if from nowhere) *as a consumer*, a place defined, in Iain Chambers's words, by a sense of homelessness.

(Frith 1992: 180)

And the rootless, whether as academics or as 'fans', cluster around pop music in particular, but also other forms of popular culture (television or sports) not as arenas which should be critically confronted, but as places within which they might hide from the ghastly realities of thought or commitment. The Williams–Hebdige split is one which is central to all thinking about popular culture, though interestingly both authors dissent equally from the dominant and the purely chaotic interpretations of culture. This creates a division between the problems of classifying social and intellectual movements which try to define culture. If both authors define themselves in relation to home, it is a home which is defined in relation to their appreciation of what constitutes movement. For Williams, rootlessness and exile are conditions of modernism, not of 'postmodernism' which he took as a contemporary anti-historical conformism. Speaking of the 'classic' modernists and their 'ideological victory', he wrote

They were exiles one of another, at a time when this was still not the more general experience of other artists, located as we would expect them to be, at home, but without the organizaion and promotion of group and city – simultaneously located *and* divided. The life of the émigré was dominant among the key groups, and they could and did deal with each other. The self-referentiality, their propinquity and mutual isolation all served to represent the artist as necessarily estranged, and to ratify as canonical the works of radical estrangement. So to *want* to leave your settlement and settle nowhere like Lawrence or Hemingway, becomes presented, in another ideological move, as a normal condition.

(Williams 1989b: 35)

Williams asks, against this, to 'counterpose an alternative tradition taken from the neglected works left in the wide margin of history ... to a modern *future* in which community may be imagined again' (1989b: 35).

In contrast, Hebdige takes the postmodern condition as an extension of modernity, and popular culture to contain a tension between rootlessness and a reclaiming of time and space.

126

The dilemma opened up with modernity will never be resolved. The rhythm will not stop. But in the end we are – as Gramsci said – *all* of us philosophers, which means we are all homesick, yearning backwards to the source ('philosophy is homesickness' [Novalis]). We all come down to earth in time; we all come back 'home': to that bounded space, that space which grounds us in relation to our own lives and to history. And to learn our place in time, to learn to live inside a situation requires us at once to 'draw the line(s)', to acknowledge the need to live within our limits and yet, at the same time, to attend to what is gathering 'beyond the boundaries', to respond as best we can to what is gathering, to yearn responsibly across it towards the other side.

(Hebdige 1988: 244)

Thus Frith is only partly correct about the distinction between Williams and Hebdige. Because he speaks out of a cerebral condition of rootlessness, and out of a tradition of popular culture which is both global and based on the particularities of unique times and spaces, Hebdige is conscious of the need for 'home', if not 'community' in Williams's sense. Hebdige's work is dominated by conflicting images that come from popular music, photography, film, rock video and fashion. Williams's work moves out from a careful political reading of published texts to television and drama as performances/productions. And yet, neither of these are apologias for rootlessness, nor are they complicit in unthinking eulogies of the avant-garde. Much of Hebdige's work is about coming to terms both with family, roots, childhood (see, in particular his article 'Some Sons and their Fathers', Hebdige 1986) but a family which has been mediated by contrasting images from the media. In this Hebdige presents us with a problem. His work is populist in the best sense of the term. All of the mass media represents the culture of the people, but, as with Benjamin's concern with the politics of culture, *how* the culture is transmitted, manipulated and resisted is an equal problem.

Whatever Baudrillard or *The Tatler* or Saatchi and Saatchi, and Swatch have to say about it, I shall go on reminding myself that this earth is round not flat, that there will never be an end to judgement, that the ghosts will go on gathering at the bitter line which separates truth from lies, justice from injustice, Chile, Biafra and all the other avoidable disasters from all of us, whose order is built upon their chaos. And that, I suppose, is the bottom line on Planet One.

(Hebdige 1988: 176)

Or, as Leonard Cohen sings in 'Everybody knows'

Everybody knows that the deal is rotten
Ole black Joe still pickin' cotton
For your bibs and bows
Everybody knows.

(Leonard Cohen, 1993: 361)

And this brings us back both to the political economy of popular culture and to the inbuilt tension between culture as novelty and culture as a reconstruction of past times (which is often a projection of past on to the future). The political economy of popular culture is bound up with an international political economy, but it is also bound up with the political economy of the everyday, of how we choose to watch or listen to or make culture. In one sense, from the Frankfurt School onwards, the spectre of a mass culture that dictated tastes and genres and ideologies because it was an *industry* has been more than borne out. The domination of a cultural industry, dictated through the USA in software and through Japan in hardware, was superbly brought out at the GATT negotiations in late 1993 where the Americans demanded that there should be an open field in culture. That only the French (successfully) tried to resist the multicultural domination (though using the weak Canadian precedent in the Free Trade agreements) speaks volumes of how countries are prepared to sell out their cultural autonomy for a mess of economic pottage.

But the issues are much more complex than how our histories are being Disneyfied or turned into Super Nintendo games. In *Towards 2000* (1985) Raymond Williams, while noting how the economy is becoming more international (Japanese cars, German kitchen equipment, New Zealand lamb, Californian carrots, Mexican honey, French cheese, Spanish wine)[8] tried to argue for a community of actual social identities (family, nation, street, city) in conjunction with the 'emotional communities' (peace, ecology, feminism) as the basis for a new society where people actually live. As sloppy as the argument appears on paper (and Williams is never more vapid than when he tries to merge economics and politics), what he does touch on is the conflict between the specific local identities and the transnational ones and how the concerns for peace, the environment and women's rights provide the clues to how culture is being redefined. If Williams is classically Durkheimian in his views about human nature – 'It is human nature to belong to a society, and to find value in belonging to it. We are born into relationships, and we live and grow through relationships.' Everything else is anomic, boyo (Williams 1985: 179) – it is a Durkheimianism which tries to find alternatives. Williams wants to find the alternative political economy that will give civil society a fresh meaning. Ultimately, therefore, Williams puts political economy and social relationships before the artefacts of culture. 'Culture', as he said in an early piece, 'is ordinary.' But more than that, the voice of the people is always the same.

> The technical means are difficult enough, but the biggest difficulty is in accepting, deep in our minds, the values on which they depend: that the ordinary people should govern; that culture and education are ordinary; that there are no masses to save, to capture, or to direct, but rather this crowded people in the course of an extraordinarily rapid and confusing expansion of their lives. A writer's job is with individual meanings, and making these meanings common. I find these meanings in the expansion, there along the journey where the necessary changes are writing themselves into the land, and where the language changes but the voice is the same.
>
> (Williams 1989a: 18)

In this sense of the common voice, the voice of the autodidact is clear against the voice of the cultural monopolies. But it was, always, the voice of a unique minority, of people who had attended the WEA and the extra-mural classes, people whose unique education and connection with social movements had provided for them the role of the intellectual who is grounded in the workplace, the family and the local community. Hebdige's problem is much more direct: who speaks out of a totally media-possessed culture? How can we feel or hear the vibrant voice? Who speaks for the crazies, the poets, the ones from the 'other side' now that the multinational monopolies have taken over? But even if we take these as workable sites, there is no sexuality, eroticism or religion in Williams, and Hebdige pushes us slowly into the 'other side', but holding back, as it were, because, exile that he wants to make himself out to be, he is not sure of the grounds of the erotic. But nobody is sure what are the grounds of the erotic in popular culture, which is probably why Madonna has been able to gain such incredible mileage over the past few years. Although much of popular culture, particularly popular music, is a play on the erotic, Madonna, because of the clear transgression of her performances, becomes the favourite subject-matter of academic and non-academic theorists of popular culture.[9]

But this sense of popular culture as the site of political resistance, whatever grounds we choose as the basis, seems to ignore one feature which is itself a consequence of both the economic and the political. In *Problems in Materialism and Culture* Williams argued:

> in East and West, if in different ways, a potentially lethal combination of abstract desire and practical cynicism seems now to be overtaking actual majorities, as a consequence not only of repeated disappointments but of the (in itself correct) identification of their causes as systematic: an unbearable state of mind in itself, where

no alternative is really believed in, and quickly convertible to violent reaction or to projection of the systematic failure to the human species and order – a projection which even the waiting formulae of religion can only temporarily hold.

(Williams 1980: 268)

If this is taken further, then one of the important features of contemporary popular culture must be that of the periodical explosions which erupt to take the culture to new highs or lows. The *specific* point at which Williams made his comment was in the aftermath of the Soviet invasion of Afghanistan and the election victory of Margaret Thatcher. But in many respects 'abstract desire and practical cynicism' is precisely what many have categorized as the postmodern condition: as Terry Eagleton wrote six years after Williams, 'Capitalist technology can be viewed as an immense desiring machine, an enormous circuit of messages and exchanges in which pluralistic idioms proliferate and random objects, bodies, surfaces come to glow with libidinal intensity' (Eagleton 1986: 142). If so, then the highs and lows appear to be less dramatic because ultimately they are programmed into the machine.

The problem then becomes that of how the popular reasserts itself against the mechanizations of desire and the sleep of reason. It is not that people are unconscious of there being a problem, but that their senses of the roots of the problem are invariably diametrically opposed to each other. In an issue of *The Independent on Sunday* (16 January 1994) there are two articles which, in juxtaposition, illustrate part of the problem. Michael Portillo, chief secretary to the Treasury and Member of Parliament for Enfield Southgate, and darling of the Thatcherite caucus, gave a talk to the Conservative Way Forward conference. *The Independent on Sunday* reprinted it in full ('Poison of a New British Disease', *IOS*, 16 January 1994: 2). The core of the problem was not in the institutions of the society, the politicians, or their policies. It was in the people themselves:

> The chattering classes have succumbed to masochism and defeatism.... Britain has become a nation of pressure groups.... For decades we have allowed ourselves to fall prey to cynics, egalitarians and socialists.... A fine tradition of national tolerance has been corrupted into a new tendency to nihilism.... So we must change things.

One is reminded of Brecht's poem on the 1953 Berlin uprising:

> After the uprising of the 17th June
> The secretary of the Writers' Union
> Had leaflets distributed in the Stalinallee
> Stating that the people

Had forfeited the confidence of the government
And could win it back only
By redoubled efforts. Would it not be easier
In that case for the government
To dissolve the people
And elect another?

(Brecht 1976: 440)

In the same issue of *IOS*, Neal Ascherson ('Sleazy Government, Public Apathy, and Nothing Left to Believe In') writes the counter-version:

Fifteen years in power corrupt a party. Everybody can see that now, when they look at this government, and everybody should have expected it. But the seaminess of the Major government is made far worse by the thick, sleek varnish of arrogance laid over it, and that is the result of public indifference. Lying over arms to Iraq, swindling the homeless to buy votes, observing one standard of sexual morality for themselves but quite another for the rest of us . . . they thought that all of these practices would be shrugged off by a public that no longer believed in politics anyway.

(Ascherson 1994: 20)

Curiously, in both stories, it is the people that are at fault. In Portillo's version the *wrong* elite has taken over. In Ascherson's account, an 'apathetic public' has been complicit in allowing 'Thatcherism, greed and the lust for power' to plunge Britain into the cesspit. Portillo blames the problem on the 'chattering classes' who have led the people astray, Ascherson on 'Thatcherism' which has done essentially the same. The people, it seems, are feckless and untrustworthy.

In both of these cases a form of cultural populism is invoked. For Portillo, there is a culture of the people which is beyond that of the media and the manipulators of public opinion (though this, presumably, does not include the Tory Party), while for Ascherson the culture of the people has been suppressed precisely because of the Tory Party. 'La Malaise Anglaise', which the French used to call it in the 1970s, might in either case be cured by the 'people' reinventing themselves or at least rediscovering their real purpose. These arguments are based on treacherous quicksand. If anything had been developed by the work of the British cultural critics of the 1960–90 period it was that there were no 'people' in any collective sense out there. The 'people', like the Marxist 'masses', were figments of ideological imaginations. We might be able to speak of 'climates of opinion', even better 'hegemony', or even 'ideology', which narrows it down to the specifics of a particular set of controlling ideologies, but otherwise both Portillo and Ascherson (here) write in reified codes (though Ascherson, clearly, in all of his writing, reveals a sense of how limited a value those codes have in reality).[10]

WHO ARE THE PEOPLE?

The 'people' are much more complex, and their relationships with the ideas, codes, sign-systems that drift through the culture are based on their own commonsensical reality. It is therefore not surprising that the study of popular culture should have become, ultimately, a concern with the great sweep of ideas, economic events, technologies, political sign-systems that have come to dominate the world of the 1990s (and, here, Portillo and Ascherson are symptoms of the concern), but that, deep down, the real issue is how the 'popular' can be considered in its segments, made *by* the segments. In the previous chapter I concluded with how the politics of representation became the politics of identity. In the next chapter I play with the concept that politics, technology and the external crises of identity affected the sense of what cultural studies might be about. Here I would like to conclude with another conference which tried to reclaim popular culture for a transatlantic group of people whose culture had always been appropriated – as simultaneously marginal and central.

> The wave of black people running from want and violence crested in the 1870s; the '80s; the '90s was a steady stream in 1906 when Joe and Violet joined it. Like others, they were country people, but how soon country people forget. When they fall in love with a city, it is forever, and it is like forever. As though there never was a time when they didn't love it.
>
> (Morrison 1992: 33)

Cultural studies in Britain, as it has been discussed here, was conceived out of political and social movement, but a movement which was rapidly marginalized. This did not mean that the movements died but rather that the momentum for movement was relocated internationally (a problem which Portillo, for all his Spanish ancestry, finds hard to take). The Campaign for Nuclear Disarmament became the *European* campaign; the British ecological campaign became Greenpeace; Amnesty International and PEN (International Association of Poets, Playwrights, Editors, Essayists, and Novelists) were formed; British activists worked with Charter 77 and Helsinki Watch. *Index on Censorship* was founded. We all broke bread and drank beer with Vaclav Havel and Boris Kagalitski. The British concerns about a meaning for life were internationalized. But these were largely *European*-centred activities. What about cultural studies as a global activity?

Lawrence Grossberg and his colleagues at the University of Illinois organized two conferences on cultural studies in the 1980s which pulled together a number of theorists from Britain, Australia, the USA and Canada using academically respectable radical authors in order to create (presumably) a kind of Cultural Studies Fourth (or Fifth) International. The two volumes have become treasure-troves of summaries of the various authors' more substantial work.[11] The political implications of this as far as cultural studies are concerned is discussed in the final chapter. But, in terms of social movement, it is difficult to see this as little more than a meeting of avant-garde intellectuals who read the same books (more or less) and who were all involved in pedagogy and who want to get published. But social movement?

Popular culture presumably comes from the 'people'. The intellectual study of popular culture should not only recognize that, but also try to return its findings back to the people from whom the ideas came, so that there is at least a modicum of discourse. But who are the 'people'? Anthropologists would probably argue that they are those who have language, customs and history in common. Each of these terms is clearly contentious, as the history of anthropology has demonstrated over the past 100 years. And yet, and yet ... there are people who claim to speak the same language, share the same customs and have experienced the same history. This goes for women, for blacks, for gays. ...

How do we take someone else's phraseology, their movement and inject ourselves into it? In December 1991 a conference was held in New York at the Dia Centre for the Arts and the Studio Museum in Harlem on 'Black Popular Culture'. The speakers were (almost) all the good and best in black scholarship: Stuart Hall, Cornell West, bell hooks, Henry Louis Gates Jr, Michelle Wallace (who was responsible for the production), Houston A. Baker Jr, Isaac Julien, Manthia Diawara, Paul Gilroy and Angela Y. Davis. It was, in many ways, a transatlantic retake of the earlier conferences held in Paris and Rome in the late 1950s (the International Conferences of Negro Writers and Artists) though the speakers there included Jacques Rabemananjara, Leopold Senghor, Frantz Fanon, Aimé Cesaire, George Lamming, Cheikh Anta Diop, Richard Wright, Eric Williams, Hampate Ba, Ezekiel Mphalele, Sekou Touré, St Clair Drake, and, of course, in Rome, the Pope (John XXIII) and Ignazio Silone. The difference between the two sets of conferences was not only the auspices, but also the terminology. The Paris and Rome conferences were not only based in Europe but also African, literary, as well as historical in their impetus (Americans, such as Richard Wright or St Clair Drake, or Caribbeans, such as Fanon, Cesaire or Lamming, were there because they were already attached to European countries). Beyond this, because many of the participants were politicians in a nascent African or Caribbean movement, there was a sense of *élan* about what they were there for. Fanon delivered what were to be the central theoretical chapters of *Wretched of the Earth* (1962). Not surprisingly, the New York conference took place in the wake of an increased centrality of blacks in American culture: in film, music, theatre, dance, sport and some sporadic incursions into mainstream politics. Whereas in the late 1950s the impending liberation of Africa and the Caribbean was centre-stage, by the 1990s, American blacks had gone some way towards liberating themselves *as Americans*, and liberated Africa had turned in on itself, providing, at best, the baseboard for discovering roots, much as the Welsh, the Irish or Scots did when they were firmly ensconced in American culture.[12]

The New York conference did not do what it might have been expected to do. Black culture, after all, had, through Hollywood and Tin Pan Alley, taken the world by storm. Since 1959 (the date of the Rome conference) not only had jazz become accepted as mainstream music, but also a whole slew of black impersonators (from Elvis, Frank Sinatra and Janis Joplin onwards), black rock musicians (where are Jimi Hendrix and Billie Holiday now that we need them?), black comedians (Flip Wilson, Bill Cosby, etc.), black actors (from Sidney Poitier to Denzil Washington), black directors (Spike Lee, of course), blacks *as* the establishment (the Marsalis brothers, Mayor Dinkins), blacks as anorexic and both gender and colourblind (Michael Jackson), blacks as Nobel Prizewinners (Toni Morrison), blacks as respectable academics (Henry Louis Gates Jr). The list is endless.

What the New York conference did was to take us back to the politics of identity. In this sense, it was a very American conference, because the framework of the concerns was not the globalization of blackness (though Stuart Hall, Manthia Diawara and Paul Gilroy touched on those issues, but they are not Americans) but the politics of representing the I (eye) who stares at you, eyeball to eyeball. It is, in many senses, the politics of confrontation, though a confrontation which is possible only from a very tenuous moral, political and economic vantage-point. This, unlike the Conservative 'Democrats' of North America, is confrontational because, if they *know* that they are right, the blacks are caught on the ambiguity of an American-chauvinism and a need for cameraderie with blacks elsewhere.

Not that all problems are ignored. In many respects the attempt to take apart the black involvement in American popular culture is one of the finest examples of a group of intellectuals coming to terms with a social movement of which they are a part, though not all of the issues were taken up at this conference. The issue of nihilism in black culture was taken up by Cornel West, and the wider issues of black ethnocentrism by Coco Fusco and Manning Marable. Henry Louis Gates discusses why a film like Isaac Julien's *Looking for Langston* could have been made only by British blacks, leading 'away from the ensolacement of identity politics, the simple exaltation of identity' (Henry Louis Gates Jr 1992: 81). He goes on:

the importance of open-textured films such as *Looking for Langston* is in presenting an aesthetics that can embrace ambiguity. Perhaps it is not without its reverential moments, but neither is it a work of naive celebration. It presents an identitarian history as a locus of discontinuities and affinities, of shared pleasures and perils. Perhaps the real achievement of this film is not simply that it rewrites the history of African-American modernism, but that it compels its audience to participate in the writing.

(Gates 1992: 83)

If many of the papers at the conference deal with the nuts and bolts questions of becoming a black producer, or of black television, or the symbolic content of Spike Lee's films, they are central to disclosing the populist in the popular, and, perhaps even more significantly, the lives of the people in the idea of popular culture. As Stuart Hall remarked in his essay,

First ... popular culture, commodified and stereotyped as it often is, is not at all, as we sometimes think of it, the arena where we find out who we really are, the truth of our experience. It is an arena which is *profoundly* mythic. It is a theatre of popular desires, a theatre of fantasies. It is where we discover and play with the identifications of ourselves, where we are imagined, where we are represented, not only to the audiences out there who do not get the message, but to ourselves for the first time. As Freud said, sex (and representation) mainly takes place in the head. Second, though the terrain of the popular looks as if it is constructed with single binaries, it is not. I reminded you about the importance of the structuring of cultural space in terms of high and low, and the threat of the Bakhtinian carnivalesque. I think Bakhtin has been profoundly misread. The carnivalesque is not simply an upturning of two things which remain locked within their oppositional frameworks; it is also crosscut by what Bakhtin calls the dialogic.

(Hall 1992b: 32)

In one paragraph, Hall flips the discussion from black popular culture in America, through to Russia, to every structuralist discourse on identity and cultural politics, in order to situate it as part of a wider socio-cultural movement, a movement which is based on the importance of dialogue. The importance of this is that it involves black studies both in the study of what Cornel West (1992) calls 'the institutions of caring' and in the ethnographic approaches of some of the British work. To do this, as Hall argues, the discussion must be dialogic, and that dialogue has to draw on a debate with theorists from anywhere in the world who might be useful.

The point is taken up by Manthia Diawara (1993b) in another article

135

but published in *Borderlines* magazine and *Afterimage* after the conference. Referring directly to the 'Black Popular Culture' conference, and to the involvement of the British delegates, Diawara welcomes the challenge for black Americans to engage with British cultural studies but wants this opening out of discourse to be grounded in a consciousness of what is happening in the USA.

> We must ground our cultural studies in material conditions. We cannot wait for Hall or Gilroy or Boyce or Julien to tell us how to do this. On the contrary, we have to elaborate the US context in light of the work of Hall and other British scholars, not to find replications of their ethnographies or abstractions. We must read their work in such a way that they do not recognize themselves. Cultural studies in our hands should give new meaning to terms such as hybridity, essentialism, ambivalence, identity politics, and the black community.
>
> (Diawara 1993b: 25)

The point surely raises a much more substantial one. On what grounds would blacks or any other ethnic, or gender, or religious, or class group, grounding themselves in their own material conditions, establish a common cause with anyone in any part of the world? The serious issue is that we connect only when we have the energy to connect, have a language that allows us to establish the point of contact. The promise of popular culture was that it was to be a language across the world, an Esperanto that connected the world in a false economy of linguistic spacelessness. But that was always a language to be negotiated. If we want to talk to each other, in what language do we want to communicate? Popular culture, because it was in a language that fed off music and a common repertoire of the language of the everyday, established its own lexicon.

Ultimately, the reasons for cultural studies taking popular culture as one of its main regions of study was precisely because it had the potential to be international and therefore to become mythic. The differences between the ways that American blacks and the British looked at the problem are illuminating both for the different geographical and political places from which they speak in the world, but also for their appreciation of how much of other people's experiences count in making sense of their own. In the identity hunt, for the American blacks neither the actual experiences of other blacks in the world nor even a theoretical exploration of how to make sense of those experiences are as important as the minute retelling of their own experiences. For the British blacks, both the experiences of others and the theoretical exercises are crucial.

If cultural studies is to contribute to the understanding of ourselves in the world, then surely the comments of non-American blacks are crucial in formulating that understanding. It is they who have been obliged to live through the transmission of American popular culture (much of it derived from or created by American blacks). That a dialogue is possible is suggested by the Black Popular Culture conference. That there is much more room for discussion is surely evident, but it is one which has to recognize that, for the rest of the world, Bill Cosby, Richard Pryor, Denzil Washington, Diana Ross, Sammy Davis Jr, even Billie Holiday and Spike Lee are part of the problem. And *that* recognition would have to take us back to the political economy of popular culture before we could even begin to have a 'global' discourse.

NOTES

1 See 'Post-Glasnost: the Culture of Vertigo' (Davies 1992) for a summary of some of the issues prior to the collapse of the Berlin Wall. But see, in particular, Sheila Fitzpatrick (1970) for an account of the cultural policies as they developed in post-1917 Russia.
2 Several books provide overviews, but see in particular Jameson (1971; 1972; 1990), Buck-Morss (1977; 1989) and Eagleton (1990).
3 On this project, *The Economist* (10–16 July 1993: 72) had the following to say:

When Euro Disney's beleaguered managers last surfaced, it was to announce a FFr1.1 billion ($201m) loss for the half-year to the end of March. No surprise there. It also said that it and its American parent, Walt Disney, were 'exploring potential sources of financing' for the amusement park near Paris. On July 8th Euro Disney said that the main source, for now, would be Walt Disney. This amounts to an admission that the ambitious project is effectively bust.

The news item goes on to give figures showing how 'bust' is 'bust'.
4 The major books by Bakhtin, published in English, are listed in the bibliography.
5 See the debates between Hall, Collins and others in the journal *Theory, Culture and Society* through the 1980s. A collection of these is found in Collins *et al.* (1986).
6 For a zany account of this entire process, see David Rieff, 'Multiculturalism's Silent Partner' (1993).
7 The saga of Philip Larkin's Life is revealed by Andrew Motion in *Philip Larkin: A Writer's Life* (1993) and also by Larkin himself in *Selected Letters of Philip Larkin* (ed. Thwaite 1992). The two books should be read together: Motion never quotes from the letters in the Thwaite collection, but does from another 120 not used by Thwaite. There are few quotes from letters *to* Larkin. The political, sexual and racist attitudes are all there, however.

> Prison for strikers
> Bring back the cat
> Kick out the Niggers
> What about that.

Or why he did not want to take out a woman:

I *don't* want to take out a girl and spend circa five pounds when I can toss myself off in five minutes, free, and have the rest of the evening to myself.

For Larkin's idea of jazz there is his collection, *All What Jazz* (1980).

8 In the third chapter of *Towards 2000* (1985), Williams elaborates on the confusing sign-systems of the contemporary nation. He might have added that none of this is particularly new: Indian, Sri Lankan or Kenyan tea, Arab or Brazilian or Colombian coffee, Mexican or Peruvian potatoes and tomatoes, oranges from South Africa, Spain (marmalade!) and Israel, American tobacco, maize and peanuts, Indian flax, Canadian beaver and mink coats, port from Portugal, spices from the Middle East, had all been here before and integrated into national cultural habits. It was as if the Irish potato famine never happened.

9 Robin Potter, a PhD student at York University writing her thesis on Madonna, in 1993 found over 10,000 books, researched articles and monographs on the subject – and that is only the English language tally.

10 Neal Ascherson should not, of course, have been given such short shrift as he is here. Ascherson, following that other Scot, James Cameron (whose columns in the *News Chronicle* and the *Guardian* became the models for journalists everywhere as the ideal for speaking and thinking the truth around the world) is the voice of of a humane, critical conscience in British journalism. Also, he *reads*. His collected articles, *Games and Shadows* (1988) gives a sense of his writing while a correspondent for the *Observer* in the 1980s on every topic concerning the state and nationalism, from Poland and Scotland to Stonehenge and Thatcher. But why are these two Scots so important? Probably because, although most journalists talk about George Orwell as a model, none of them has the guts, intelligence or political acumen to take him seriously.

11 See Nelson and Grossberg (1988) and Grossberg *et al.* (1992) for the volumes.

12 The transcripts of these conferences may be found in *Présence Africaine*, 8/9/10 (1956) and 24/25 (1959), and in Dent (1992).

8

NARRATIVE AND ENTROPY

Those I love know how I should run my life, they know what's right
in life, they know their hierarchy of values. Only I blunder around
in uncertainty.

(Klima 1990: 98)

THE INSTITUTIONALIZATION OF CULTURAL STUDIES

Therefore and however, let us return to the narrative before concluding
with a rethinking of the route that cultural Marxism took. By the late
1980s cultural studies was institutionalized, internationalized and, from
some perspectives, apparently depoliticized. The academic institutionalization was clearly a consequence of the cultural void that Perry Anderson
had noted in his article, 'Components of the National Culture' (1964).
Cultural studies, because of its immediacy and its European theory, had
a presence which appeared to shatter the pretences of insular academia.
And, in many ways, because it was concerned with the media, it was able
to use the media to get its points home.[1] It was strategic that the Open
University was staffed by people associated with segments of the New
Left and that journals like *New Society*, *New Statesman*, *City Limits*,
Marxism Today, *The Listener* and the various *Times* supplements had
many contributors who saw the media as the site of a voice/pen from
which academia could be exposed and (hopefully) a new readership might
be galvanized.[2] The left certainly produced 'organic intellectuals' – but
for whom? The temptation was to be culturist for the sake of culturism,
for New Left Marxism was, by the 1980s, vying for a different hegemonic
position, that is as the arbiters of aesthetic taste and lifestyle for a
largely bourgeois audience. The new universities of the 1960s had created
interdisciplinary faculties of the humanities and social sciences, and many
of the polytechnics, following degree-granting status in the early 1970s,
established programmes in communication, humanities and cultural studies. None of this is to argue that cultural studies became part of the
establishment, but rather that there was an established area of scholarship

into which it easily might be inserted, or with which it might compete on academic, rather than political, terms. That there might be different kinds of cultural studies with different political agendas is becoming clear once again.[3] Auberon Waugh has argued an extreme elitist version of seeing culture as an essential element in class struggle[4]. But even in academia cultural studies is not the preserve of the left. Noel Annan, quoted in the epigraph to Chapter 4, saw himself as the continuity of a Bloomsbury culturalist tradition. At the University of East Anglia (UEA) in Norwich, for example, the School of English and American Studies has for many years been the centre of programmes in cultural studies, whose concerns are about as random and 'liberal' as the American Popular Cultural Association, where anything that is shared by any group of people is 'popular' and worth studying.[5] As David Punter argues in an East Anglia collection on cultural studies, 'we need to be reluctant to offer a definition of culture; to define it is already to collude in a hierarchy of meaning' (Punter 1986: 14)[6]

The institutionalization of cultural studies necessarily brought with it a publishing industry. Although the output from CCCS dwindled in the 1980s, the Open University, Verso, Commedia, Methuen, Macmillan and Routledge produced a steady supply of texts on aspects of cultural studies. Several new journals appeared, notably *Cultural Studies*, *New Formations*, *News From Nowhere*, *10/8*, *Block*, *Textual Practice*, and *Theory, Culture and Society*. Cultural studies was exported – to Australia, Canada, Italy and the United States, in most cases emerging out of departments of communications or English. For the most part, the work fed into an international caravan of travelling scholarship which debated the finer points of deconstruction, modernism, postmodernism, gender, neo-colonialism, post-Marxism, even post-feminism. Such political roots that cultural studies might have had were rarely in evidence, though *Arena* in Australia, *Borderlines* in Canada, and *Social Text* in the United States retained a dogged sense of purpose.[7]

Thus the debates on Marxism and culture which had been central to the left's sense of practice in Britain became part of a peripatetic avant-garde that migrated to summer events in Bologna, Rome, Paris, Prague, Bordeaux, Oxford, New Orleans, Toronto or Urbana. Although the theoretical advantages that came from appropriating European theory and testing it against British experiences were evident enough in the 1970s, by 1990 it seemed that critical theory had become a performance for the academic cognoscenti, and the debates could be appreciated only by an international bourgeoisie. To understand why, it is important to return to Britain and see what had happened to the left's use of its own cultural analysis.

THATCHERISM, FORDISM AND POST-FORDISM

In different ways, the arrival of 'Thatcher' had been predicted by Stuart Hall, Tom Nairn, Raymond Williams and Perry Anderson. The collapse of the old consensus was on the cards after Macmillan's resignation in 1962. It was a central theme of *Policing the Crisis* (Hall *et al.* 1978b), *The May Day Manifesto* (Williams 1968), Anderson's articles on Sweden, and *The Break-Up of Britain* (Nairn 1977). From 1956 to Thatcher's election in 1979, Britain lurched from one crisis of economy, law'n'order, external relations, purpose, to another. All of these were carefully monitored by the left. What happened after the Thatcher coup was a redefinition both of the rules of the game and of what constituted hegemony. In his collected essays, *The Hard Road to Renewal*, Stuart Hall argued that 'Since the break-up of the great Liberal formation in the early years of this century, the British political system has shown an increasing tendency, in periods of crisis, to turn to Caesarist solutions' (Hall 1989a: 66). He saw 'Thatcher' as the culmination of this process.[8,9]

Stuart Hall's great achievement was, as we have seen, to teach a whole generation of students how to read politically. He holds in British cultural analysis the unique position of being the consummate political pedagogue and, in many respects, the weather-vane of discourses in political theorizing. His article, 'Encoding/Decoding' (1980a), ostensibly a piece about television (and in spite of a number of serious counter-critiques) was perhaps *the* most important guide to any student, anywhere, on how to interpret the material at hand, encompassing a Marxist theory of production, a structuralist theory of the text, and a phenomenological sense of knowing.[10] More than any of Raymond Williams's studies or the many long essays in *NLR*, this was the pedagogical piece that turned people on to critical/cultural theory. It was a piece that they could take out of the classroom and apply to whatever they were about. They could apply it to the state, to the welfare office or to the local school board. Above all, they could apply it to the language and performances of politicians. Textual analysis, critical theory and political critique were fused.

But a few things changed between 'Encoding/Decoding' and the moment of 'Thatcher'. The first was that the Thatcher regime looked as if it would last forever and thus became the 'common sense' of continuity (Anderson's warnings about heterogeneous culture and discontinuous time went unheeded). The second, picking up from the 'fragments' of culture (including blacks, Asians, Celts and women), was that a theory was obviously needed to include them all, as well as the working class. Ernesto Laclau and Chantal Mouffe, using a paradigm of a discursive 'civil society', seemed to provide an indication of why reconnecting the fragments was important by using a Foucauldian notion of decentred politics, though, unlike Marcuse, without 'necessary' violence. The third

141

was that even though culture might ultimately be seen to be about artefacts and meta-languages, which might be read *electronically* as bric-à-
brac anywhere, the centre-placing of culture in society had become very
much a political and economic reality. And the fourth was that, ultimately,
if political economy was not to be appealed to 'in the last resort' then
political economy itself had to be rethought.

And yet all of the ingredients for a new political economy derived
from our reading of contemporary cultural studies have been in place for
some time. In *Comments on the Society of the Spectacle* (1990), Guy
Debord, the central theorist of the Situationist International in the
1960s, wrote, developing on the themes of an earlier book,

> It is sometimes said that science today is subservient to the impera-
> tives of profit, but that is nothing new. What is new is the way the
> economy has now come to declare open war on humanity, attacking
> not only our possibilities for living, but our chances of survival. It
> is here that science – renouncing the opposition to slavery that
> formed a significant part of its own history – has chosen to put itself
> at the service of spectacular domination.

(Debord 1990: 39)

What Debord calls the 'Society of the Spectacle' is, of course, a complex
one involving not only a vast array of new technologies (computers,
television, video, modems, compact discs, faxes, and a variety of repro-
ductive and surveillance mechanisms) but also their rapid centralization
through military economies, multinational corporations, and government
bodies. These processes, political, economic and technological, are central
to understanding such nebulous and vacuous themes as George Bush's
'New World Order' which never spelt out the political and economic
ramifications of its imperialist rhetoric, but rather dwelt on the consumerist *élan* of the processes.

The left critique of a consumerist economy leant heavily on a Gramscian cultural reading of the transitions from a market to a multinational
to a technologically driven society. Perry Anderson (1992a: 8–9) saw three
phases within which 'the political culture of the left' had appropriated
Gramsci. The first was the so-called 'Nairn-Anderson thesis'. This is
summarized by David Forgacs (whom Anderson bases his interpretation
on) in an article in *NLR* (Forgacs 1989) which might be itemized as:

1 peculiarities of national history
2 a strategic interpretation of the left's prospects by combining a long-
  term historical analysis along with a 'diagnosis of the present situation'
  (Forgacs 1989: 75)
3 making a distinct break with economism by

(a) severing a 'direct and instrumental connection between the economic base and the political superstructure', and

(b) emphasizing the cultural and ideological aspects of political domination

4 displaying a peculiar awareness of the process by which historically contingent relations of social domination are eternalized as 'common sense'

5 the failure of the labour movement to see how it could move from an economic-corporatist system to place itself at the front of a new social movement.

The second Gramscian phase was the reflection on popular culture, rather than state forms. As Forgacs writes, 'Gramsci ... was reintroduced into British Marxism *after* its honeymoon with Althusserian structuralism; he emerged in a new guise as a "post-Althusserian" ' (1989: 83). It was this reintroduction of Gramsci that acted as the basis for Hall's analysis of Thatcherism and which ultimately led to the development of Gramsci's concept of *Fordism* into *Post-Fordism*. The second analysis was

predicated on the end of the conventional wisdom that there is a simple, irreversible correspondence between the economic and the political, or that classes, constituted as homogeneous entities at the economic or 'mode of production' level, are ever transposed in their already unified form onto the 'theatre' of political and ideological struggle. They therefore insist that political and ideological questions be addressed in their full specificity, without reduction.

(Hall 1988: 4)

'Thatcherism' destroyed the residual idea that there was any kind of correspondence between economic class and either political or popular culture, nor indeed between the identification of class interests and the state.

It is therefore a complicated matter to say in any precise sense which class interests are represented by Thatcherism (multinational capital 'lived' through the prism of petty-bourgeois ideology) since it is precisely class interests which, in the process of their 're-presentation', are being politically and ideologically redefined.

(Hall 1988: 5)

What Thatcherism did was to redefine the idea of culture:

So, one thing we can learn from Thatcherism is that, in this day and age, in our kind of society, politics is either conducted ideologically, or not at all. Thatcherism has put in play a range of different social and economic strategies. But it has never for a moment neglected the ideological dimension. Privatization, for example, has many economic and social payoffs. But it is never advanced by Thatcherism without being constructed ideologically ('Sid', the 'share-owning democracy' etc). There is no point in giving people tax cuts unless you also sell it to them as part of the 'freedom' package.

(Hall 1988: 274)

If a monetarist definition of culture had taken over ('value for money') it was one which required of the left a rethinking of its own strategy, which had assumed, since the end of the nineteenth century, that capitalism would collapse under the weight of its own inbuilt contradictions. But,

the contradictory capacity, for a time, of the system to pioneer expansion, to drive and develop new products and maximize new choices, while at the same time creaming off its profit margins, was seriously underestimated. Thus the left has never understood the capacity of the market to become identified in the minds of the mass of ordinary people, not as fair and decent and socially responsible (that never was), but as an expansive popular system.

(Hall 1988: 215)

This, of course, also goes for popular pleasures.

while the recession prevents the mass of people from participating to the same degree on a regular or stable basis, it certainly does not prevent them, when they can, from wanting – and often having – not yesterday's but today's goods, both for themselves and their children. Television is now a majority interest and video could soon be. Britain is the largest market for personal computers, just as, for better or worse, the move to computer languages and thinking through video games is a mass, not a minority privileged interest, for children and young people.

(Hall 1988: 215)

Almost all of this analysis is applicable in a general sense to the USA, Canada, New Zealand, Australia, and most of western Europe, whatever the nuanced versions within those societies. But in order to make sense of the politico-cultural, it was, of course, also important to develop an interpretation of the economic changes which was culturist rather than purely economic. Hence there was the third Gramscian phase – the debate around Fordism and post-Fordism.

In his collection of essays on twentieth-century culture, Peter Wollen (1993) described Fordism in the following way:

Fordism meant more than the mass production of standardized objects. It meant a form of production. This involved bringing together three principal elements: first a hierarchy of standardized segmented and subsegmented parts, all interchangeable, plus a parallel hierarchy of machine tools (themselves made up from standardized parts) which both formed and assembled the parts into the finished product; second a fully Taylorized workforce, themselves performing segmented and standardized repeated actions (a de-skilled labour force, controlled by an elite of engineers, supervisors and designers); third, a continuous, sequential assembly-line, with a tempo determined by time and work studies, which transferred the parts through the whole process, designed so that the worker never had to move, even to stoop to pick something up.

(Wollen 1993: 36)

In addition, Fordism required a captive market (and hence a protectionist market) and thus virtually had to eliminate opposition to the product by an advertising system of conditioning demand and by buying up and neutralizing competitors (e.g. General Motors, Standard Oil and Firestone Tyres 'bought up and then dismantled the electric trolley and transit systems in 44 urban areas' – Murray 1989: 39). In many respects the identification of capitalism with Fordism is also an identification of Fordism with modernism.

These structures and their culture are often equated with industrialism, and regarded as an inevitable part of the modern age. I am suggesting that they are linked to a particular form of industrialism, one that developed in the late 19th century and reached its most dynamic expression in the postwar boom. Its impact can be felt not only in the economy, but in politics (in the mass party) and in much broader cultural fields – whether American football, or classical ballet (Diaghilev was a Taylorist in dance), industrial design or modern architecture. The technological *hubris* of this outlook, its Faustian bargain of dictatorship in production in exchange for mass consumption, and above all its destructiveness in the name of progress and the economy of time, all this places Fordism at the centre of modernism.

(Murray 1989: 41)

Over time, and particularly after the 1950s, Fordism transformed itself. What had been seen as the model of instrumental reason in industry became consumerism for the sake of it. The functional cars of, first, the Model T and, then, the Model A Fords were replaced by ornate, flashy, fuel-wasteful, badly constructed automobiles with built-in obsolescence. But these represented the last gasp of Fordism. The introduction of automation began to transform the productive process in the 1960s, and the decline of economic growth in the 1960s and 1970s changed the nature of consumer demand. Even more crucially, new industries came into existence with the growth of new information technology and electronics. Symbolically 'Japanization' had taken over. The total automation of the motor industry had not only marginalized places like Detroit and Flint, Michigan, but also internationalized the production of cars. Beyond that, the computer itself transformed virtually every area of communications in a way not foreseen by the critical theorists of the period from 1930 to 1960. Walter Benjamin's analysis of mechanical reproduction was essentially Fordist: he could not have anticipated the computer. Marshall McLuhan saw himself as the prophet of the end of Fordism: but his technological revolution was based on a sense of print and television. Post-Fordism was a new social system within which the communications industries had moved to the centre of the world. (For a cultural critique of all this see Wollen 1993: 35–71.)

The implications of this new cultural political economy may be seen world-wide, in the Third World, eastern Europe, Canada, Australasia and, of course, Britain, where the Society of the Spectacle has superseded the taken-for-granted nature of local economies and, ultimately, local polities. 'Thatcher' was not only an enabling mechanism to allow the Society of the Spectacle to take over in Britain but also in a perverse way a catalyst to the exalting of the nation-state. In that sense she was the precursor of the Yeltsins, Mulroneys, Wallesas, Langes, Antalls, and others, who saw the 'market' as being supreme, but who ultimately wanted to have their nationalist cake too. The effect of all this has been a split consciousness in how culture is conceived in relation to political economy. Abandoning the base-superstructure model ultimately meant that either the culture of the everyday or textual reading of cultural artefacts took priority in cultural analysis. Thus decentred politics made some kind of sense, but in relation to what model of political economic theory? Because, meanwhile, culture, as media, was commandeered by forces much wider than the interpretation of everyday culture, base/superstructure, as Baudrillard had warned us, was now in a much more compromising relationship.

THE GULF WAR AND THE COLLAPSE OF THE SOVIET UNION

The Gulf War suggested the route to a new political economy based on cultural analysis. Simon Frith, in *Sound Effects* (1983), showed us how rock music had moved from a decentred, yet internationalist, performance/creative British moment to one which was taken over progressively by the multicultural agencies. John Keane, employing a longer time-span in *The Media and Democracy* (1990), has argued that the free press has declined in the west in the last two hundred years as the multinationals have taken over. The experience of the Gulf War displays something remarkably different, but building on these analyses.

From the Crimean War in the 1860s to the 1990s, the issue of how the photograph, the hologram, the paintbrush or the pen would report on war has been a central feature of how we plan for or represent war. And yet, up to and beyond the Vietnam War, no one thought of how to plan a war through the media. The Gulf War was not only a media war, but also a war which had several trial runs, not least of which was Chile, the Grenada 'war' in 1983, and also the simulated runs throughout the 1980s, through computers and their spin-offs, video war games and the production of Hollywood films which systematically argued pro and con war as the solution to all our problems. The 'Cold War' was implanted into our consciousness, long after it was, logistically, over. Most of the films and television programmes that 'We' had made since the early 1960s were a kind of guerrilla warfare against their definition of what the media might be about, using whatever funding equipment might be available. We were lodged in the toe-nails between 'nay-toe' and 'double-your-toe'. Now that nay-toe seems to have won, we have to rethink the economic political strategy.

The execution of the Gulf War was one which used not only the full might of technical warfare, but also that of media violence. Quite apart from whether it was a 'just' war, the 'last crusade' or any of the other euphemisms applied to it, it was significantly a cultural war using the new technologies of simulacrum and violence. It was both, as in the past, a war to end all wars, the inevitable rhetoric of all multicultural conflicts, but now the ultimate presentation of Walter Benjamin's spectacle of destruction as being the aesthetics of power. Not only was war beautiful, but also it was beautiful because our children saw it as the consummate realization of all that they had seen to be aesthetic in their video games where Michelangelo, Donatello, Leonardo and Raphael emerged out of the sewers of the holocaust to determine how we would live ever after, as Turtles (an endangered species after the Gulf oil-spill). The Gulf War was the ultimate in the aestheticization of power. War became beauty, the ultimate beauty of winning with only the modicum of casualties on *our* side, unlike the First World War or Vietnam, where no one won, but many of 'us' died. 'We' won in the Gulf, of course, because we had played the video games before, though, in the long run, Saddam Hussein outsmarted everyone by recognizing that this was a no-win situation.

Coincidentally with the Gulf War, there was the collapse of Communism in Russia and the rise of separatist nationalism in Europe as Yugoslavia broke apart and atavistic xenophobia became a substitute for discourse. There were two major lessons here, which fed directly into the ongoing concerns of the cultural left. The crumbling of the Soviet political economy as such was no great surprise, nor was there any mourning for it. Virtually every left-wing group in Britain had, for different reasons, written-off the Soviet Union as a revolutionary force since the late 1950s, including the CPGB, whose theoretical journal, *Marxism Today*, became in the 1980s the mouthpiece of the consumerist *nouveaux riches*. The various neo-Trotskyist groups (in particular the International Socialists and their successor, the Socialist Workers Party),[11] the Socialist Party of Great Britain, the International Marxist Group, the Militant Tendency in the Labour Party, etc., as well as various unattached socialists, had been highly critical of all aspects of Russian Communism. Throughout the 1980s the *New Left Review* monitored the break-up of Yugoslavia (in a series of articles by Branka Magas) and also the collapse of Communist power in Russia (in articles by Boris Kagarlitski). The real problem with the collapse of Soviet Communism was that it happened in conjunction with the apparent collapse of the left everywhere (Labour or Socialist parties in Australia, New Zealand, Britain, France or Scandinavia had become willing agents of whole-scale marketization) and these events coincided with the growth of the international domination of multi-national corporations. Whether it was considered left or not, the Soviet Union as well as China represented a competing political and economic system to that of the rest of the world, and social democracy seemed to represent a principled corrective to unbridled capitalism. The complete collapse of both alternatives left the issue of critical opposition in effect in political limbo. Books such as Raymond Williams's *The Long Revolution* (1961) and *The May Day Manifesto* (1968) had assumed both that the Soviet system would persist in one form or another and that the gains over the years of socialist democracy could be built on, even if the struggle would be a long one. By the end of the 1980s both of these assumptions were shown to be ill founded. The new politics everywhere were clearly going to be dominated by what everyone came to call 'the market', in spite of the fact that the late 1980s also saw an unbridled and unprincipled misuse of 'the market' and that this orgy of junk bonds, defence spending, bank log-rolling would ultimately put even 'the market' itself in peril, not to speak of the minimal aspects of social welfare and education. If new political movements emerged out of all this, they were clearly not going to be based on any socialist, let alone Marxist, theory. *Solidarnosc* disappeared as a political force in Poland almost as soon as the Wall came down; the various separatisms and nationalisms that emerged in eastern Europe had virtually nothing in common with what anyone in the west would have thought of as 'socialism'; Sarajevo (copying Belfast, Beirut and Jerusalem) became the symbol of how multicultural-ism could be crushed by religious/ethnic separatism; the rump of the Russian Communist Party re-emerged as crypto-fascist Slavs.[12] In the west, France generated Le Pen's party, Britain the highly conservative Liberal-Democrats, and Canada *two* forms of reaction – an evangelical-based

148

western party and the Separatist Bloc Quebecois. Even if Japan, Italy, Canada and the United States threw out the political gangs that had dominated politics with market-driven economies for a decade or more, they did not generate new radical movements. In fact, the new regimes quickly fell into line with the dominant commercial wisdoms.

Meanwhile there emerged the classic *social* dichotomy of the early 1990s. The breadlines got longer, the unemployed rates were higher, the bankruptcies more systematic, the hospitals and schools underfunded, the prisons overfunded. As the nationalized industries were privatized, the basic work was siphoned off to countries with cheaper labour costs: our loss was their gain. There were also more television channels, more theme parks, more videos, fewer public libraries, more and better computers. . . . The information, communication explosion was coupled with a poverty of basic, human resources, and the absence of any mechanism by which they could be democratically acquired.

POSTMODERNISM

Much of the writing in the period since the collapse of the Wall has been concerned with many of these issues, and in many ways the discourses around postmodernism not only anticipated them but also flippantly made it more difficult to come to terms with them. The postmodern debate was in many respects a nervous tick in the body politic, which put together a whole range of topics that might otherwise be never seen to cohere. What, for example, do people as different as Charles Jencks, Jean-François Lyotard, Andreas Huyssen, Jean Baudrillard, David Harvey, Arthur Kroker, Jacqueline Rose or even Fredric Jameson and Angela McRobbie have in common except that they use postmodernism as part of their self-description? That the term postmodernism was coined in the early 1970s within literary and architectural criticism (and quickly taken up by philosophy) as a response to new styles of writing or designing is well accepted,[13] even though when it 'began' (posthumously, as it were) is an ongoing sick joke – Augustine's conversion to Christianity from Manicheanism? The expulsion of Jews and Arabs from Spain? Walter Benjamin's suicide on the Spanish frontier, or Mayakovsky's before Stalin got him? The Death of Lorca? Of Kennedy? Of Jim Morrison? As Raymond Williams said in 'When was Modernism?' (Williams 1989: 51), 'Modernism being the terminus, everything afterwards is counted out of development. It is *after*; stuck in the past.' So when *was* Postmodernism, Zaïre, Wales, Israel, Canada, me, you? Postmodernism is stuck in the intermediate present and future.

And yet this omnibus phrase should be taken as having its own political and cultural epistemic value. In many respects, it responded to a perceived void in critical theory, one that had difficulty coming to terms with earlier openings that had subsequently been subverted. The cultural issues that had to be confronted were themselves substantial: the architectural legacies of the modernists, notably through the symbolic presence of Le Corbusier; the terminal sense of art and aesthetics in the face of new technologies; the realization that most forms of literature, art, history, language, politics, pedagogy, law, philosophy and science were both gender and ethnically coded; the apparent collapse of the meta-narratives (utopian and dystopian); the perception that the politics of the nation-state (or even the para-nation) was increasingly subject to economic forces over which it had little control; the development of a range of communications that provided more information but at the same time decentred any collective options; the increasing uncertainty (for all of the above reasons and increased migration) of knowing where was home. Obviously no one social theory could adequately account for all of these human conditions. In fact, if we take any of the literature on postmodernism as an indication, it takes various sets of these issues as its own motif of postmodernism. If there is an attempt to create a grand theory that encompasses all (Lyotard, Baudrillard, Kroker, Laclau and Mouffe are examples) they are immediately seen to be partial or, in the case of Baudrillard or Kroker, plainly silly: the apocalyptic sense of terminal closure produces an extra-terrestrial element which has no place in either Marxism or any critical social theory.

The issue with postmodernism is surely not that things have changed (they always do) but why this term has taken on a life of its own in order to package so many discrete issues? The answer, of course, is that, even though the postmodern is ostensibly against the meta-narratives, it needed a meta-narrative to collect the pieces together. The appeal of postmodernism is therefore two-faced: the conservatives can see it as a confirmation of the dead-end of the (old) democratic routes (and thus a confirmation of a status quo), while the new radicals see it as unfolding new openings. That a 'movement' can be everything to everyone suggests a problem of definition against the stubborn realities of the everyday. Within the British appropriation of postmodernism (and from Jencks to Harvey to Laclau and Mouffe, to Prince Charles and Gerry Adams or Ian Paisley, the British are as much responsible for Pomo as are the French) it is clear that the issues are to do with how we read our history and how we bring it to the present. Gillian Rose (1988), in a piece on postmodernism and the Tower of Babel, uses architecture and philosophy as the trope to make sense of what Pomo is all about, in a tone which is similar to Raymond Williams:

Paradoxically, the claim advanced formerly by modern and now by postmodern architecture and philosophy, that each alone offers a genuine 'opening' disowns previous openings – attempts to renegotiate potentiality – by characterizing the other position without differentiation as 'total', 'closed', 'functionalist', 'rationalist', 'dominatory', instead of drawing on the experience of those openings and their subsequent subversion, instead of comprehending illusion: the relation between the limit of the meaning at stake and its configuration or form ... the use of architecture in philosophy bolsters a tendency to replace the concept by the sublimity of the sign.

(Gillian Rose 1988: 368)

So ideas are replaced by symbols: the struggle to create a language of discourse is replaced by code-words, slogans. The implication is that new openings are already foreclosed because concepts have been replaced 'by the sublimity of the sign'. If this is so, then the condition of postmodernity is ultimately one where, because of the bricolage effect of collecting ideas, art, bits of history from here and there, the evaluation of what these add up to is random and piecemeal, highly relativistic. One of the features of this random collection is that the packagings are highly ideological, and fraudulently so. David Harvey in *The Condition of Postmodernity* (1990), discusses the 'casino capitalism' of the Reagan/Thatcher years:

The emergence of this casino economy, with all of its financial speculation and fictitious capital formation (much of it unbacked by any growth in real production) provided abundant opportunities for personal aggrandizement. ... On the back of this boom in business and financial services, a whole new Yuppie culture formed, with its accoutrements of gentrification, close attention to symbolic capital, fashion, design, and quality of urban life.

The obverse side of this affluence was the plague of homelessness, disempowerment, and impoverishment that engulfed many of the central cities. 'Otherness' was produced with a vengeance and a vengefulness unparalleled in the post-war era.

(Harvey 1990: 332)

It was precisely these casino capitalists and their political front-men who advised the governments of eastern Europe on 'privatization' and who built a whole creed around the 'free' market equalling 'democracy'.

The other fraudulent collecting of historical and symbolic artefacts, but this time on the left, is based on the reading of difference. One of the great issues of contemporary western society is the way that gender and multiculturalism have come to be seen as major themes in knowledge and the distribution of jobs and other social/cultural resources (topics which are central to the theme of this book). But one of the central issues is how such a topic should be handled as public policy. There are two strategies here (which are not necessarily complementary). The first relates to the workplace. For many years (since the 1960s in the USA and somewhat later elsewhere) there have been policies of affirmative action which have encouraged employers to give priority to 'minority' groups (blacks, Chicanos, Puerto Ricans, disabled people, women, native Indians, and so on in a widening sweep), though Britain is distinctive in having virtually no affirmative legislation. Bitter disputes have accompanied such measures, but, in general, they have entered into the mainstream of labour legislation as a fact of life. In fact, it is possible to say – as David Rieff has argued in an article in *Harper's* (1993: 62–71) – that the multinational corporations are delighted with affirmative action because it allows them to hire cheap labour, to create an international labour force as well as fragmenting it so that it cannot unionize, and to present a positive image to the world. The socio-political contexts within which these decisions are made are at least as important as the campaigns that accompany them. After the many colours of Benetton. . . .

The other aspect of the multicultural debate is much more serious because it centres on knowledge itself. What knowledge is relevant to whom? There is a dead, white or black, male or female, 'other' knowledge which we might or might not appropriate to our everyday concerns. How do we know? The double-bind within which American educators find themselves is succinctly stated by Robert Hughes in his *Culture of Complaint: The Fraying of America* (1993). Within that scenario two opposed camps seem to contend for primacy in defining what counts as 'relevant' knowledge, both of them operating at the level of slogans and of the symbolic. Allan Bloom's *The Closing of the American Mind* (1987), for all its invocation of Socratic dialogues, ultimately is a prelude to the preservation of a particular 'canon' of literature and thought which is seen as central to 'western civilization'. The subsequent debates on what that 'canon' consists of have filled many volumes of *The American Scholar, Commentary, The New Republic* and *The Public Interest* as well as academic journals, and have taken up much conference space at the Modern Languages Association. On the other side (the 'left'? side), another campaign, starting with contemporary popular culture and the culture of experience, has argued for a curriculum which is based on the logistics of everyday life. As Hughes puts it,

> In cultural matters the old division of right and left has come to look more like two Puritan sects, one plaintively conservative, the other posing as revolutionary but using academic complaint as a way of evading real engagement in the real world. Sect A borrows the techniques of Republican attack politics to show that if Sect B has its way, the study of Plato, Titian and Milton will be replaced by indoctrination programs in the works of obscure Third World authors and Californian Chicano muralists, and the pillars of the

West will forthwith collapse. Meanwhile Sect B is so stuck in the complaint mode that it can't mount a satisfactory defense, since it has burnt most of its bridges to the culture at large (and denies, in its more narcissistic moments, that the general intelligent reader still exists – though the worse problem is the shortage of general intelligent *writers*).

(Hughes 1993: 67)

A further problem, which moves deeper into how pedagogy can function at all, is that the educational ministries of some states in the USA and one or two provinces in Canada have issued instructions to universities (generally called 'zero-tolerance') in which anything said or portrayed in the classroom that seems to denigrate or offend any religious, gender or ethnic group is liable to a complaints procedure with all the legal ramifications entailed. As a Canadian professor of journalism has written:

Is this a case of academic freedom colliding with human rights? That's a point made in some public discussions, but it seems to me entirely mistaken. Freedom is itself one of the human rights and can't be separated from the others. The exercise of freedom within the universities is essential to everyone.

Somehow, the past 20 years of rights-seeking have brought us to the point where protecting the feelings of students appears to be more important than almost anything else. Somehow, we have acquired the crazy idea that self-esteem is a gift that institutions can bestow by making rules and codifying decency.

(Fulford 1994)

It is important to set these North American stories together against the British readings of the times within which we live because, although there is some common concourse between the two countries, the different ways within which the condition of postmodernity has been interpreted are crucial to understanding the nuanced realities. The Back To Basics campaign by the John Major government in Britain was not, of course, a campaign to restore 'the classics' but more to restore 'the British way of life', a miasma of nationalism, family values, Protestant rectitude and a nostalgia for the movies that the BBC had been churning out for foreign export and which would allow the Protestant Irish (and the American literati) to feel that 'England' was always all what they had imagined it to be. Allan Bloom's 'Basics' were in many ways more civil and liberal, though couched in a symbolic elitism for all that.

The 'postmodern' reading of contemporary culture forces us all to find certainties where we may. These searches for certainty are not, by any means, pleasant. None of us has found a space which allows us to connect to others in such a way that the politics of identity or experience can be connected to other experiences, other identities. One of the crucial features of the British social scientists' 'turn' to culture was to explore a route which allowed for a common democratic sensibility and not only a respect for distinction, but also a space where those distinctions might be played out within a frame of discourse which allowed an appreciation of experience as well as the experiences of all those 'dead' others whose thoughts had framed our own (the work of Williams or Thompson or Hall was nothing if not that). In this it was quite unique in its attempts at combining narrative and theoretical engagement. The British 'take' on culture was to persuade us to take ongoing theorizing as part of understanding the way we live now.

But if the British account was to connect the academic with the world beyond it (this was, after all, the roots of cultural studies), then the connection, via a political economy and a sociology of culture, was much more problematic. The new political economy of culture is not about the decentred political sites that we inhabit, *as such*, but about the ways that the media has become part of the new economic rule that makes it difficult for any of us to create our own culture. Curiously enough, although the world appears to be becoming decentred (the former Soviet Union is the best example) it is a decentredness which displays its impotence against the control by the new media technologies. The new political economy would have to be one that tried to make sense both of the arrogation of power to the new media/military bodies that would commandeer the lives of everyone not yet immediately under their control and to incorporate into that analysis the various strategies that are used to resist them. The impotent rage of the various nationalisms is hardly a defence against anything: the Disneyfication of their cultures will proceed remorselessly unless a strategy for cultural independence is based on more than random violence and being sucked into a world of unthinking marketization. If, as some scholars from the Birmingham Centre argued in the mid-1970s, resistance comes from understanding rituals, now it is even more important to know what the local and international rituals are.

The Gulf War, as James Der Derian has argued in a piece entitled 'Videographic War' (1991), was based on simulations of war using video games and unmanned weapon-systems in which the whole panoply of recent 'state of the art' technology was employed not only to demoralize a Third World country, but also to ensure that there were virtually no casualties on the American side and maximum casualties among the Iraqis. The logical conclusion of this is that, not only is the simulation more significant than the real, but also the simulations are consciously used to determine the real. The same is true of shopping centres, newspaper sales, marketing in general, and the state of politics. The computer has become the determinant of what is real, and also the signification for the aesthetics of everyday life. Not 'what should be, is, and is therefore beautiful' (the bizarre logic of the old Soviet system) but 'what is, should be, and is therefore necessarily beautiful' (the even more bizarre logic of an amnesic multi-media). Both versions are historically vacuous, yet make perfect sense within their sealed-off political economies.

CULTURAL STUDIES; ABSOLUTE AND RELATIVE

In an interesting critique of cultural studies in Britain, Angela McRobbie (1991) has argued that the current crisis is based on those who 'endorse an economic Marxism, where culture is seen to reflect, or express, or to exist in a mimetic relation to, "the base" ' and those who can 'testify to the unadulterated pleasures of visiting, for example, the IKEA furniture warehouse on the North Circular Road in London, or indeed the Armani Emporium in Knightsbridge without putting those pleasures in their social or historical context'. There is some sense in making fun of a trendy appropriation of the glitter of the marketplace and it is precisely the marketplace (as well as the workplace or the powerplace) that is not being taken seriously in much of the current floundering in cultural thinking.[14] But the implications of such a critique are surely wider. It is not that the base/superstructure analysis is wrong, but that it has not integrated the cultural critique into the world we live in now. It is a position which has not thought through multinational corporations, technology, video games and the simulacrum of reality into its analysis. 'Post-Fordism' is a formula which is wasted if it does not return us to the political economy of the culture that we are obliged to inhabit and make.

The problem with all this is that the substantive work in British cultural studies during the 1970s promised something rather different. The thrust of the work on feminism, race, subcultures, the police, ideology, economism was precisely directed against a society that was market-driven. If in some ways this could be interpreted as a 'consumerist' cultural critique, that was only part of the analysis. By far the most telling work concerned itself with the power structure, traditional culture and the components of civil society. Both *Policing the Crisis* (Hall *et al.* 1978b) and *Resistance through Rituals* (Hall and Jefferson 1976) certainly dealt with consumerism, but as an aspect of resistance. Hegemony, as Lawrence Grossberg put it, summarizing Hall, was 'a struggle over "the popular", a matter of articulating relations, not only within civil society (which is itself more than culture) but between the State (as a condensed site of power), the economic sector and civil society.'[15] The analysis thus incorporated cultural studies into a critique of political-economic forces, which was, as Hall argued, related both to the symbiosis between the media and the masses and between political leadership and popular articulation. These concerns provide the crux of what Angela McRobbie has described as the 'middle ground' of cultural analysis. Continuing to explore these issues, she says,

> would entail a return to an integrative mode of analysis and would avoid the temptations of the 'textual trap'. In a sense it was the appeal of textual analysis in media and cultural studies in the early 1980s which allowed the neo-marxist critics to appear to be providing all the answers when they entered the field of debate on post-modern culture.
>
> (McRobbie 1991: 15)

As with aesthetics, so with cultural studies as a whole, the route to a critique was complicated by methodological entrapments, which, as with positivistic empiricism, rapidly took on the nature of a dominant theoretical paradigm. The slippage from structuralism to post-structuralism to postmodernism was a direct one, and one which took place by failing to develop a theory of culture in society which was other than piecemeal. What Eagleton writes of Foucault's *The Use of Pleasure* might stand for many of the encounters with British culture in the 1980s:

> As with Nietzsche, Foucault's vigorously self-mastering individual remains wholly monadic. Society is just an assemblage of autonomous self-disciplining agents, with no sense that their self-realization might flourish within bonds of mutuality. The ethic in question is also troublingly formalistic. What matters is one's control over and prudent distribution of one's powers and pleasures; it is in this ascetic that true freedom lies, as the freedom of the artefact is inseparable from its self-imposed law.
>
> (Eagleton 1990: 393)

But if postmodernism produced a sense both of the autonomy of the individual (and hence of the decentredness of what Raymond Williams called 'militant particularism') and of the in-built self-defined temporality of all cultural objects, so it bypassed any sense of the past (except as artefact) or of the self (except as self-fulfilling actor) or of politics (except, as with Lyotard, as failed utopias that send us back to a clean slate). Opposed to this there is a reading of history which is not merely of history as artefact, but of a developing social structure and hegemony, and of lived, everyday experiences. In forgetting this, much of contemporary criticism chooses to bypass history, except as the nightmare from which it wants to awake. And, curiously, the work of the major sociological writers – Marx, Weber, Durkheim, Simmel, Parsons – has been absent from this rethinking of history. Textuality (and, hence, the dispossessed artefact) has become all.

But, of course, texts are lived and woven into a tapestry of an ongoing narrative. The crucial issue was how theory was read to establish their saliency for understanding British culture. Drawing on a somewhat different tradition (that of Talcott Parsons), Roland Robertson has written of 'the responses to and interpretation of the global system as a whole' (Robertson 1988: 20). By this he means that people everywhere have to 'sift the global-cultural scene for ideas and symbols considered to be relevant to their own identities. This consumption and syncretization of culture is, perhaps, the most neglected aspect of the revitalization of culture as a sociological motif' (1988: 21). However banal this may sound, it does suggest both that there is a whole range of theory (in sociological, anthropological, philosophical, political and economic traditions) which has received short shrift from those writing in cultural studies, and also that theoretical connectedness between the individual and the global totality have been only hinted at in neo-Marxist cultural writing.[16] British cultural studies has continued to display its own national proclivities. As Robertson puts it:

> The British concern has been not so much with the relationship between socially shaped interests and knowledge (the German focus) or between social structure and modes of thought (the dominant French perspective) but with *the natural intimacy* of culture and social relationships and structures – culture as the *way of life* of a people (as in the work, inter alia, of Leavis, Eliot, E. P. Thompson and Raymond Williams).
>
> (Robertson 1988: 13)

If the emphasis of cultural studies in various societies is so different, then of course the factors that govern the conceptions of culture must also be different. Thus any attempts to learn from other societies' modes of enquiry will necessarily be transmuted into the cultural matrices of that society. The questions of cultural relativism and of cultural dominance are therefore crucial not only in understanding what culture means but also whether it is an interpellation in the structural processes or necessarily a precondition for them.

One of the major questions in thinking about cultural studies is therefore how it (or any kind of theoretical work) moves from one country to another. In looking at British cultural theorizing, it has been striking how certain writers from Europe or North America have been adopted and developed in Britain, while others have been published, but then largely ignored. It is a topic which has been noted by many writers, and to some extent theorized over by Edward Said in relation to Lukács, Goldmann and Raymond Williams (see Said 1983: 226–47), and by Perry Anderson (1992a; 1992b) while wider implications are developed in James Clifford (1988; 1992). Benjamin was developed, but not Adorno or Lukács, Barthes but not Baudrillard, Gramsci but not Eco, Althusser but not Bourdieu or Henri Lefebvre. The ways in which particular theorists were used

157

as seeds for British theorizing depended on several factors, for example the availability of texts in English in particular publishing sequences and under specific auspices, the projects of particular groups of scholars and activists in relation to their own sense of social movement, the development of national and international political and economic processes. The reception of the British work in other countries has, of course, gone through similar modalities, though, in the case of cultural studies, there is an important peculiarity. Cultural studies, as the earlier chapters tried to show, emerged out of educational and political movements, and, in its development, displayed the cut and thrust of the debate that we would expect in such movements. When this material travels to other countries, certain ideas and personalities are transposed, but not others. More than this, the transposition that takes place segments the thinkers from movement and even from each other. The most dramatic example is that of the United States.

There is a tendency in most countries, when ideas are picked up from elsewhere, to graft them onto ongoing local preoccupations. This is inevitably, and candidly, a partial appropriation, and is perhaps best instanced in the United States by the way in which E. P. and Dorothy Thompson became important figures in *that* social history movement. On the other hand, the way in which cultural studies as a Thing has been co-opted by certain groups in the United States raises quite a different issue. It is, of course, taken everywhere as an *academic* development, rather than a political or educational one, forgetting that many of the debates in Britain took place in the pages of *New Left Review, Marxism Today*, and a host of non-academic magazines and journals. It is also a development which is launched through conferences, and conferences which are put together in such a manner that the proceedings are being structured as *textbooks*, even before the conference takes place: the performances are orchestrated, dialogue is 'conducted', the score is edited in advance. Thus who will be part of this Thing called cultural studies have been selected much in the same way as a rock extravaganza sponsored by Coca-Cola decides who is already significant enough or who has great potential to be marketed now. One can imagine a committee of all that are great and good in cultural studies sitting down and defining the new wave. If the avant-garde does not exist in art any more, it can be made to exist in academia.

The grandest version of these caravanserai is the one co-ordinated from the University of Illinois at Urbana-Champaign. The first of the conferences was held in the summer of 1983 on 'Marxism and the Interpretation of Culture'; and the publication deriving from it was edited by Cary Nelson and Lawrence Grossberg under that title and issued in 1988. The second, held in April 1990, was on 'Cultural Studies Now and in the Future'. The subsequent book, *Cultural Studies*, was edited by Lawrence Grossberg, Cary Nelson and Paula Treichler, and published in 1992. Both conferences included an impressive collection of academics from Europe, the United States, Australia and Canada. The advantage of both conferences was clearly that they were able to gather together a large number of people with something to say and provide a forum within which, if not a debate, at least the simulacrum of a debate was possible. The whole point was to collect illustrious names, define the 'field', and produce the definitive 'reader'. The disadvantage was that the great array of speakers allowed for little discussion and that both Marxism and cultural studies were ripped out of context to be recontextualized as universal themes. (A year before the second Illinois conference, another conference was held in Ottawa, Canada, on 'Relocating Cultural Studies'. Although this was a partial accounting of cultural studies in Canada, it did provide a context within which the issues could be raised. Even Lawrence Grossberg and Tony Bennett, who were visiting speakers, could themselves be contextualized. And there *was* discussion. For a book version see Blundell *et al.* 1993).[17] Although it would be fun to list who was included or excluded in each conference (no Thompson or Williams or Worsley or Geras in the first one, no Bourdieu or Featherstone or Eco or Aronowitz or Kroker in the second one), the clear feature was that both conferences tried to set particular agendas of what cultural studies is *about*, and they did this by establishing cultural studies as the simulacrum of a social movement, located in academia and striving for respectability. It was, in a sense, an extension of the Perry Anderson version of the New Left: a publishing venture by academics in the know. At both of the Illinois conferences there were interventions by participants who felt that they were being marginalized. In 1983 a group of blacks and women organized a counter-conference; in 1990 bell hooks – who was subsequently written into the book script (hooks 1992: 338–46) – intervened:

> I feel all the more like an outsider here, at this conference that seems to me so much mirroring of the very kinds of hierarchies that terrorize and violate.
>   The problem is we can't even dialogue in this space. The challenge to us here *is* to try to disrupt and subvert and change that and not sit here and be passively terrorized. We need to actualize the politics that we are trying to evoke as being that radical moment in cultural politics.
>
> (hooks 1992: 171)

bell hooks was responding to a talk by John Fiske, though she was ultimately responding to the entire structure of the event.

This bludgeoning of cultural studies into a definition of who is, and who is not, important seems a peculiarly American trait. The sense of movement which was present in the British and French and Italian and Russian equivalents is sidelined – to what? In his quirky account of

American intellectual life, Russell Jacoby bemoaned the death of the American intellectual as possessing 'a voice and presence that younger intellectuals have failed to appropriate' (Jacoby 1987: ix) and also the idea of the intellectual being appropriated by academia. The book is, of course, a wake – for the Jewish, bohemian, diasporic, New York intelligentsia. Even though journals like *New Republic, The Nation, Dissent, Tikkun, Harpers, MS*, the *Village Voice* or even the *Utne Review* have tried to keep alive the idea of the intellectual as someone who connects with a public wider than the purely academic, its audience is dispersed, fragmented. There are no intellectual coffee-shops in Urbana, and the ones in San Francisco are tourist traps. The 'movements' that surround these magazines are suburban, middle class, or they lead a shadow life on *Internet*. Was the New York intellectual related to anything else? Of course, there was a grounding in a connected hinterland of migratory experience (Irving Howe's work is a crucial path) and a trajectory that reached back into the sidewalk contestation between Jews, blacks and WASPS, when neighbourhood contestations were feasible. In those streets there were intellectual *giants*. But now, as Jacoby mourns,

One thousand radical sociologists, but no Mills; three hundred literary critics, but no Wilson; scads of Marxist economists but no Sweezy or Braverman; urban critics galore but no Mumford or Jacobs.

(Jacoby 1987: 234)

This sense of trying to find the intellectual Big Men is reproduced, once again, in the attempt by the Illinois school to buy them into the States. But now (and this partly gives the game away to Jacoby) they are bought from elsewhere into academia, just as structuralism, post-structuralism, modernism, expressionism, surrealism, etc. were brought in order to validate American liberalism and to add a creative panache to a spread-eagled culture. This is, of course, a kind of Disneyfication of the left, trucked around, as Walter Benjamin noted ruefully, as the symbols of a decaying civilization, much as the statues of Marx, Lenin and Kadar now adorn the Marxist theme park outside Budapest. Mike Davis, in the first chapter of *City of Quartz*, has shown how pathetic was this importation into the cultural history of Los Angeles (Davis 1990: 15–97). The new importation is to appropriate the avant-garde Big Men into the academic theme parks where they will be neutered and congealed. A previous importation, via Talcott Parsons, was to create a grand theory which would depoliticize everything that the various Europeans stood for and, out of their work, create a grand imperial social system. Within this appropriation, Weber's deconstructive doubts about any kind of vocation, Durkheim's agonies over the Dreyfus case, or Marx's crisis over culture were notable by their absence. Simmel's phenomenology was sideswiped. C. Wright Mills, a notable opponent of this systematization, was ignored

160

by all Americans who thought about European ideas. We can, perhaps, understand this with the structural-functionalists, but cultural sociology? As far as most people on the British left were concerned, the American influence started with Mills.

One of the most trenchant critiques of the American tendency in cultural studies is offered by Alan O'Connor (1989a) in a short article which specifically centres on the work of Grossberg, though similar critiques have been offered by Marcus (1986a) and Nugent (1986). After noting how Grossberg's 'conceptual suggestions amount to a kind of theoretical *bricolage*', O'Connor argues that Grossberg has combined an Althusserian concern with 'cultural apparatuses' with an emphasis on postmodern theorizing. The reasons are not far to seek. Americans have difficulty in

> reading the cultural studies style of theorizing through concrete examples when most of the examples are specific to British society.... The more general overviews and discussions of theory obviously cross the Atlantic better. This has led to a tendency to falsely unify the field around a small number of articles by Stuart Hall. Given Hall's strong advocacy of collective and committed intellectual work, this is an ironic development.
>
> (O'Connor 1989a: 407)

The second reason relates to

> the relative isolation of cultural studies scholars in the United States and the relative absence of a Left intellectual tradition. Cultural studies in the United States is being sponsored by scholars who rarely have any connection to existing political and cultural movements and are somewhat surprised that this might even be possible.
>
> (O'Connor 1989a: 407)

In the final section of his article O'Connor itemizes the 'misreadings' by Grossberg of the work, among others, of Williams, Hebdige and Hall, while making a plea for American academics taking a more active part in alternative radio and television.

Within the United States, there has been some resistance to such a definition of cultural studies. Stanley Aronowitz (1993) has argued forcefully for an indigenous American version of cultural studies which takes oppositional social movements as its base, while Douglas Kellner (1990) and John Downing (1984; 1990) have provided spirited accounts on how the media can be radicalized. Along with the Black Popular Culture project, these indicate alternative roots towards creating a cultural studies which are based on political commitment and action, and which involve more than being seen as an academic avant-garde and more than simply Disneyfying European cultural studies.

CULTURAL STUDIES AND BEYOND

IN THE COLONIES

In Canada, Australia, tropical Africa and Latin America, cultural studies have their own momentum, but also working under the imperial posturings of American academia. The Australian case is particularly poignant. The first cultural studies journal anywhere to designate itself as such was the *Australian Journal of Cultural Studies (AJCS)*, which was established in 1983 'in a joint institutional arrangement between Murdoch University and the Western Australian Institute of Technology (both in Perth, Western Australia) with members of the editorial board drawn from other new tertiary institutions' (Craik 1993: 3). The journal, coming from the margins of Australian academic life, was distinctive

> in addressing Australian themes and issues, as well as presenting cultural studies debates for Australian readers, the journal also developed a distinct mode of writing and analysis. This has been described by Meaghan Morris as inventive and open.
>
> (Craik 1993: 4)

What *AJCS* did was to build on a tradition of Australian cultural studies that had been developed in technical colleges, new universities, teachers' training colleges and various socialist groups in contradistinction to the academic culture of established Australian universities and to the work that came out of Britain, the United States and France. It drew on literary, anthropological, sociological and political theory traditions in order to publish articles 'dealing with the theory and practice of culture, the reception and creation of texts, and the particular ways in which the Australian culture endows its members with a cultural identity, Australian ideologies and myths' (*AJCS* editorial statement). Its dynamism was recognized by the British publishing house Routledge, who proposed that it be turned into an international journal, *Cultural Studies*. Reluctantly the *AJCS* board agreed, though on the understanding that one issue (out of three per year) should be edited in Australia, one in Britain/Europe and one in the United States. The first issue came out in 1987 but by 1992 its editors were Lawrence Grossberg and Janice Radway in the United States, and the idea of continentally edited issues was replaced by 'occasional' issues representing 'other cultures'. The 'Americanization' which the *AJCS* board had feared had become reality. In Australia, or anywhere else, no one reads *Cultural Studies* except academics.

One of the themes in Australian cultural studies is a tension between the academic and the popular and between theory and practice. But it is also bound up with a sense of play, and an overwhelming sense of the ironic as an important element in communication. If Meaghan Morris stands at the pinnacle of Australian cultural writing it is, perhaps, because she displays the liveliness of a culture at home with itself. Her career –

writing for a large number of independent publications (*Local Consumption*, *Intervention*, *Working Papers Collective*, *On the Beach*, *Tension*, *Art and Text*), playing with theory as 'an invitation to make up answers as I go along' (Morris 1988), an attitude not far different from Stuart Hall's 'I am not interested in Theory, I am interested in going on theorizing' (Hall 1986a: 60), and her status as a freelance writer – marks a sense of cultural studies that takes the antipodal as its point of departure and criticism.

> She speaks as the antipodes' antipode. An antipode, after all, exists relative to some vector from a site of power and presence. As the sites of discursive power multiply, so too do the antipodean points each identifies as the other pole, towards which it orients itself. These traceries intersect and overlap, making possible a mobile, antipodean strategy – in theoretical practice at least.
>
> (Wark 1992: 445)

Australians, like Canadians, are conscious of there being many Australias, of the enormous problems of understanding themselves, let alone providing a unified cultural front to the world. In this the relations between Australian cultural studies and that in the USA or Britain closely parallel Australia's international relations. At a conference (held in Freemantle, Western Australia, in 1991) called 'Dismantle Freemantle', Meaghan Morris summarized the dilemma:

> Settler subjectivity – primarily but not exclusively articulated in Australia by Anglo-Celtic people – is oddly placed by contemporary cultural studies. The old dominions (like Australia, Canada, New Zealand) mess up the maps, drawn in Britain and the United States, that determine what counts as 'sterling' in global intellectual exchange. To use an Australianism, dominion subjects are 'whingeing whites' of international cultural studies. Doubtlessly postcolonial, prematurely postmodern, constitutively multicultural but still predominantly white, we oscillate historically between identities as colonizer and colonized. Economically, we are perhaps more aware of being (re)colonized now than at any time in the past, and yet this awareness – with its intimations of a hostile future context for current forms of cultural activism – is becoming more difficult to communicate internationally as the old political empires disintegrate. So we are sometimes caustic Cassandras in Anglophone cultural studies: accustomed to being objects as well as subjects for global 'restructuring' programmes, always thinking ... in terms of identity *in* exchange, we are practised and prescient readers of prevailing trends in international trade. We rarely expect to affect them.
>
> (Morris 1992: 471)

Even though this piece was published in *Cultural Studies* – 'Because of its cost, subscriptions in sterling, and its method of distribution, *Cultural Studies* is a journal that few Australians will ever read' (Morris 1992: 475) – Morris supports the 'expatriation' of the journal. Of course, Australians go on doing cultural studies, but the argument is incisive. To go on doing it new alliances are needed which will not draw Australian work into the imperialism of the Other.

The Canadian, African and Latin American cases are equally important, but for different reasons. Because of their proximity to the United States, these countries have been subjected to more direct influence than most others. Like any other country, they have their own indigenous traditions of cultural studies which do not fall squarely within the American sense of what counts as cultural studies. In the cases of the various countries that comprise 'Latin' America, a cultural studies has emerged which is much more rooted in the life of the everyday than anything that passes for cultural studies in the USA. From Octavio Paz's *Labyrinth of Solitude* (1967), to Gabriel García Márquez's various essays and novels, to the work of Jesus Martin-Barbero and the work of the Mattelarts and Nestor Garcia Canclini, to William Rowe and Vivian Schelling's *Memory and Modernity: Popular Culture in Latin America* (1991) there has been a steady stream of books and articles and radio programmes which try to define the culture of 'Latin' America as retrieving memory against the impositions of a predatorial, imperial culture. These writings are partly discourses within Latin America and partly discourses directed against those who would define the culture of the Latinos and the Central and South American Indians. Ultimately, the idiom of the cultural accounts is unique, even if the writers from Latin America are familiar with the discourses in Europe and the United States. After the overturning of the Dorfman-Mattelart thesis of Latin Americans being dupes of American cultural imperialism (see Dorfman and Mattelart 1975) there has been a systematic exploration of popular culture as a reclaiming of memory and as a site for political action. It is a gritty, seasoned, street-fighting cultural studies, which bears little resemblance to much that has emerged in the United States, except, to some extent, among American blacks. (For a tentative bibliography, see endnote.)[18] After reading this material the revolt in Chiapas, where destitute and unemployed Mexican Indians took up arms against the government, came as no surprise. One way of doing this so that it connects with the concerns of those who live in the west is indicated by Emily Hicks in her book *Border Writing* (1991), which suggests that all of the Latin American cultures are central to the Americans' understanding of themselves.

Canada, too, has cultural studies, but it is a term which is systematically contested for several reasons. The first is that everything in Canada can be defined as cultural rather than political or economic. This society, whose economics is dictated by the country to the south of it, exists only as culture. Its major critical theorists were centrally concerned with culture in all of its aspects. The recognition of the significance of cultural issues is evidenced in constant debates about television, radio, funding for the arts, bilingualism, multiculturalism, first nations, immigration policies, federal–provincial relations, the importance of gender in the Charter of Rights and Freedoms, and so on. Cultural studies (in the British sense) is therefore a grafting on to an ongoing series of debates that are much wider than academia. Even the availability, distribution and taxing of cigarettes is a major cultural issue, across provincial boundaries and involving the role of first nations in Canada. Law and the weather (because they unite and divide the country) are central features of the definition of what culture is all about. European and American theorists are read as avidly as they are in Australia, but, like Australia, they are given particular twists of their own, and because Canada has better relations with publishers in Britain and France than most of the USA, more of this material is read and criticized as part of a national intellectual exercise. Even if it shares some of the same problems as the USA or Britain, the unique twists of Canadian culture require particular ways of studying them. The journals and magazines that have emerged to articulate the issues are idiosyncratic, quirky, mischievous. The academic departments within which the work is done (if it is done in academic departments at all) include departments of English, political science, sociology, social and political thought, French, communications, anthropology, fine arts. There is only one department of cultural studies in Canada (an undergraduate one at Trent University). Most people who 'do' cultural studies in Canada have some similarity with Americans (the country is large, there is little central sense of an intellectual core) but ultimately they are much more politically aware and more conscious of the importance of relating culture to movement, even if that movement sometimes seems anarchistic.[19] Unlike US cultural studies, the Canadian has been written as much by people who lived outside academic life as in it, and if there are any big names, they are buried in the collectives that go on making cultural critique possible.

It is not that the 'big names' are not there, but that they are appropriated as others' big names. For example, the great quartet of Toronto critical theory – Northrop Frye (author of *The Great Code*, *Fearful Symmetry* and *The Bush Garden*), Marshall McLuhan (author of *The Guttenberg Galaxy* and *Understanding Media*), C. B. McPherson (author of *The Political Theory of Possessive Individualism*) and Harold Innis (*Empire and Communication* and the *Bias of Communication*) – are prejudged by those outside Canada as being American, or even stateless. The same could be said of the creative writers and artists. Who thinks of Margaret Atwood as Canadian? Or Leonard Cohen? Or Glenn Gould? Or Oscar

Peterson? Canadian culture is a vacuum sucked dry by those who would possess it by denying its origins.

Much more critical than these are the discourses that spin around the journals which are invariably the locus of serious theorizing. Apart from the obvious journals which cater to the academic in-groups, there are other journals which (thanks to the energy of local groups and minimal funding policies of federal, provincial and municipal groups) act as the galvanizing force on what that culture might be creatively about. In many ways, Canadian funding from the 1960s onwards was composed of a concern with thinking about the nature of the culture. A country which was strung together by trade routes, refusing to be part of the USA, and which, through the inheritance of a French colony, and a series of reservations occupied by aboriginals, as well as offshore rocks populated by Irish, Scots and Cornish/Devon fisherpeople, became an instant multi-cultural space. It was bound to see culture as central to its being. The politics of Canada has, in most respects, reflected this. The fragility of identity has always been routed through the various communication systems – across, through and into those which declared that this was a non-space, the inheritor of other peoples' sense of what was communicable. Identity was ultimately a negotiated space, a search for the space where the air is clear (*las region mas trasparente*, as Carlos Fuentes wrote of a similar search in Mexico) or where the lark is always singing. If it is the alternative to Grand Central Station in New York where immigrants sat down and wept realizing that the New World was no better than the Old, it was invariably the space which permitted everyone to recollect all the former spaces. The political decentredness of Canada, its ten provinces (one as big as the Isle of Wight) claiming exclusive jurisdiction, while the real cultural units (the French Canadian, the various aboriginal groups, the huge Italian or Chinese communities in Toronto or Vancouver) and the political/economic ones (for example, the multinational corporations, the USA and Japan) which have no representation, anywhere, in any halls of government, create a space for mischief and confusion. Does Canada really exist? Or is it all a space in the mind?

In one of the major books on cultural studies in Canada (Blundell *et al.* 1993), Will Straw, now professor of Communications at McGill University, suggests how the tradition of cultural studies initially imported from Britain and subsequently fused with both social science and humanities traditions within Canada has created a discourse, hinged on certain institutions (McGill and Concordia in Montreal, York in Toronto and Simon Fraser in Vancouver) which has its major impact through magazines which 'have grown within the overlapping spaces of graduate student cultures, editorial collectives and the parallel gallery system, and have not, for the most part, been attached to university or commercial publishers' (Straw 1993: 101). He goes on to argue that 'the range of publications, sense of sustained dialogue and presence of shared concerns which seemed to many Canadians to characterize cultural Studies in Australia has offered a more appealing and viable model than either those of Great Britain or the United States' (Straw 1993: 101).

Thus, if we take the Canadian encounter with its own culture as another mode of doing cultural studies, then the preoccupations of the major theorists, the various academic institutional arrangements, and the social movements related to magazines (rather than journals) show distinctive alternatives to the British preoccupations with their own end of a millennium. The ties that connect Canada with other Commonwealth countries (in particular, Australia, New Zealand, South Africa, Zimbabwe, Kenya – all countries with a settler heritage) are much stronger than those with Britain and the USA, while the connections with geographical vastness makes Russia a more vital comparison. As Jody Berland writes about the weather in Canada:

> If pleasure is increasingly the matrix against which experience is assessed, weather is the condition through which we negotiate such experience against the seasonal and cultural vocabulary of a place. Each region has its jokes and prohibitions, its seasonal festivities, its home remedies, its fears and forecasts that have become proverbs over time. These form the ambivalent pleasures of memory and place, of topophilia: the pleasure of the located body.
>
> (Berland 1993: 223)

But if vastness, weather, multiculturalism, bilingualism and an immediate proximity to a major imperial power all contain the specific essences of Canada, an even more damaging strike against claiming any universalism for cultural studies is surely to be found in Africa. Apart from some academics in South Africa (and, interestingly enough, linked to faculties of education), the influence of British or American cultural studies in Africa is minimal. In cultural studies, as in everything else, Africa has provided the scene for whole-scale plundering, and to document *that* element would take another book. What is important, though, is to recognize Africans have themselves established a tradition of critical cultural studies which further emphasizes just how institutionalized and academic cultural studies in the west has become. If we examine some of the major African writers on culture (whether they live in Africa or in exile) it is clear that their work, contrasted with American, British or Canadian, is the essence of political commitment, and for the most part is written by people who do not have fixed academic appointments, if any, and who sometimes write from gaol. There are too many cases to be explored here, but, for example, let us take the Kenyan novelist/playwright/essayist Ngugi Wa Thiong'o as something of an example of the perils of creating cultural studies in Africa (and similar accounts could attend the writing of people from other countries, such as Nawal el Saadawi, the feminist Egyptian novelist, or Wole Soyinka, the Nigerian playwright and Nobel Prizewinner).

Ngugi's work shows a sweep of all that is possible and impossible in Africa. A Gikuyu, born in Limuru, the centre of the so-called 'White Highlands' of Kenya, though in reality the land was stolen from the Gikuyu by the British, the scope of his work includes several plays, novels and two important books of cultural criticism, as well as autobiographical accounts of his imprisonment and expulsion from Kenya. None of these works should be separated from each other, though as a cultural theorist his experiences in establishing the Kamiriithu Community Education and Cultural Studies Centre near Limuru between 1977 and 1982 is centre-piece in the problems of establishing anything like cultural studies in Africa. The Centre was destroyed, burned down, razed by President Moi's government in 1982. Ngugi's cultural studies is committed to helping us to construct something out of those ruins. His book, *Decolonizing the Mind* (1988), was initially delivered as a series of lectures at the University of Auckland, and in his introduction, Ngugi is gracious in thanking, not only the univerisity administrators, but also the Samoans and Maoris who hosted him and introduced him to their cultures. But, beyond this, Ngugi's work is both a personal and recondite attempt at coming to terms with the shifting centre of all of our cultures. His novel, *Matigari*, published in 1986 in Kikuyu, is the saga of a former 'Mau Mau' freedom fighter coming from a long internal exile back into mainstream Kenya trying to persuade the people he meets to explore 'freedom, truth and justice'. The book was so powerful that President Moi heard rumours that a man called Matigari was wandering round Kenya demanding truth and justice. Moi ordered that Matigari be arrested. When the police informed the President that Matigari was a fictional character in a book, the book itself was then banned.

Ngugi's work displays two themes that have informed the writing of this book. The first is that if cultural studies is to be more than merely another appendix to academic life, it must be part of a thorough rethinking of all the constituents of a culture. That task is dangerous and highly political. Ngugi's attempt at creating a Kenyan cultural studies centre at Kamiriithu was destroyed by dictatorial vandalism. Essentially Ngugi and his colleagues found it important to contest the neo-colonialism of Kenya in all its forms: its use of language, its attitude to its own nature, its political and social institutions, its sense of the cultural forms within which Kenyans moved and had their beings. The destruction of Kamiriithu was ultimately the destruction of Kenya. As Ngugi moved into exile, firing off volleys in Kikuyu or Swahili, while the Kenyan elite spoke English, the transformation of Kenya into a European parkland supervised by addle-brained megalomaniacs gained pace. If the ultimate destruction of

British cultural studies by a regime that was intent on making one idea (the market) supreme seems comparable, there is a major difference. The Kamiriithu space was dead before it started. Both the British and the Kenya authorities had decided to bury the idea of a critical culture long before Ngugi got into the act. At least the Birmingham Centre and History Workshop and *Screen* drew on traditions which had antecedents. In Kenya there have been no major acquisitions for university libraries since 1986. Kenyan cultural studies (within Kenya) is now based on two projects. The first task, therefore, is the reclamation of everyday traditions, lives, mores, jokes and stories in what is called 'oral literature' (not quite what History Workshop in Britain does, but so close that they should talk to each other), and the other is a project on theatre and law by a group of travelling actors (called Theatre Workshop). The future of Kenya and its people is hinged on continuing to do both of these projects: rediscovering the roots of the everyday and connecting those roots to the realities of working politics. Only in such a way will a Kenyan civil society ever begin to exist.

But Ngugi's other feature is that he had to go away to continue the work that the regime in Kenya denied. Thus, like most of the writers discussed in this book, he became an exile. But his task remained centrally cultural studies in Africa. His collection of articles, *Moving the Centre: The Struggle for Cultural Freedoms* (1993), is an exercise not only in thinking about the cultural forms that have been imposed on Kenya (schoolboy stories from England, Karen Blixen, the black faces with white masks that dominate Kenyan politics), but also in how African writing in Kenya is received and transmitted. In his exile, Ngugi is aware that centres of critical awareness exist in London, Auckland, Yale and Paris, but that such awareness is nothing if they are not connected to a realization that languages must speak to languages without any imperialist connotations.

> I have nothing against English, French, Portuguese, or any other language for that matter. They are all valid in as far as they are languages and in as far as they do not seek to oppress other nations, nationalities, and languages. But if Kiswahili or any other African language were to become the language of the world, this would symbolise the dawn of a new era in human relations between the nations and peoples of Africa and those of other continents. For these reasons I for one would like to propose Kiswahili [which has no history of oppression or domination of other cultures] as the language for the world.
>
> (Ngugi 1993: 41)

If cultural studies is about refocusing our concerns about how the centre operates, it might be worthwhile to think about what the marginal opposition would look like if it comprised the centre. Ngugi's burnt theatre glows brighter in the dark.[20]

CULTURAL STUDIES AND BEYOND

If there has been a crisis in cultural studies where the attempts to create an international movement based on the United States have looked more and more like American imperialism, we should not be surprised. The resources are greater and the imperial sense of appropriation is as great in academic life as they are anywhere. The *advantage* of the USA is, of course, that it allows work that was foreclosed elsewhere to continue (though in a situation which sunders it from the context which initially gave it meaning). The *disadvantage* is that it uses this privilege to impose its own meaning on all the others outside its boundaries. This, ultimately, means that it renders a disservice both to itself (it has no mechanism for hearing what the others are saying so that their conversations could be valuable to American discourses) and, of course, to the others because they have to go on struggling to rearticulate what they had once said and to go on thinking, creating, writing.

The entropy to which the title of this chapter refers does not relate to cultural studies as such, but to the slippage that occurs when discourses and practices are hijacked by others to turn them into code-words which have meaning only inside a small group of academic cognoscenti. The discourses in Britain (round post-Fordism, for example) were directed towards understanding what was happening and also galvanizing practice. To turn them into a sterile academic linguistic and textual exercise is to commit a serious disservice to the originators of the discourse. Cultural studies is not at the top of a pyramid in creating a new academic 'discipline': rather, it is a guerrilla warfare against all such appropriations.

In the 1920s and 1930s the Russians invented a discipline called Kul'turologyia (culturology) which was suppressed as an ongoing enterprise by Stalin in 1937, but was resurrected after the collapse of the Wall in 1989. In the same period the Frankfurt School developed in Germany, until Hitler forced it into exile, only to re-emerge in Frankfurt after its American exile in the 1950s. In the 1960s cultural studies emerged in Britain, until it suffered emasculation at the hands of a deeply reactionary political establishment, and many of its authors dispersed to UCLA or Australia. In the late 1940s, first existentialism, then structuralism, and ultimately post-structuralism debated culture as myth, resistance and anti-text until, ultimately, the culture of the market took over and the discourses could only be sold to Harvard or Yale as the highest academic bidders. Ngugi Wa Thiong'o wanders the United States, Britain or New Zealand in search of the lost Kamiriithu Centre.

What an amazingly reactionary way of looking at these processes!

Reactionary, of course, because it assumes that, like a garden, someone grew it, someone else came and cut down the plants, then some friends of the gardeners took some of these cuttings and grafted them on to plants elsewhere, and then, much later, someone else decided to bring them home when the ground was clear. In many ways all these metaphors derived from horti- or agri-culture do the study of culture a disservice. None of the forms of cultural studies should be compared to well-tended gardens. Rather (if we keep to botany) they should be seen as weeds which encroach on other peoples' cultivations. They are therefore cut back, frequently, by those who do not want the gardens to be taken over. But these weeds are crafty, like ivy, and know they can never be eliminated, and that they will grow more resilient strains because the savage pruning gives them strength beyond the pampered perennials. As Walter Benjamin was aware, progress is a machine: real culture is the ivy cracking open the concrete. Which is why culturology, existentialism, cultural studies and post-structuralism were not moments that we can try to recreate, here or anywhere. They were examples to us of being our own weeds against the machinic society within which we found ourselves. If we try to cultivate them, they become part of the mechanized landscape. We must, as Arthur Koestler and Franz Kafka tried to say, become the ghosts in the machine.

The rationalism that we inherited from our ancestors had two major aspects. The first, which has become the paramount one, stressed technology, mechanism, bureacracy and, ultimately, imperialism in the bid to display to the world the values of a reasonable and orderly world. The other side of reason was that we could live rationally and argue against all of that without recourse to transcendentally framed ethics. This meant finding out exactly what was going on and working out a counter-strategy in order to consolidate a foundation for political action. Cultural studies is the latest version of this sense of the rational.

As such it has a major creative mandate.

NOTES

1 That all products of the left were of benefit to the media is questionable, however. Richard Gott (in response to a piece by Christopher Hitchens) has commented on the International Socialists (IS) of the 1960s and their subsequent transition to the media:

Of all the leftist sects that emerged in that period to take advantage of the global revolutionary upheaval that shook established institutions in every country, the IS was possibly the most pernicious, the most arrogant, and the most blindly sectarian. Inspired by deranged fakirs, of whom Peter Sedgwick was but one outstanding example, the IS dragged half a generation into a one-way alley of political despair, mixing half-baked Marxist incantations with sentimental appeals to a vanishing labourism. This, says Hitchins, was politics 'without illusions'. Maybe. But the result of their final disillusionment is a world now peopled with ex-IS graduates, a cynical, sardonic, amoral generation, without faith or optimism and prey to the enthusiasms of the Thatcher era – and plentiful in the higher reaches of the media.

(Gott 1993)

This wide-ranging denunciation should be taken with a grain of salt, but it gives an indication that the net social effect of left-intellectual activity was not always what it might have appeared.

2 By the early 1990s, however, things had changed considerably. *Marxism Today, City Limits, New Society* and *The Listener* were no more, the *New Statesman* was on its last legs, and the *Times Literary Supplement* (whose publishing house was owned by Rupert Murdoch) was edited by the Tory Ferdinand Mount.

3 Once *again*, because a cultural studies of the right was always present in the works of the literary critics and many poets and novelists. Raymond Williams's *Culture and Society* was an attempt to counter this tradition.

4 In an article in the *Spectator*, celebrating his fiftieth birthday, Auberon Waugh, the maverick conservative cultural critic and son of Evelyn Waugh, wrote:

But there is still a struggle which is worth our powder and shot . . . and that is the class struggle. By this I do not mean that we should stand shoulder to shoulder in an effort to drive the workers back to their hovels. Those battles have all been lost. The new class struggle is to reassert the ascendancy of the bourgeois culture in all the fields where it is being crushed by the Murdoch-Thatcher juggernaut: in political and administrative leadership, arts, education, entertainment, television and newspapers. By 'bourgeois culture' in this context I mean the standards of intelligent, liberally-educated people such as still hold the strings of power in most of Europe.

(Waugh 1989)

5 The best known book from Norwich is Malcolm Bradbury's *The History Man*, the image of which all lecturers at UEA must spend their days trying to live down. The American Popular Cultural Association was an offshoot of the Modern Languages Association. Operating from Bowling Green, Ohio, it is a largely untheoretical exercise in eclecticism. Its journals are the *Journal of Popular Culture* and the *Journal of American Culture* and it operates the Bowling Green State University Popular Press.

6 In *Politics and Letters*, however, Raymond Williams admitted to the impossibility of ever defining culture: 'I've only become more aware of its difficulties, not less, as I've gone on. You know the number of times I've wished that I had never heard of the damn word' (Williams 1979: 154).

7 In the United States a series of journals emerged in the 1980s that might be called cultural studies journals. Three earlier journals (*Telos, New German Critique* and *Yale French Studies*) which specialized in European studies were joined by *Cultural Critique, Social Text, October, Communication Inquiry* and the *International Journal of Politics, Culture and Society*. In 1988 *Public Culture* appeared from the University of Pennsylvania. In Canada, the *Canadian Journal of Political and Social Theory* started publication in the late 1970s and *Borderlines* in 1984. *Studies in Political Economy* and *Labour/Le Travail* were high on political commitment but low on cultural studies.

8 Hall, like everyone else, was caught in the dilemma of not knowing whether Thatcherism was an epistemic moment, or simply a temporary state on the road from one form of hegemony to another:

172

To a significant extent, Thatcherism is about the remaking of common sense: its aim is to become the 'common sense' of the age. 'Common sense' shapes our ordinary, practical, everyday calculation and appears as natural as the air we breathe. It is simply 'taken for granted' in practice and thought, and forms the starting-point (never examined or questioned) from which every conversation begins, the premises on which every television programme is predicated. The hope of every ideology is to naturalize itself out of History into Nature, and thus to become invisible, to operate unconsciously. It is Mrs. Thatcher's natural idiom of speech and thought – some would say her only idiom. But common sense, however natural it appears, always has a structure, a set of histories which are traces of the past as well as the future.

(Hall 1988: 8)

9 In an active, politically engaged career, it is doubtful whether Hall has not studied, written about, taught or turned into an arena of political struggle every major theory that has emerged since the early 1960s. For the nearest thing to a *Festschrift* see *Communication Inquiry* (1986) 10(1).

10 The article may be found in Stuart Hall *et al.* (1980: 128–38).

11 For a spirited discussion on the history and politics of the IS groups see the *London Review of Books*, 6 and 27 January 1994. A review by Christopher Hitchens of two Socialist Workers Party books is followed three weeks later by critical rebuttals by no fewer than seven writers/activists.

12 In a series of interviews with the intelligentsia in eastern Europe in 1986–92, I was able to monitor the uncritical pro-western stance of many 'dissident' writers, film directors and playwrights in Russia, Hungary, Czechoslovakia and Poland. Equally it was unnerving to see the rabid slavism of representatives of the higher reaches of the Writers' Union in the USSR. For two different accounts of these visits see my articles, 'Post-Glasnost: the Culture of Vertigo' (1992) and 'The Return of Virtue: Orwell and the Political Dilemmas of Central European Intellectuals' (1989a).

13 In his edited collection of articles, *The Post-Modern Reader* (1992), Charles Jencks provides a credible account of the origins and use of the term, as well as a series of articles that either spell out what the authors think postmodernism is about or are critical of its use as a blanket terminology. There is a little in this for everyone, if the issue of postmodernism is taken merely as an academic discourse. But if postmodernism is agit-prop as well as theorizing, surprisingly there are few examples (apart from images) of it in practice. Arthur Kroker's work (e.g. *The Hysterical Male*, 1991) deserves a place, and so surely does Krzysztof Wodiczko's Homeless Vehicle Project (see Hebdige, 1993) but accounts of similar interventions have been around for a long time. The collection is also curiously ethnically dead, and almost entirely without contributions from the Third World.

14 Charlie Leadbeater's comments in *Marxism Today* puts an interesting gloss on this problem:

Thatcher's ideology of individual choice runs far beyond consumerism. To argue that the Left needs an alternative individualism is not a plea for greater attention to consumer choice. It is an argument for putting individual interests at the centre of socialist strategy. For that is how Thatcher has succeeded, by articulating a vision of how society should be organized which has individual morality at the centre.

(Leadbeter 1989: 141)

Thus Thatcher, the theorist, replaces Tom Paine, Rousseau, Marx and all the older theorists of a social contract. But if any theorist has taken over here, it is surely Adam Smith. A stronger reading of the problems of consumerism would require a rethinking of Meaghan Morris's 'Things to Do with Shopping Centres' (1988) or Erica Carter's 'Alice in the Consumer Wonderland' (1984).

15 See Grossberg (1986: 69).

16 The connections that might exist are in many respects foreclosed by the nature, and intended audiences of the journals that have emerged since the early 1980s, all of them with their nuanced sense of readership: *Third Text; Cultural Studies; Historical Sociology; Theory, Culture and Society; Media, Culture and Society; News from Nowhere; Humour* and *New Formations*. The responsibility of *New Left Review* has therefore never been greater in attempting to make the connections from a radical perspective. None of us is sure whether it knows how to meet that responsibility.

17 I was present at all these conferences and therefore the degree of discussion and debate owes something to my observation as a participant-observer. But, in most respects, the texts speak for themselves.

18 *Borderlines* magazine published a special issue on cultural studies in Latin America (edited by Alan O'Connor and Michael Hoechsmann) as issue no. 27 (1993), which included a superb bibliography as well as articles by some of the major cultural studies authors. *That* bibliography should be consulted, but, in particular, the following English originals or translations are important: Canclini (1993), Mattelart and Mattelart (1990), Yudice, Franco and Flores (1992), Rowe and Schelling (1991) and Martin-Barbero (1993).

19 The critical introductory books to Canadian cultural studies would include: Susan Crean and Marcel Rioux, *Two Nations* (1993); Valda Blundell *et al.* (eds), *Relocating Cultural Studies* (1993); Arthur Kroker, *Technology and the Canadian Mind: Innis, McLuhan, Grant* (1984); John Fekete, *The Critical Twilight* (1977); Northrop Frye, *The Bush Garden* (1971); Tony Wilden, *The Imaginary Canadian* (1985); Michael A. Weinstein, *Culture Critique: Fernand Dumont and the New Quebec Sociology* (1985); Daniel Francis, *The Imaginary Indian: the Image of the Indian in Canadian Culture* (1992); Ioan Davies and Kathleen Herman (eds), *Social Space: Canadian Perspectives* (1971); Gaile McGregor, *The Wacusta Syndrome* (1985); Alexander Wilson, *The Culture of Nature* (1991); Brian Fawcett, *Cambodia: A Book for People who Find Television Too Slow* (1986); Kari Levitt, *Silent Surrender* (1974). See also the special issue on cultural studies in Canada of the *Canadian Review of Sociology and Anthropology* (1991) 28(2).

20 This endnote cannot do enough service to those who have educated me. But in particular I would like to thank Mwikali Kieti and her brother Musyoki who took me to Kamiriithu and beyond, to Ato Sekyi Otu, my colleague and friend of over twenty years with whom I read and discussed Ngugi, and Handel Kashope Wright, a co-editor of *Borderlines*, who wrote the marvellous review of Ngugi which inspired this section of the book (see Wright 1994).

ENVOI

In the 1960s the BBC produced three plays by the Yorkshire playwright David Mercer called *The Generations* (1964), a saga which took the central character from a working-class background, through a New Left political commitment in London, to ultimately being killed in a cross-fire as he scaled the Berlin Wall. Mercer's end was less dramatic. By 1984 he was dead of a heart attack after partaking of alcohol while on Antabuse. Perhaps we should remember him as the Malcolm Lowry of the New Left, and the symbolism of his plays – industrial workers, lonely Orwellian socialist intellectuals in rooming-houses in London or Paris, relationships with middle-class copy-writers, telephone-operators ('a working-class virgin mind'), eastern European dissidents, the acting out of Charlie Chaplin and the Marx Brothers – are the symbolism of the search for the Sacred Bottle of Rabelais, found somewhere in Brendan's hole, which must be close to Newfoundland. In *A Suitable Case for Treatment* (made into a film as *Morgan*) the hero lives in a car outside his wife's apartment while she gets it on with his pin-striped publisher. Morgan creeps into the apartment, dressed as a gorilla, and carves hammers and sickles on the rug. But the Sacred Bottle keeps things lubricated.[1]

This story is told as a warning for the perils of creating anything like a culture of the left. There are other stories of which most of us must be at least dimly aware, but Mercer was probably the last of a generation who took state media culture (the BBC, the National and Royal Shakespeare Theatre companies) as well as the European and Hollywood film establishments (Joe Losey, Alain Resnais) by storm, only to slip from fame as Thatcher took over and Mercer died. Who reads his plays now or watches his films?

Mercer, like many other playwrights of the time (Arnold Wesker, Trevor Griffiths, John Osborne, John Arden and Shelagh Delaney) took his politics from a fusion of class, marginality (ethnic or cultural) and a gut reading of the politically absurd. If there was any theory (political or dramaturgical) it came from a sense of social movement and wrestling with the work of Brecht. The plays were innovative in incorporating

175

images from the media and using them as the 'alienation effect' to the narrative of the performance. Unlike the plays of Harold Pinter and Tom Stoppard, they were not intellectual in that they demanded a knowledge of earlier texts or a command of literary or other cultural theories (though they were replete with references to them). Most of the plays were modernist in spite of themselves, inhabiting a world where fixed certainties were being challenged, but where the impulse was to reclaim a moral ground within terms that were comprehensible to those who felt that their world was slipping away or had been commandeered by others. The plays of Mercer were a stab at situating that anguish, and in *Flint*, a play first produced in 1970, it is delivered as a confrontation between a policeman (Hounslow) and a clergyman (Flint) who is suspected of burning down his church:

HOUNSLOW: No one knows what it's like to be a policeman anymore. Not even the police. Was it Oscar Wilde who talked about life imitating art? The Superintendent is a shocker in that respect. (*Pause.*) No, madam, I'm an old and useless dog in the department. On the verge of retirement. I often look at it this way. If our unit was a monastery, set down on some icy mountain. And the Super an Abbot. *I'd* be the old St Bernard they push off into the snowstorm without his little barrel of brandy. (*Pause.*) That's me in a nutshell.
· · · · ·

FLINT: The brandy would be for the snowbound traveller, Inspector – not for the St Bernard dog. It would hardly be an injustice directed against *yourself.*
· · · · ·

HOUNSLOW: I'm not a churchgoer myself.
FLINT: This is not an epoch of widespread belief, Inspector. Don't get to feel isolated.
HOUNSLOW: Millions of Catholics in Latin America. Praying. Lighting candles. Crawling up and down church steps on their knees. (*Pause.*) I should think it's hard for your revolutionary, is Latin America. (*Pause.*) In Western Europe now, I blame affluence for the decline of faith.
FLINT: I didn't burn the church down, you know.
(*Pause.*)
HOUNSLOW: Myself, I believe in God all right. But I can't take your modern church. Christmas is a commercial farce, isn't it? And take last Easter. I've got two boys and a girl, came late in life. What's Easter to them? Chocolate rabbits, eggs, chickens. I even saw a chocolate frog in one shop, Kilburn way. (*Pause.*) I do have irreverent thoughts about it all. Imagine if you were there on crucifixion day. Calvary. (*Pause.*) You walk up to the foot of the cross. You cup your hands to your mouth and call up. (*Cups his hands to his mouth.*) 'Jesus', you shout. (*Hands*

down.) 'Yes?' he says. (*Hands to mouth.*) 'I've brought your chocolate rabbit' you say. (*Pause.*) That's going to cheer him up isn't it? *That's* a rare old Christian message, isn't it?

FLINT: There are many paths to grace, Inspector. And irreverence may be one of them.

(Mercer 1970: 57–9)

As this was being written and produced, Jim Morrison was dying in Paris, Jimi Hendrix in London, the Beatles were breaking up: a whole tradition of rock music had more-or-less come and gone. The comedy that had fuelled BBC television and radio (*Beyond the Fringe, That Was The Week That Was*, the Goons, Tony Hancock, Marty Feldman) was institutionalizing itself as a semi-permanent Bakhtinianization of British culture in the work of the Monty Python troupe, to culminate in the 1980s in the work of Rowan Atkinson and *Not the Nine O'Clock News*. In the 1970s it seemed that every pub in Britain had either a comedy group in tow or a rock band. In addition theatre seemed to be everywhere. The 'fringe' extended from Deptford and Battersea to Leeds and Glasgow. Britain looked like a society in which culture was a dynamic that generated itself in critically playing out its tensions as performance. Not everyone saw it that way, of course. Christopher Brooker in various books and columns in *Private Eye* and the *Daily Telegraph* tried to show how all of this was self-indulgent, and that the root causes of the 'decline' of culture were to be found in architecture and urban design.[2]

It was ultimately clear that Britain in the 1960s and 1970s had created a context within which two forms of oppositional culture could emerge. The first was directly out of the privileged classes, and those who, by educational or media happenstance, were associated with it. Class-fixated as British culture is, at least since the advent of the Irish authors of the late nineteenth and early twentieth centuries, the privileged classes have not produced any form of culture which commands the attention either of the British or of the rest of the world. What has happened to the sites of privilege is that they have been shored up by those from outside who found that the cut and thrust of English discourse was conducive to creating their own sense of culture. Thus the major institutions (the universities, the art institutions, the theatres, etc.) were the spaces that could be inhabited because of their arrogant tolerance of dissent, the depth of the historical experience that they could command as archival artefact. If the 'English' had constructed an empire and a series of institutions with which to manage it, they had lost any sense of their own culture, except as archive. As Gertrude Stein (1937) wrote (looking at Oakland, California) 'there is no There *there*'. The real English culture (as opposed to the historical, Disneyfication of Merrie England) is that of the immigrants (internal and external) who grasped on to the absurdity of it all and called themselves British: Bernard Shaw, Oscar Wilde, D. H. Lawrence, Raymond Williams, Tom Stoppard, Salman Rushdie and Harold Pinter. The other part of this is the establishment figures who tried to create a dissident culture within the establishment: Thomas Hardy was perhaps the last real one, but, subsequently, E. M. Forster, Evelyn Waugh, Graham Greene, Virginia Woolf, the Attenboroughs, David Lean, the Dimblebys, though as we reach the end of this line we move rapidly to the nadir of re-creating the lost noble moments of a dead culture.

The other culture is a subterranean one, as Dick Hebdige wrote in *Subculture*, 'the teddy boys and mods and rockers, the skinheads and the punks – who are alternately dismissed, denounced and canonized; treated at different times as threats to public order and as harmless buffoons' (Hebdige 1979: 2) or as Greil Marcus wrote in *Lipstick Traces*:

> Every new manifestation in culture rewrites the past, changes old maudits into new heroes, old heroes into those who should never have been born. New actors scavenge the past for ancestors, because ancestry is legitimacy and novelty is doubt – but in all times forgotten actors emerge from the past not as ancestors but as familiars. In the 1920s in literary America it was Herman Melville; in the rock 'n' roll 1960s it was Mississippi bluesman Robert Johnson of the 1930s; in the entropic Western 1970s it was the carefully absolutist German critic Walter Benjamin of the 1920s and 1930s. In 1976 and 1977, and in the years to follow, as symbolically remade by the Sex Pistols, it was, perhaps dadaists, lettrists, situationists, and various medieval heretics.
>
> (Marcus 1986b: 21–2)

This reading of culture is one which tries to place the slave, the seaman, the exile, the unemployed youth, and, ultimately, the vast array of ignored women at the centre of history. David Mercer and the late modernists of the 1960s tried to rethink the codes of modernity as they were being washed away by the crumbling of the edifices that the modernists themselves had created. The fragile traces of the meaning of an established culture were being eroded by the ambiguity of the proponents of that culture, whether on the so-called left or the right.

The shift in British culture was from a confident imperial centre to one which was ultimately confronted by its own conquests. Not surprisingly, therefore, thinking about that culture involved a new form of theorizing – the inside making sense of its new naked self and the outside grasping what might be salvageable of what had made it marginal. If this pull-and-push effect had a strange effect on the polity of Britain it had even stranger effects on the cultural productions. In a stable, self-confident society, the theory that animates any cultural production is derived directly from the hegemony of that society, even if that hegemony contains within itself a series of contestable differences. Hegemony is the language of a society where everyone agrees on common meanings. Empire creates that *lingua franca*. When empire collapses, the languages dissolve into the livable units. The death of the British empire has been slow and torturous, but the voices that rise out of its ashes are not simply the cries of the oppressed, but the cries of the *de*pressed. The dry anguish of a burnt-out hegemony speaks with forked tongue.

The depressed invoke psychology as their metaphor, a psychology conjoined with detective stories, the 'Where, in these marvellous ruins of history, did we go wrong?' and 'Who, of all those mischievous and nasty people whom we knew were lurking around, did this to us?' syndrome. Those of us who were both oppressed and depressed by the empire (God! and did we not read Iris Murdoch and Doris Lessing close together?) feel some release that it has all gone (at last!).

There are two images that make some kind of sense as we try to grab spaces beyond simply enjoying the 'subsequent performances' of ancient texts. The first reaches out of the work of Angela Carter where our previous texts are consciously re-made, re-lived and re-written so that they become integral to our present, and ultimately therefore giving acoustics to the laughter of the world:

> Fevvers' laughter seeped through the gaps in the window-frames and cracks in the door-frames of all the houses in the village; the villagers stirred in their beds, chuckling at the enormous joke that invaded their dreams, of which they would remember nothing in the morning except the mirth it caused. She laughed, she laughed, she laughed.
>
> (Carter 1985: 294–5)

And thus the circus, the transvestite, the clown, the acrobat and the stripper are returned to the centre of the world, so that representation is ultimately a game of the stage, the bedroom and the streets, all at the same time, but also *funny* . . .

If this is a literate, intellectual happiness, it is a happiness, a laughter, which is possible only because one is literate, intellectual. Angela Carter's laughter is Rabelaisian because she has read him as a woman (as well as Chaucer, Boccaccio and Bakhtin) and come through to the other side.

The other way of routing the post-imperial culture is through the creative works of the colonized. The work of Salman Rushdie and Hanif Kureishi provides one such avenue. But, of course, so also do the films by the various black collectives (*Sankofa*, *Ceddo* and the *Black Audio Film Collective*).[3] In all of these cases, something quite distinctive has happened. The colonial nostalgia that animates such films as *Cry Freedom*, *Out of Africa* or *A Passage to India* is counterposed by *Sammi and Rosie get Laid*, *Twilight City* and *Passion of Remembrance*. And, crucially, these narratives are woven within a theoretical tapestry which owes everything to the cultural critique initiated by the New Left. If David Mercer and Arnold Wesker's work contested existing theories (socialist, communal, etc.) which seemed to them not to make sense of particular versions of home and politics, the work of Angela Carter, Salman Rushdie and the Black Film collectives has grown from a theorizing which seems to make sense of the crises of multiple identities. We have a conundrum here. The earlier work, which arguably helped to foster the New Left, was possibly weak in its theoretical force. The newer work, while arguably theoretically forceful, may be lacking a sense of political agency. But this is a conundrum which is at the heart of British culture as a whole. Hopefully, this book goes a little way in helping us to understand the issues.

NOTES

1 Mercer's plays were published initially by Calder & Boyars, but after Jonathan Calder and Marian Boyars terminated their dynamic relationship, latterly in his life by Methuen and now by Faber, if they publish him at all. See, in particular, the collections *The Generations* (1964), *Three Television Plays* (1966), *On the Eve of Publication and Other Plays* (1970) and *The Bankrupt and Other Plays* (1974). *Morgan – a Suitable Case for Treatment* appears in its original television version in *Three Television Plays*.

2 See, for example, Christopher Brooker's books on the 1960s and 1970s, *The Neophiliacs* (1969) and *The Seventies* (1980), which collect his journalism, and his BBC TV documentary, *City of Towers* (1979), which provided grist to the Prince of Wales's campaign against 'modern' architecture. One of the curious features of Brooker's diatribe against people doing their own thing in the 1960s was that ultimately he found, in the campaign against urban design, a cause which put him firmly in the same camp as Peter Fuller.

3 For debates around the emergence of Black Film in Britain see Kobena Mercer (ed.) (1988) *Black Film: British Cinema*, ICA Documents 7, London: Institute of Contemporary Arts. See also Isaac Julien and Colin MacCabe (1991) *Diary of a Young Soul Rebel*, London: British Film Institute, the account of making the film *Young Soul Rebels*, with the screenplay by Paul Hallam and Derrick Saldaan McClintock.

REFERENCES

Ahmad, Aijaz (1992) *In Theory: Classes, Nations, Literature*. London: Verso.

Alexander, Sally (1984) 'Women, Class and Sexual Differences in the 1830s and 1840s: Some Reflections on the Writing of a Feminist History', in Lovell (1990).

Althusser, Louis (1971) *Lenin and Philosophy and Other Essays*. London: New Left Books.

——(1977) *For Marx*. London: Verso.

Anderson, Benedict (1983, revised 1991) *Imagined Communities*. London: Verso.

——(1990) *Language and Power: Exploring Political Cultures in Indonesia*. Ithaca, NY: Cornell University Press.

Anderson, Perry (1964) 'Components of the National Culture', *New Left Review* 50: 3–18. Reprinted in Anderson (1992a) and in Cockburn and Blackburn (1969).

——(1969) 'Components of the National Culture', in Cockburn and Blackburn (1969): 214–86.

——(1974a) *Lineages of the Absolute State*. London: Verso.

——(1974b) *Passages from Antiquity to Feudalism*. London: Verso.

——(1980) *Arguments Within English Marxism*. London: Verso.

——(1984) 'Modernity and Revolution', *New Left Review* 144: 114–23. Reprinted in Anderson (1992b) and in Nelson and Grossberg (1988).

——(1990) 'A Culture in Counterflow', *New Left Review* 182: 85–137.

——(1992a) *English Questions*. London: Verso.

——(1992b) *A Zone of Engagement*. London: Verso.

Annan, Noel (1990) *Our Age*. London: Weidenfeld & Nicolson.

Appiah, Kwame Anthony (1990) *In My Father's House: What does it Mean to be an African Today?* London: Methuen.

Appignanesi, Lisa (ed.) (1987) *Identity*, ICA Documents 6. London: Free Association Books.

Archer, Robin, Bubeck, D., Glock, H., Jacobs, L., Moglen, S., Steinhouse, A. and Weinstock, D. (eds) (1989) *Out of Apathy*. London: Verso.

Arnold, Matthew (1869) *Culture and Anarchy*. London: Smith, Elder.

Aronowitz , Stanley (1993) *Roll Over, Beethoven*. New York: Westview Press.

Ascherson, Neal (1988) *Games and Shadows*. London: Radius.

——(1994) 'Sleazy Government, Public Apathy, and Nothing Left to Believe in', *The Independent on Sunday* 16 January: 20.

Auty, Giles (1993) 'The Enemy Within', *Spectator* 31 July: 34.

Bakhtin, Mikhail (1981) *The Dialogic Imagination*, trans. Caryl Emerson and Michael Holquist. Austin: University of Texas Press.

181

——(1985) *Rabelais and his World*, trans. Helene Iswolsky. Bloomington: Indiana University Press.

Barrett, Michele (1988) 'The Place of Aesthetics in Marxist Criticism', in Nelson and Grossberg (1988: 697–714).

Bazin, Andre (1971) *What is Cinema?* Berkeley: University of California Press.

Bell, Daniel (1960) *The End of Ideology*. New York: Free Press.

——(1976) *The Cultural Contradictions of Capitalism*. New York: Basic Books.

Benjamin, Walter (1970) *Illuminations*, trans. Harry Zohn. London: Jonathan Cape.

Bennett, Tony (1979) *Formalism and Marxism*, London: Methuen.

Bensmaia, Reda (1987) *The Barthes Effect: The Essay as Reflective Text*, trans. Pat Fedkien. Minneapolis: University of Minnesota Press.

Berger, John (1960) *Permanent Red*. London: Methuen.

——(1972) *Ways of Seeing*. Harmondsworth: Penguin.

——(1985) *The Sense of Sight*. New York: Pantheon.

Berger, Peter, and Luckman, Thomas (1966) *The Social Construction of Reality*. London: Allen Lane.

Berland, Jody (1993) 'Weathering the North', in Blundell *et al.* (1993).

Bernstein, Basil (1971a) *Class, Codes and Control*, vol. 1. London: Routledge.

——(1971b) 'Education Cannot Compensate for Society', in Cosin *et al.* (1971: 61–6).

Bhaba, Homi (1987) 'Interrogating Identity', in Appignanesi (1987: 5–12).

Bianchini, Franco (1987) 'GLC R.I.P. Cultural Politics in London, 1981–1986', *New Formations* 1: 103–17.

Blackburn, Robin (1988) *The Overthrow of Colonial Slavery*, London: Verso.

Blake, David (1989) 'Communist Parties Play the Name Game', *Sunday Correspondent* 26 November: 8.

Bloom, Allan (1987) *The Closing of the American Mind*. New York: Simon & Schuster.

Blundell, Valda, Shepherd, John, and Taylor, Ian (1993) *Relocating Cultural Studies: Developments in Theory and Research*. New York: Routledge.

Bourdieu, Pierre (1971a) 'Intellectual Field and Creative Project', in Young (1971: 161–88).

——(1971b) 'Systems of Education and Systems of Thought', in Young (1971: 189–207).

——(with Jean-Claude Passeron) (1977) *Reproduction*, trans. Richard Nice. London: Sage.

——(1984) *Distinction*, trans. Richard Nice. Cambridge, Mass: Harvard University Press.

Bradbury, Malcolm (1974) *The History Man*. Harmondsworth: Penguin.

Brecht, Berthold (1976) *Poems*, 3 vols, trans. by various hands. London: Eyre/ Methuen.

Brooker, Christopher (1969) *The Neophiliacs*. Harmondsworth: Penguin.

——(1980) *The Seventies*. Harmondsworth: Penguin.

Brown, Richard (ed.) (1973) *Knowledge, Education and Cultural Change*. London: Tavistock.

Buck-Morss, Susan (1977) *The Origin of Negative Dialectics*. Hassocks: Harvester.

——(1989) *The Dialectics of Seeing*. Cambridge, Mass: MIT Press.

Burgin, Victor (1986) *The End of Art Theory*. London: Macmillan.

Calvino, Italo (1972) *Imaginary Cities*. London: Secker.

Cameron, James (1988) *Games and Shadows*. London: Radius.

Canadian Review of Sociology and Anthropology (1991) Special Issue on Cultural Studies in Canada, 28(2).

Canclini, Nestor Garcia (1993) 'Studies of Communication and Consumption: Interdisciplinary Work in Neoconservative Times', trans. Cyndi Meillon, *Borderlines*: 27: 8–12.

Carasso, Jean-Pierre (1970) *La Rumeur irlandaise: guerre de religion ou lutte de classe?* Paris: Maspero.

Carter, Angela (1985) *Nights at the Circus*. London: Picador.

Carter, Erica (1984) 'Alice in the Consumer Wonderland', in McRobbie and Nava (1984).

Caudwell, Christopher (1937) *Illusion and Reality*. London: Macmillan.

——(1938) *Studies in a Dying Culture*. London: Macmillan.

Cesaire, Aimé (1956) *Cahiers d'un retour au pays natal* (*Return to my Native Land*). Paris: Présence Africaine.

Chakrabarty, Dipesh (1992) 'Postcoloniality and the Artifice of History: Who Speaks for "Indian" Pasts?', *Representations* 37: 1–26.

Centre for Contemporary Cultural Studies (1968–9) *Fifth Report 1968–9*, Birmingham: CCCS.

Chun, Lin (1993) *The British New Left*. Edinburgh: Edinburgh University Press.

Clarke, John, Critcher, Chas, and Johnson, Richard (eds) (1979) *Working Class Culture*. London: Hutchinson.

Clarke, Simon (1979) 'Socialist Humanism and the Critique of Economism', *History Workshop Journal* 7: 138–66.

Clifford, James (1988) *The Predicament of Culture: Twentieth-Century Ethnography, Literature and Art*. Cambridge, Mass: Harvard University Press.

——(1992) 'Travelling Cultures', in Grossberg *et al.* (1992: 96–116).

Cockburn, Alexander, and Blackburn, Robin (eds) (1969) *Student Power*. Harmondsworth: Penguin.

Cockburn, Claud (1975) *I, Claud*. Harmondsworth: Penguin.

Cohen, Derek (1993) 'The Question of Shylock', *Brick* 46: 32–9.

Cohen, Leonard (1993) *Strange Music: Selected Poems and Songs*. Toronto: McClelland & Stewart.

Cohen, Stan, and Taylor, Laurie (1978) *Escape Attempts*. Harmondsworth: Penguin.

Collins, R., Curran, J., Garnham, N., Scannell, P., Schlesinger, P., and Sparks, C. (eds) (1986) *Media, Culture and Society: A Critical Reader*. London: Sage.

Communication Inquiry (1986) Special Issue on Stuart Hall, 10(1).

Cordell, Alexander (1959) *Rape of the Fair Country*. London: Gollancz.

Corrigan, Philip (1990) *Social Forms/Human Capacities: Essays in Authority and Difference*. London: Routledge.

Corrigan, Philip, and Sayer, Derek (1985) *The Great Arch*. Oxford: Basil Blackwell.

Cosin, B. R., Dale, I. R., Easland, G. M., and Swift, D. F. (eds) (1971) *School and Society*. London: Routledge.

Coward, Rosalind, and Ellis, John (1977) *Language and Materialism*. London: Routledge & Kegan Paul.

Craik, Jennifer (1993) 'Cashing in on Cultural Studies: Future Fortunes', unpublished paper presented to the Symposium on Cultural Studies in Asia, the Pacific, and the US, 16–18 September.

Crean, Susan, and Rioux, Marcel (1983) *Two Nations*. Toronto: James Lorimer.

Crosland, Anthony (1956) *The Future of Socialism*. London: Jonathan Cape.

Crossman, R. H. S. (ed.) (1950) *The God that Failed*. London: Hamish Hamilton.

REFERENCES

Davies, Ioan (1980) 'Approaching Walter Benjamin: Retrieval, Translation and Reconstruction', *Canadian Journal of Political and Social Theory* IV(i): 59–74.
——(1989a) 'The Return of Virtue: Orwell and the Political Dilemma of Central European Intellectuals', *International Journal of Politics, Culture and Society* 3(1): 107–28.
——(1989b) 'Lenny Bruce: Hyperrealism and the Death of Jewish Tragic Humor', *Social Text* 22: 92–114.
——(1990) *Writers in Prison*. Oxford: Basil Blackwell.
——(1992) 'Post-Glasnost: The Culture of Vertigo', in Reichardt and Muskens (1992: 85–98).
Davies, Ioan, and Herman, Kathleen (eds) (1971) *Social Space: Canadian Perspectives*. Toronto: New Press.
Davis, Mike (1990) *City of Quartz*. London: Verso.
Debord, Guy (1990) *Comments on the Society of the Spectacle*. London: Verso.
de Lauretis, Theresa (1987) *Technologies of Gender: Essays on Theory, Film, and Fiction*. Bloomington: Indiana University Press.
——(1988) 'Displacing Hegemonic Discourses: Reflections on Feminist Theory in the 1980s', *Inscriptions* 3/4: 127–44.
Dent, Gina (1992) (ed.) *Black Popular Culture: A Project by Michelle Wallace*. Seattle, Wash: Bay Press.
Der Derian, James (1991) 'Videographic War', *Alphabet City* I(i): 4–12.
Derrida, Jacques (1976) *Of Grammatology*, trans. Gayatri Chakravorty Spivak. Baltimore, Md: Johns Hopkins University Press.
Diawara, Manthia (1993a) *African Cinema*. Bloomington: Indiana University Press.
——(1993b) 'Black Studies, Cultural Studies: PERFORMATIVE ACTS', *Borderlines* 29/30: 21–30.
Dorfman, Ariel, and Mattelart, Armand (1975) *How to Read Donald Duck*. New York: International General.
Douglas, Mary (1966) *Purity and Danger*. London: Routledge.
Downing, John (1984) *Radical Media: The Political Experience of Alternative Communication*. Boston, Mass: South End Press.
——(1990) 'Alternative Media and the Boston Tea Party', in Downing *et al.* (1990: 180–91).
Downing, John, Mohammadi, Ali, and Srebeny-Mohammadi, Annabelle (eds) (1990) *Questioning the Media: A Critical Introduction*. Newbury Park, Calif: Sage.
Eagleton, Terry (1983) *Literary Theory: An Introduction*. Oxford: Basil Blackwell.
——(1986) *Against the Grain: Selected Essays*. London: Verso.
——(1987) 'The Politics of Subjectivity', in Appignanesi (1987: 47–8).
——(1990) *The Ideology of the Aesthetic*. Oxford: Basil Blackwell.
Easthope, Anthony (1988) *British Post-structuralism*. London: Routledge.
Ehrmann, Jacques (ed.) (1970) *Literature and Revolution*. Boston, Mass: Beacon.
Fanon, Frantz (1962) *Wretched of the Earth*, trans. Constance Farrington. London: McGibbon & Kee.
Farson, Dan (1987) *Soho in the Fifties*. London: Michael Joseph.
Fawcett, Brian (1986) *Cambodia: a Book for People who Find Television Too Slow*. Vancouver: Talonbooks.
Fekete, John (1977) *The Critical Twilight*. London: Routledge.
Fiske, John (1988) 'Meaningful Moments', *Critical Studies in Mass Communication* 6: 246–50.
Fiske, John, and Hartley, John (1978) *Reading Television*. London: Methuen.

Fitzpatrick, Sheila (1970) *The Commissariat of the Enlightenment*. Cambridge: Cambridge University Press.

Forgacs, David (1989) 'Gramsci and Marxism in Britain', *New Left Review* 176: 70–88.

Forrester, John (1987) 'A Brief History of the Subject', in Appignanesi (1987: 13–16).

Foucault, Michel (1985) *The History of Sexuality II: The Use of Pleasure*, trans. by Robert Hurley. New York: Random House.

Francis, Daniel (1992) *The Imaginary Indian: The Image of the Indian in Canadian Culture*. Vancouver: Arsenal Pulp Press.

Fraser, Ronald (1986) *In Search of a Past*. London: Verso.

Frith, Simon (1983) *Sound Effects: Youth, Leisure and the Politics of Rock'n'Roll*. London: Constable.

——(1988) 'Art Ideology and Pop Practice', in Nelson and Grossberg (1988: 461–70.

——(1992) 'The Cultural Study of Popular Music', in Grossberg *et al.* (1992: 174–86).

Frye, Northrop (1971) *The Bush Garden*. Toronto: Anansi.

Fulford, Robert (1994) 'Defending the Right to be Offensive', *Globe & Mail*, 2 February: C1.

Fuller, Peter (1980) *Beyond the Crisis in Art*. London: Writers & Readers.

—— (1990) *Images of God*. London: Hogarth Press.

Garfinkel, Harold (1967) *Studies in Ethnomethodology*. Englewood Cliffs, NJ: Prentice-Hall.

Gates, Henry Louis Jr (1992) 'Black Pleasure, Black Joy', in Dent (1992: 1–19).

Gellner, Ernest (1959) *Words and Things*. London: Victor Gollancz.

Genosko, Gary (1992) 'Gramsci's Organic Army', *Research and Society* 5: 58–67.

Geras, Norman (1971) 'Louis Althusser: An Assessment', *New Left Review* 71: 57–88.

Gilroy, Paul (1987) *There Ain't No Black in the Union Jack*. London: Hutchinson.

Goldmann, Lucien (1964) *The Hidden God*. London: Routledge & Kegan Paul.

Gorak, Jan (1988) *The Alien Mind of Raymond Williams*. Columbus, Mo: University of Missouri Press.

Gott, Richard (1993) Letter in *London Review of Books* 27 January: 4.

Gould, Julius (1977) *Attack on Higher Education: Marxist and Radical Penetration*. London: Institute for the Study of Conflict.

Gramsci, Antonio (1971) *From the Prison Notebooks*, trans. Quentin Hoare and Geoffrey Nowell Smith. London: Lawrence & Wishart.

——(1985) *Selections from Cultural Writings*, trans. William Boelhower. Cambridge, Mass: Harvard University Press.

Grossberg, Lawrence (1983) 'Cultural Studies Revisited and Revised', in M. Mander (ed.) *Communications in Transition*. New York: Praeger.

——(1984a) 'I'd Rather Feel Bad than Not Feel Anything at All: Rock and Roll, Pleasure and Power', *Enclitic* 8: 94–110.

——(1984b) 'Strategies of Marxist Cultural Interpretation', *Critical Studies in Mass Communication* 1: 392–421.

——(1986) 'History, Politics and Postmodernism: Stuart Hall and Cultural Studies', *Communication Inquiry* 10(2): 61–77.

——(1993) 'The Formations of Cultural Studies: An American in Birmingham', in Blundell *et al.* (1993: 21–66).

Grossberg, Lawrence, Nelson, Cary, and Treichler, Paula (eds) (1992) *Cultural Studies*. New York: Routledge.

Hall, Stuart (1980a) 'Encoding/Decoding', in Hall *et al.* (1980: 128–38).

——(1980b) 'Cultural Studies at the Centre: Some Problematics and Problems', in Hall *et al.* (1980: 15–47).

——(1980c) 'Cultural Studies – Two Paradigms', *Media, Culture and Society* 2 (2), reprinted in Collins *et al.* (1986).

——(1981a) 'Notes on Deconstructing "The Popular" ', in Samuel (1981: 227–40).

——(1981b) 'In Defence of Theory', in Samuel (1981: 378–85).

——(1986a) 'On Postmodernism and Articulation: An Interview', ed. Lawrence Grossberg. *Communication Inquiry* 10(2): 45–60.

——(1986b) 'The Problem of Ideology: Marxism without Guarantees', *Communication Inquiry* 10(2): 28–45.

——(1987) 'Minimal Selves', in Appignanesi (1987: 44–6).

——(1988) 'The Toad in the Garden: Thatcherism among the Theorists', in Nelson and Grossberg (1988: 35–73).

——(1989a) *The Hard Road to Renewal*. London: Verso.

——(1989b) 'The "First" New Left: Life and Times', in Archer *et al.* (1989: 11–38).

——(1992a) 'Cultural Studies and its Theoretical Legacies', in Grossberg *et al.* (1992: 277–294).

——(1992b) 'What is "Black" in Black Popular Culture', in Dent (1992: 21–33).

Hall, Stuart, and Jacques, Martin (eds) (1989) *New Times*. London: Lawrence & Wishart.

Hall, Stuart, and Jefferson, Tony (eds) (1976) *Resistance through Rituals*. London: Hutchinson.

Hall, S., Lumley, B., and McLennan, G. (eds) (1978a) *On Ideology*. London: Hutchinson.

Hall, S., Critcher, C., Jefferson, T., Clarke, J., and Roberts, B. (1978b) *Policing the Crisis*. London: Macmillan.

Hall, S., Hobson, D., Lowe, A., and Willis, P. (eds) (1980) *Culture, Media, Language*. London: Hutchinson.

Halliday, Michael (1969) 'Relevant Models of Language', *Educational Review* 22(1).

Harlow, Barbara (1987) *Resistance Literature*. New York: Methuen.

——(1992) *Barred: Women, Writing and Political Detention*. Hanover, Conn: Wesleyan University Press.

Harris, David (1987) *Openness and Closures in Distance Education*. Barcombe: Falmer Press.

——(1992) *From Class Struggle to the Politics of Pleasure: The Effects of Gramscianism on Cultural Studies*. London: Routledge.

Hartley, John (1988) 'The Real World of Audiences', *Critical Studies in Mass Communication* 6: 234–8.

——(1992) ' "Dismantling" Fremantle', *Cultural Studies* 6(3): 307–10.

Harvey, David (1990) *The Condition of Postmodernity*. Oxford: Basil Blackwell.

Hayman, Ronald (ed.) (1977) *My Cambridge*. London: Robson.

Hebdige, Dick (1979) *Subculture: The Meaning of Style*. London: Methuen.

——(1986) 'Some Sons and their Fathers', *TEN/8* October.

——(1987) *Cut 'n' Mix*. London: Commedia.

——(1988) *Hiding in the Light*. London: Commedia.

——(1993) 'Redeeming Witness: In the Tracks of the Homeless Vehicle Project', *Cultural Studies* 7(2): 173–223.

Heftler, Victoria (1993) 'Finding a Familiar Face in the Crowd: "History from

Below", "Orientalism" and the Politics of Knowledge', unpublished paper, York University.

Hicks, Emily (1991) *Border Literature*. Minneapolis: University of Minnesota Press.

Hirschkop, Ken (1989) 'A Complex Populism – The Political Thought of Raymond Williams', *News From Nowhere* 6: 12–22. Oxford: Oxford English Ltd.

Hobsbawm, Eric (Francis Newton) (1959) *The Jazz Scene*. London: McGibbon & Kee.

——(1977) *Revolutionaries*. London: Quartet.

Hobson, Dorothy (1982) *Crossroads – The Drama of a Soap Opera*. London: Methuen.

Hoggart, Richard (1957) *The Uses of Literacy*. London: Chatto & Windus.

——(1978) *An Idea and its Servants: UNESCO from Within*. London: Chatto and Windus.

hooks, bell (1992) 'Representing Whiteness in the Black Imagination', in Grossberg *et al.* (1992: 338–46).

Hughes, Robert (1993) *Culture of Complaint: The Fraying of America*. New York: New York Public Library and Oxford University Press.

Jakobson, Roman (1930) 'The Generation that Squandered its Poets', in Ehrmann (1970: 119–25).

Jacoby, Russell (1987) *The Last Intellectuals*. New York: Basic Books.

James, C. L. R. (1963, reissued 1983) *Beyond a Boundary*. New York: Pantheon.

Jameson, Fredric (1971) *Marxism and Form*. Princeton, NJ: Princeton University Press.

——(1972) *The Prison-House of Language*. Princeton, NJ: Princeton University Press.

——(1981) *The Political Unconscious*. Ithaca, NY: Cornell University Press.

——(1983) 'Pleasure: A Political Issue', in *Formations: Of Pleasure*. London: Routledge & Kegan Paul.

——(1990) *Late Marxism: Adorno, or, The Persistence of the Dialectic*. London: Verso.

Jencks, Charles (ed.) (1992) *The Post-Modern Reader*. London: Academy Editions.

Johnson, Richard (1978a) 'Thompson, Genovese and Socialist Humanist History', *History Workshop Journal*, 6 (autumn): 79–100.

——(ed.) (1978b) *Making Histories*. London: Hutchinson.

——(1979) 'Culture and the Historians', in Clarke *et al.* (1979: 41–71).

——(1981) 'Against Absolutism', in Samuel (1981: 396).

——(1986/7) 'What is Cultural Studies Anyway?', *Social Text* 16: 38–80.

Johnson, Richard, Baron, Steve, Finn, Dan, Grant, Neil, and Green, Michael (eds) (1981) *Unpopular Education: Schooling and Social Democracy in England since 1944*. London: Hutchinson.

Jones, Jack (1938) *Off to Philadelphia in the Morning*. London: Murray.

Keane, John (1990) *The Media and Democracy*. Oxford: Polity.

Kellner, Douglas (1990) *Television and the Crisis of Democracy*. Boulder, Co: Westview.

Kettle, Arnold (1968) *An Introduction to the English Novel*. London: Hutchinson.

Klima, Ivan (1990) *Love and Garbage*, trans. Ewald Osers. Harmondsworth: Penguin.

Kracauer, Siegfried (1960) *Theory of Film: The Redemption of Physical Reality*. London: Oxford University Press.

Kristeva, Julia (1980) *Desire in Language*, trans. Thomas Gora, Alice Jardine and Leon Roudiez. New York: Columbia University Press.

REFERENCES

Kroker, Arthur (1984) *Technology and the Canadian Mind: Innis, McLuhan, Grant*. Montreal: New World Perspectives.

——(1991) *The Hysterical Male: New Feminist Perspectives*. Montreal: New World Perspectives.

Kundera, Milan (1984) 'A Kidnapped West, or Culture Bows Out', trans. Edmund White, *Granta* 11: 93–118.

Lacan, Jacques (1977) *The Four Fundamental Concepts of Psycho-analysis*, trans. Alan Sheridan. London: Hogarth Press.

——(1982) *Feminine Sexuality*, trans. Jacqueline Rose and ed. Jacqueline Rose and Juliet Mitchell. New York: W. W. Norton.

Laclau, Ernesto, and Mouffe, Chantal (1985) *Hegemony and Socialist Strategy*. London: Verso.

Larkin, Philip (1980) *All What Jazz: A Record Diary 1961–1971*. London: Faber & Faber.

——(1992) *Selected Letters of Philip Larkin*, ed. Anthony Thwaite. London: Faber & Faber.

Lawrence, D. H. (1957) *Collected Poems*. London: Heinemann.

Leadbeater, Charlie (1989) 'Power to the Person', in Hall and Jacques (1989: 137–149).

Levine, Donald (ed.) (1971) *George Simmel on Individuality and Social Forms*. Chicago: University of Chicago Press.

Levitt, Kari (1974) *Silent Surrender*. Toronto: James, Lewis & Samuel.

Lewis, C. S. (1980) *The Chronicles of Narnia: The Lion, the Witch and the Wardrobe*. London: HarperCollins.

Littlewood, Joan (1994) *Joan's Book*. London: Methuen.

Llewellyn, Richard (1939) *How Green was My Valley*. London: Michael Joseph.

Lloyd, A. L. (1944) *The Singing Englishman*. London: Workers' Music Association.

——(1952) *Come All Ye Bold Miners: Ballads and Songs of the Coalfields*. London: Lawrence & Wishart.

——(1967) *Folk Song in England*. London: Lawrence & Wishart.

Lovell, Terry (1980) *Pictures of Reality: Aesthetics, Politics and Pleasure*. London: British Film Institute.

——(ed.) (1990) *British Feminist Theory*. Oxford: Basil Blackwell.

Lukács, Gyorgi (1971) *History and Class Consciousness*, trans. Rodney Livingston. London: Merlin.

MacCabe, Colin (1975) 'The Politics of Separation', *Screen* 16(4): 46–51.

——(1986) *High Theory/Low Culture*, Manchester: Manchester University Press.

McCole, John (1993) *Walter Benjamin and the Antinomies of Tradition*. Ithaca, NY: Cornell University Press.

McGregor, Gaile (1985) *The Wacusta Syndrome: Explorations in the Canadian Landscape*. Toronto: University of Toronto Press.

McGuigan, J. (1992) *Cultural Populism*. London: Routledge.

McLellan, David (1973) *Karl Marx: His Life and Thought*. London: Macmillan.

McRobbie, Angela (1991) 'New Times in Cultural Studies', *New Formations* 13: 1–18.

McRobbie, Angela, and Nava, M. (eds) (1984) *Gender and Generation*. London: Macmillan.

Mandel, Ernest (1962) *Marxist Economic Theory*, trans. Brian Pearce, 2 vols. London: Merlin.

——(1975) *Late Capitalism*, trans. Joris De Bres. London: New Left Books.

Marcus, Greil (1986a) 'Critical Response', *Critical Studies in Mass Communication* 3: 77–81.

——(1986b) *Lipstick Traces: A Secret History of the Twentieth Century*. Cambridge, Mass: Harvard University Press.

Marcuse, Herbert (1978) *The Aesthetic Dimension*. Boston, Mass: Beacon.

Martin-Barbero, Jesus (1993) ' Communication: A Strategic Site for the Debate on Modernity', trans. Michael Hoechsmann. *Borderlines* 27: 47–52.

Marx, Karl (1973a) *Grundrisse* trans. Martin Niklaus. Harmondsworth: Penguin.

Marx, Karl (1973b) *Surveys from Exile: Political Writings Volume 2*, ed. David Fernbach. Harmondsworth: Penguin.

Mast, Gerald, and Cohen, Marshall (eds) (1979) *Film Theory and Criticism*. New York: Oxford University Press.

Mattelart, Michele, and Mattelart, Armand (1990) *The Carnival of Images: Brazilian Television Fiction* Boston, Mass: Bergin & Garvey.

Mayhew, Henry (1861) *London Labour and the London Poor*. London: Charles Griffin.

Mercer, David (1964) *The Generations*. London: Methuen.

——(1966) *Three Television Plays*. London: Methuen.

——(1970) *On the Eve of Publication and Other Plays*. London: Methuen.

——(1974) *The Bankrupt and Other Plays*. London: Methuen.

Metz, Christian (1974a) *Film Language: A Semiotics of the Cinema*, trans. Michael Taylor. New York: Oxford University Press.

——(1974b) *Language and Cinema*, trans. Donna Jean Umiker-Sebeok. The Hague: Mouton.

Miller, Jonathan (1986) *Subsequent Performances*. London: Faber & Faber.

Minh-ha, Trinh T. (1989) *Woman Native Other*. Bloomington: Indiana University Press.

Mitchell, Juliet (1966) 'Women: The Longest Revolution', *New Left Review* 40: 11–37.

——(1971) *Women's Estate*. Harmondsworth: Penguin.

——(1974) *Psychoanalysis and Feminism*. Harmondsworth: Penguin.

Morley, David (1986) *Family Television: Cultural Power and Domestic Leisure*. London: Commedia.

Morris, Meaghan (1988) 'Things to Do with Shopping Centres', in Sheridan (1988).

——(1992) 'Afterthoughts on "Australianism" ', *Cultural Studies*, 6(3): 468–75.

Morrison, Toni (1992) *Jazz*. New York: Knopf.

Motion, Andrew (1993) *Philip Larkin: A Writer's Life*. London: Faber & Faber.

Mudimbe, V. Y. (1988) *The Invention of Africa*. Bloomington: Indiana University Press.

Murray, Robin (1989) 'Fordism and Post-Fordism', in Hall and Jacques (1989: 38–53).

Nairn, Tom (1977) *The Break-Up of Britain*. London: Verso.

——(1988) *The Enchanted Glass: Britain and its Monarchy*. London: Century Hutchinson.

Nelson, Cary, and Grossberg, Lawrence (eds) (1988) *Marxism and the Interpretation of Culture*. London: Macmillan.

Ngugi Wa Thiong'o (1986) *Matigari*. London: James Curry.

——(1988) *Decolonizing the Mind*. London: James Curry.

——(1993) *Moving the Centre: The Struggle for Cultural Freedoms*. London: James Curry.

Nichols, Bill (ed.) (1976) *Movies and Methods*. Berkeley: University of California Press.

Norris, Christopher (1991) 'Old Themes for New Times: Basildon Revisited', *Socialist Register* 52–77.

Nugent, S. L. (1986) 'Critical Response', *Critical Studies in Mass Communication* 3: 82–5.

O'Connor, Alan (1989a) 'The Problem of American Cultural Studies', *Critical Studies in Mass Communication* 6: 405–13.

——(1989b) *Raymond Williams: Writing, Culture, Politics.* Oxford: Basil Blackwell.

O'Connor, Alan, and Hoechsmann, Michael (eds) (1993) Special Issue on Cultural Studies in Latin America. *Borderlines* 27.

Orwell, George (1937) *Road to Wigan Pier.* London: Gollancz.

Osborne, Peter (1989) 'Aesthetic Autonomy and the Crisis of Theory', *New Formations* 9: 31–50.

Palmer, Brian (1981) *The Making of Edward Thompson.* Toronto: New Hogtown Press.

Paz, Octavio (1967) *The Labyrinth of Solitude*, trans. Lysander Kemp. London: Allen Lane.

Pocock, J. G. A. (1985) *Virtue, Commerce and History.* Cambridge: Cambridge University Press.

Pope, Alexander (1985) *Selected Poems.* Harmondsworth: Penguin.

Portillo, Michael (1994) 'Poison of a New British Disease', *The Independent on Sunday* 16 January: 2.

Présence Africaine (1956) *First International Conference of Negro Writers and Artists.* Paris: Présence Africaine.

——(1959) *Second Congress of Negro Writers and Artists: The Unity of Negro African Cultures.* Paris: Presence Africaine.

Punter, David (ed.) (1986) *An Introduction to Cultural Studies.* London: Longman.

Reichardt, Robert H., and Muskens, George (eds) (1992) *Post-Communism, the Market and the Arts.* Frankfurt-am-Main: Peter Lang.

Rieff, David (1993) 'Multiculturalism's Silent Partner: It's the Newly Globalized Economy, Stupid', *Harpers* 287 (1719): 62–71.

Rilke, Rainer Maria (1985) *Sonnets to Orpheus*, trans. Stephen Mitchell. New York: Simon & Schuster.

Robertson, Roland (1988) 'The Sociological Significance of Culture: Some General Considerations', *Theory, Culture and Society* 5(1): 3–23.

Rose, Gillian (1988) 'Architecture to Philosophy: The Postmodern Complicity', *Theory, Culture and Society* 5(2–3): 357–72.

Rose, Jacqueline (1987) 'The Man Who Mistook His Wife for a Hat', in Appignanesi (1987: 30–3).

Rose, Richard (1976) *Northern Ireland: A Time of Choice.* London: Faber & Faber.

Ross, Andrew (1989) *No Respect: Intellectuals and Popular Culture.* London: Routledge.

Rowe, William, and Schelling, Vivian (1991) *Memory and Modernity: Popular Culture in Latin America.* London: Verso.

Said, Edward (1978) *Orientalism.* New York: Vintage.

——(1983) *The World, the Text and the Critic.* Cambridge, Mass: Harvard University Press.

——(1993a) *Culture and Imperialism.* New York: Knopf.

——(1993b) 'Interview', *The Independent on Sunday Review* 4 July: 25.

Samuel, Raphael (ed.) (1977) *Miners, Quarrymen and Saltworkers.* London: Routledge.

——(ed.) (1981) *People's History and Socialist Theory.* London: Routledge.

REFERENCES

Samuel, Raphael, MacCall, Ewan, and Cosgrove, Stuart (eds) (1985) *Theatres of the Left, 1880–1935: Workers' Theatre Movements in Britain and America.* London: Routledge.
Sarris, Andrew (1976) 'Towards a Theory of Film History', in Nichols (1976: 237–50).
Schutz, Alfred (1964) *Collected Papers,* 2 vols. The Hague: Martinus Nijhoff.
Screen Reader 1 (1977) *Cinema/Ideology/Politics.* London: Society for Education in Film and Television.
Screen Reader 2 (1981) *Cinema and Semiotics.* London: Society for Education in Film and Television.
Sheridan, Susan (ed.) *Grafts.* London: Verso.
Smith, Dorothy (1987) *The Everyday World as Problematic.* Toronto: University of Toronto Press.
Solmos, John, Findlay, Bob, Jones, Simon, and Gilroy, Paul (eds) (1982) *The Empire Strikes Back.* London: Hutchinson.
Soyinka, Wole (1988) *Art, Dialogue and Outrage.* Ibadan: New Horn Press.
Stein, Gertrude (1937) *Everybody's Autobiography.* New York: Random House.
Straw, Will (1993) 'Shifting Boundaries, Lines of Descent', in Blundell *et al.* (1993).
Thompson, Denys (ed.) (1964) *Discrimination and Popular Culture.* Harmondsworth: Penguin.
——(ed.) (1984) *The Leavises: Recollections and Impressions.* Cambridge: Cambridge University Press.
Thompson, Dorothy (1993) *Outsiders: Class, Gender and Nation.* London: Verso.
Thompson, E. P. (1955) *William Morris: From Romantic to Revolutionary.* London: Lawrence & Wishart.
——(1963) *The Making of the English Working Class.* London: Gollancz.
——(1965) 'The Peculiarities of the English', *Socialist Register 2.* Reprinted in Thompson (1978).
——(ed.) (1970) *Warwick University Ltd: Industry, Management and the Universities.* Harmondsworth: Penguin Books.
——(1977) *Whigs and Hunters.* Harmondsworth: Penguin.
——(1978) *The Poverty of Theory.* London: Merlin.
——(1980) *Writing by Candlelight.* London: Merlin.
——(1988) *The Sykaos Papers.* London: Bloomsbury.
——(1993a) *Customs in Common.* New York: New Press.
——(1993b) *Witness against the Beast: William Blake and the Moral Law.* New York: New Press.
Trotsky, Leon (1960) *Where is Britain Going?* London: Socialist Labour League.
Turner, Graeme (1990) *British Cultural Studies: An Introduction.* London: Unwin Hyman.
Walkerdine, Valerie (1990) *Schoolgirl Fictions.* London: Verso.
Wark, McKenzie (1992) 'Speaking Trajectories: Meaghan Morris, Antipodean Theory and Australian Cultural Studies', *Cultural Studies* 6(3): 433–48.
Waugh, Auberon (1989) 'Now We Are Fifty', *Spectator* 2 December: 8.
Weinstein, Michael A. (1985) *Culture Critique: Fernand Dumont and the New Quebec Sociology.* Montreal: New World Perspectives.
Wesley, Charles (1935) 'Oh Come Thou Traveller Unknown', Hymn 311, in *The Methodist Hymnal,* New York: Methodist Book Concern.
West, Cornel (1992) 'Nihilism in Black America', in Dent (1992: 37–47).
Whitty, G., and Young, M. F. D. (1976) *Explorations in the Politics of School Knowledge.* Driffield: Nafferton.

REFERENCES

Wilden, Tony (1972) *System and Structure*. London: Tavistock.
——(1985) *The Imaginary Canadian*. Vancouver: Pulp Press.
Williams, Gwyn A (1979) *The Merthyr Rising*. London: Croom Helm.
——(1985) *When Was Wales?* London: Black Raven Press (BBC Annual Wales Lectures 1978).
Williams, Raymond (1950) *Reading and Criticism*. London: Frederick Muller.
——(1958) *Culture and Society*. London: Chatto & Windus.
——(1961) *The Long Revolution*. London: Chatto & Windus.
——(ed.) (1968) *The May Day Manifesto*. Harmondsworth: Penguin.
——(1970) *The English Novel from Dickens to Lawrence*. London: Chatto & Windus.
——(1975) *The Country and the City*. London: Chatto & Windus.
——(1979) *Politics and Letters*. London: Verso.
——(1980) *Problems in Materialism and Culture*. London: New Left Books/ Verso.
——(1981) *Culture*. London: Fontana.
——(1984a) *Writing in Society*. London: Verso.
——(1984b) *Keywords*. New York: Oxford University Press.
——(1984c) 'Seeing a Man Running', in Denys Thompson (1984).
——(1985) *Towards 2000*. Harmondsworth: Penguin.
——(1989a) *Resources of Hope*. London: Verso.
——(1989b) *The Politics of Modernism: Against the New Conformists*. London: Verso.
Willis, Paul (1977) *Learning to Labour: How Working-Class Kids Get Working-Class Jobs*. Farnborough: Saxon House.
——(1978) *Profane Culture*. London: Routledge.
——(1990) *Common Culture*. Milton Keynes: Open University Press.
Wilson, Alexander (1991) *The Culture of Nature*. Toronto: Between-the-Lines.
Wolf, Kurt H. (ed.) (1950) *The Sociology of Georg Simmel*. New York: Free Press.
Wolff, Janet (1981) *Social Production of Art*. London: Macmillan.
——(1983) *Aesthetics and the Sociology of Art*. London: Allen & Unwin.
Wolff, Janet, and Seed, John (eds) (1988) *The Culture of Capital: Art, Power and the Nineteenth-Century Middle Class*. Manchester: Manchester University Press.
Wollen, Peter (1993) *Raiding the Icebox*. London: Verso.
Women's Study Group (eds) (1978) *Women Take Issue*. London: Hutchinson.
Wood, Neil (1960) *Communism and British Intellectuals*. London: Gollancz.
Worsley, Peter (1957) 'Britain: Unknown Country', *The New Reasoner* 1(4): 53–64.
——(1964) *The Third World: A New Vital Source in International Affairs*. London: Weidenfeld & Nicolson.
——(1984) *The Three Worlds: Culture and World Development*. London: Weidenfeld & Nicolson.
Wright, Haudel Kashope (1994) 'Dare We Call this African Cultural Studies?', *Borderlines* 33: 60–3.
Young, Michael F. D. (ed.) (1971) *Knowledge and Control*. London: Collier-Macmillan.
Young, Michael F. D., and Whitty, G. (eds) (1977) *Society, State and Schooling*. Barcombe: Falmer Press.
Yudice, George, Franco, Jean, and Flores, Juan (eds) (1992) *On the Edge: The Crisis of Contemporary Latin American Culture*. Minneapolis: University of Minnesota Press.
Zizek, Slavoj (1990) *The Sublime Object of Ideology*. London: Verso.

INDEX

INDEX

Wesker, Arnold 175, 180
Wesley, Charles 64 n.12
West, Cornel 133, 134, 135
Whitty, Geoff 45
Wilde, Oscar 93, 176, 178
Wilden, Tony 60, 174 n.19
Williams, Eric 133
Williams, Gwyn 23, 28 n.6
Williams, Raymond: academic career
30, 32, 50, 54–5, 58–9; background
32, 53–4; conception of culture 121,
172 n.6; Frith on 125–7; Gilroy on
97–8; Illinois conferences 159;
influence 16–17, 31, 38, 39, 46, 60,
94, 105, 119, 122, 157, 161, 178; *New
Left Review* 11; novels 4 n.1, 56;
Politics and Letters journal 54; US
reading of 122, 161; Welshness 2, 23,
50, 55–8, 61, 113, 118; works – *The
Country and the City* 16, 56; *Culture*
65 n.20; *Culture and Society* 6, 7–8,
16, 57, 172 n.3; *The English Novel*
16, 58; *The Long Revolution* 2, 16,
57, 63 n.4, 148; *May Day Manifesto*
141, 148; *Politics and Letters* 14, 34,
54, 57–8, 63 n.4, 172 n.6; *The Politics
of Modernism* 6, 126, 149–50, 156;
*Problems in Materialism and
Culture* 129–30; *Reading and
Criticism* 58; *Resources of Hope* 57,
129; 'Seeing a Man Running' 59;
Towards 2000 97, 128, 138 n.8;
Writing in Society 59–60, 63 n.4
Williamson, Judith 25
Willis, Paul 21, 46–7, 52, 120

Willmott, Peter 109
Wilson, Alexander 174 n.19
Wilson, Colin 65 n.19
Wilson, Edmund 160
Wilson, Flip 134
Winkler, R.O.C. 54
Wittgenstein, Ludwig 12
Wodiczko, Krzysztof 173 n.13
Wolff, Janet 37, 43, 64, 75, 85 n.1, 86 n.6
Wollen, Peter: Los Angeles 86 n.8;
Raiding the Icebox 83, 84–5, 86 n.4,
144–5, 146; works 72, 91
Wollstonecraft, Mary 5, 93
Wood, Neil 17 n.2
Woolf, Virginia 6, 93, 123, 178
Wootton, Barbara 18 n.8
Workers' Educational Association
(WEA) 6, 11, 15, 33, 48, 50, 129
Worsley, Peter 7, 11, 28 n.8, 159
Wright, Handel Kashope 174 n.20
Wright, Richard 133
Writers & Readers 14, 33

Yeltsin, Boris 146
York University 14
Young, Jock 87
Young, Michael Dunlop 109
Young, Michael F.D. 45, 64 n.7
Yudice, George 174 n.18
Yugoslavia 147–8

Zed 14
Zizek, Slavoj 42

10/8 140

203